Voices of Islam

VOICES OF ISLAM

Volume 3

VOICES OF LIFE: FAMILY, HOME, AND SOCIETY

Vincent J. Cornell, General Editor

Virginia Gray Henry-Blakemore, Volume Editor

PRAEGER PERSPECTIVES

Westport, Connecticut
London

Library of Congress Cataloging-in-Publication Data

Voices of Islam / Vincent J. Cornell, general editor.
  p. cm.
  Includes bibliographical references and index.
  ISBN 0–275–98732–9 (set : alk. paper)—ISBN 0–275–98733–7 (vol 1 : alk. paper)—ISBN
0–275–98734–5 (vol 2 : alk. paper)—ISBN 0–275–98735–3 (vol 3 : alk. paper)—ISBN 0–
275–98736–1 (vol 4 : alk. paper)—ISBN 0–275–98737–X (vol 5 : alk. paper) 1. Islam—
Appreciation. 2. Islam—Essence, genius, nature. I. Cornell, Vincent J.
  BP163.V65 2007
  297—dc22   2006031060

British Library Cataloguing in Publication Data is available.

Library of Congress Catalog Card Number: 2006031060
ISBN: 0–275–98732–9 (set)
     0–275–98733–7 (vol. 1)
     0–275–98734–5 (vol. 2)
     0–275–98735–3 (vol. 3)
     0–275–98736–1 (vol. 4)
     0–275–98737–X (vol. 5)

First published in 2007

Praeger Publishers, 88 Post Road West, Westport, CT 06881
An imprint of Greenwood Publishing Group, Inc.
www.praeger.com

Printed in the United States of America

The paper used in this book complies with the
Permanent Paper Standard issued by the National
Information Standards Organization (Z39.48–1984).

10 9 8 7 6 5 4 3 2 1

Contents

VOICES OF ISLAM

———————————— • ————————————

Vincent J. Cornell

It has long been a truism to say that Islam is the most misunderstood religion in the world. However, the situation expressed by this statement is more than a little ironic because Islam is also one of the most studied religions in the world, after Christianity and Judaism. In the quarter of a century since the 1978–1979 Islamic revolution in Iran, hundreds of books on Islam and the Islamic world have appeared in print, including more than a score of introductions to Islam in various European languages. How is one to understand this paradox? Why is it that most Americans and Europeans are still largely uninformed about Islam after so many books about Islam have been published? Even more, how can people still claim to know so little about Islam when Muslims now live in virtually every medium-sized and major community in America and Europe? A visit to a local library or to a national bookstore chain in any American city will reveal numerous titles on Islam and the Muslim world, ranging from journalistic potboilers to academic studies, translations of the Qur'an, and works advocating a variety of points of view from apologetics to predictions of the apocalypse.

The answer to this question is complex, and it would take a book itself to discuss it adequately. More than 28 years have passed since Edward Said wrote his classic study *Orientalism,* and it has been nearly as long since Said critiqued journalistic depictions of Islam in *Covering Islam: How the Media and the Experts Determine How We See the Rest of the World.* When these books first appeared in print, many thought that the ignorance about the Middle East and the Muslim world in the West would finally be dispelled. However, there is little evidence that the public consciousness of Islam and Muslims has been raised to a significant degree in Western countries. Scholars of Islam in American universities still feel the need to humanize Muslims in the eyes of their students. A basic objective of many introductory courses on Islam is to demonstrate that Muslims are rational human beings and that their beliefs are worthy of respect. As Carl W. Ernst observes in the preface to his recent work, *Following Muhammad: Rethinking Islam in the*

Contemporary World, "It still amazes me that intelligent people can believe that all Muslims are violent or that all Muslim women are oppressed, when they would never dream of uttering slurs stereotyping much smaller groups such as Jews or blacks. The strength of these negative images of Muslims is remarkable, even though they are not based on personal experience or actual study, but they receive daily reinforcement from the news media and popular culture."[1]

Such prejudices and misconceptions have only become worse since the terrorist attacks of September 11, 2001, and the war in Iraq. There still remains a need to portray Muslims in all of their human diversity, whether this diversity is based on culture, historical circumstances, economic class, gender, or religious doctrine. Today, Muslims represent nearly one-fourth of the world's population. Although many Americans are aware that Indonesia is the world's largest Muslim country, most are surprised to learn that half of the Muslims in the world live east of Lahore, Pakistan. In this sense, Islam is as much an "Asian" religion as is Hinduism or Buddhism. The new reality of global Islam strongly contradicts the "Middle Eastern" view of Islam held by most Americans. Politically, the United States has been preoccupied with the Middle East for more than half a century. Religiously, however, American Protestantism has been involved in the Middle East for more than 150 years. Thus, it comes as a shock for Americans to learn that only one-fourth of the world's Muslims live in the Middle East and North Africa and that only one-fifth of Muslims are Arabs. Islam is now as much a worldwide religion as Christianity, with somewhere between 4 and 6 million believers in the United States and approximately 10 million believers in Western Europe. Almost 20 million Muslims live within the borders of the Russian Federation, and nearly a million people of Muslim descent live in the Russian city of St. Petersburg, on the Gulf of Finland.

To think of Islam as monolithic under these circumstances is both wrong and dangerous. The idea that all Muslims are fundamentalists or anti-democratic religious zealots can lead to the fear that dangerous aliens are hiding within Western countries, a fifth column of a civilization that is antithetical to freedom and the liberal way of life. This attitude is often expressed in popular opinion in both the United States and Europe. For example, it can be seen in the "Letters" section of the June 7, 2004, edition of *Time* magazine, where a reader writes: "Now it is time for Muslim clerics to denounce the terrorists or admit that Islam is fighting a war with us—a religious war."[2] For the author of this letter, Muslim "clerics" are not to be trusted, not because they find it hard to believe that pious Muslims would commit outrageous acts of terrorism, but because they secretly hate the West and its values. Clearly, for this reader of *Time,* Islam and the West are at war; however the "West" may be defined and wherever "Islam" or Muslims are to be found.

Prejudice against Muslim minorities still exists in many countries. In Russia, Muslim restaurateurs from the Caucasus Mountains must call themselves "Georgian" to stay in business. In China, being Muslim by ethnicity is acceptable, but being a Muslim by conviction might get one convicted for antistate activities. In the Balkans, Muslims in Serbia, Bulgaria, and Macedonia are called "Turks" and right-wing nationalist parties deny them full ethnic legitimacy as citizens of their countries. In India, over a thousand Muslims were killed in communal riots in Gujarat as recently as 2002. As I write these words, Israel and Hizbollah, the Lebanese Shiite political movement and militia, are engaged in a bloody conflict that has left hundreds of dead and injured on both sides. Although the number of people who have been killed in Lebanon, most of whom are Shiite civilians, is far greater than the number of those killed in Israel, television news reports in the United States do not treat Lebanese and Israeli casualties the same way. While the casualties that are caused by Hizbollah rockets in Israel are depicted as personal tragedies, Lebanese casualties are seldom personalized in this way. The truth is, of course, that all casualties of war are personal tragedies, whether the victims are Lebanese civilians, Israeli civilians, or American soldiers killed or maimed by improvised explosive devices in Iraq. In addition, all civilian deaths in war pose a moral problem, whether they are caused as a consequence of aggression or of retaliation. In many ways, depersonalization can have worse effects than actual hatred. An enemy that is hated must at least be confronted; when innocent victims are reduced to pictures without stories, they are all too easily ignored.

The problem of depersonalization has deeper roots than just individual prejudice. Ironically, the global village created by international news organizations such as CNN, BBC, and Fox News may unintentionally contribute to the problem of devaluing Muslim lives. Depictions of victimhood are often studies in incomprehension: victims speak a language the viewer cannot understand, their shock or rage strips them of their rationality, and their standard of living and mode of dress may appear medieval or even primitive when compared with the dominant cultural forms of modernity. In her classic study, *The Origins of Totalitarianism,* Hannah Arendt pointed out that the ideology of human equality, which is fostered with all good intentions by the international news media, paradoxically contributes to the visibility of difference by confusing equality with sameness. In 99 out of 100 cases, says Arendt, equality "will be mistaken for an innate quality of every individual, who is 'normal' if he is like everybody else and 'abnormal' if he happens to be different. This perversion of equality from a political into a social concept is all the more dangerous when a society leaves but little space for special groups and individuals, for then their differences become all the more conspicuous."[3] According to Arendt, the widespread acceptance of the ideal of social equality after the French Revolution was a major reason why genocide, whether of Jews in Europe, Tutsis in Rwanda, or Muslims in the former Yugoslavia, has become a characteristically modern phenomenon.

The idea of equality as sameness was not as firmly established in the United States, claimed Arendt, because the "equal opportunity" ideology of American liberalism values difference—in the form of imagination, entrepreneurship, and personal initiative—as a token of success.[4] This ideology enabled Jews in America to assert their distinctiveness and eventually to prosper in the twentieth century, and it provides an opportunity for Muslim Americans to assert their distinctiveness and to prosper today. So far, the United States has not engaged in systematic persecution of Muslims and has been relatively free of anti-Muslim prejudice. However, fear and distrust of Muslims among the general public is fostered by images of insurgent attacks and suicide bombings in Iraq, of Al Qaeda atrocities around the globe, and of increasing expressions of anti-Americanism in the Arabic and Islamic media. In addition, some pundits on talk radio, certain fundamentalist religious leaders, and some members of the conservative press and academia fan the flames of prejudice by portraying Islam as inherently intolerant and by portraying Muslims as slaves to tradition and authoritarianism rather than as advocates of reason and freedom of expression. Clearly, there is still a need to demonstrate to the American public that Muslims are rational human beings and that Islam is a religion that is worthy of respect.

Changing public opinion about Islam and Muslims in the United States and Europe will not be easy. The culture critic Guillermo Gomez-Peña has written that as a result of the opening of American borders to non-Europeans in the 1960s, the American myth of the cultural melting pot "has been replaced by a model that is more germane to the times, that of the *menudo chowder*. According to this model, most of the ingredients do melt, but some stubborn chunks are condemned merely to float."[5] At the present time, Muslims constitute the most visible "stubborn chunks" in the *menudo chowder* of American and European pluralism. Muslims are often seen as the chunks of the *menudo chowder* that most stubbornly refuse to "melt in." To the non-Muslim majoritarian citizen of Western countries, Muslims seem to be the most "uncivil" members of civil society. They do not dress like the majority, they do not eat like the majority, they do not drink like the majority, they do not let their women work, they reject the music and cultural values of the majority, and sometimes they even try to opt out of majoritarian legal and economic systems. In Europe, Islam has replaced Catholicism as the religion that left-wing pundits most love to hate. Americans, however, have been more ambivalent about Islam and Muslims. On the one hand, there have been sincere attempts to include Muslims as full partners in civil society. On the other hand, the apparent resistance of some Muslims to "fit in" creates a widespread distrust that has had legal ramifications in several notable cases.

A useful way to conceive of the problem that Muslims face as members of civil society—both within Western countries and in the global civil society that is dominated by the West—is to recognize, following Homi K. Bhabha, the social fact of Muslim *unhomeliness*. To be "unhomed," says Bhabha, is not to be homeless, but rather to escape easy assimilation or accommodation.[6] The problem is not that the "unhomed" possesses no physical home but that there is no "place" to locate the unhomed in the majoritarian consciousness. Simply put, one does not know what to make of the unhomed. Bhabha derives this term from Sigmund Freud's concept of *unheimlich*, "the name for everything that ought to have remained secret and hidden but has come to light."[7] Unhomeliness is a way of expressing social discomfort. When one encounters the unhomed, one feels awkward and uncomfortable because the unhomed person appears truly alien. Indeed, if there is any single experience that virtually all Muslims in Western countries share, it is that Islam makes non-Muslims uncomfortable. In the global civil society dominated by the West, Muslims are unhomed wherever they may live, even in their own countries.

This reality of Muslim experience highlights how contemporary advocates of Muslim identity politics have often made matters worse by accentuating symbolic tokens of difference between so-called Islamic and Western norms. The problem for Islam in today's global civil society is not that it is not seen. On the contrary, Islam and Muslims are arguably all too visible because they are seen as fundamentally different from the accepted norm. Like the black man in the colonial West Indies or in Jim Crow America, the Muslim is, to borrow a phrase from Frantz Fanon, "overdetermined from without."[8] Muslims have been overdetermined by the press, overdetermined by Hollywood, overdetermined by politicians, and overdetermined by culture critics. From the president of the United States to the prime minister of the United Kingdom, and in countless editorials in print and television media, leaders of public opinion ask, "What do Muslims want?" Such a question forces the Muslim into a corner in which the only answer is apologetics or defiance. To again paraphrase Fanon, the overdetermined Muslim is constantly made aware of himself or herself not just in the third person but in *triple person*. As a symbol of the unhomely, the Muslim is made to feel personally responsible for a contradictory variety of "Islamic" moral values, "Islamic" cultural expressions, and "Islamic" religious and political doctrines.[9]

In the face of such outside pressures, what the overdetermined Muslim needs most is not to be seen, but to be heard. There is a critical need for Islam to be expressed to the world not as an image, but as a narrative, and for Muslims to bear their own witness to their own experiences. The vast majority of books on Islam written in European languages, even the best ones, have been written by non-Muslims. This is not necessarily a problem, because an objective and open-minded non-Muslim can often describe Islam for a non-

Muslim audience better than a Muslim apologist. The scholars Said and Ernst, mentioned above, are both from Christian backgrounds. The discipline of Religious Studies from which Ernst writes has been careful to maintain a nonjudgmental attitude toward non-Christian religions. As heirs to the political and philosophical values of European liberalism, scholars of Religious Studies are typically dogmatic about only one thing: they must practice *epoché* (a Greek word meaning "holding back" or restraining one's beliefs) when approaching the worldview of another religion. In the words of the late Canadian scholar of religion Wilfred Cantwell Smith, it is not enough to act like "a fly crawling on the outside of a goldfish bowl," magisterially observing another's religious practices while remaining distant from the subject. Instead, one must be more engaged in her inquiry and, through imagination and the use of *epoché*, try to find out what it feels like to be a goldfish.[10]

Through the practice of *epoché*, the field of Religious Studies has by now produced two generations of accomplished scholars of Islam in the United States and Canada. Smith himself was a fair and sympathetic Christian scholar of Islam, and his field has been more influential than any other in promoting the study of Islam in the West. However, even Smith was aware that only a goldfish truly knows what it means to be a goldfish. The most that a sympathetic non-Muslim specialist in Islamic studies can do is *describe* Islam from the perspective of a sensitive outsider. Because non-Muslims do not share a personal commitment to the Islamic faith, they are not in the best position to convey a sense of what it means to *be* a Muslim on the inside—to live a Muslim life, to share Muslim values and concerns, and to experience Islam spiritually. In the final analysis, only Muslims can fully bear witness to their own traditions from within.

The five-volume set of *Voices of Islam* is an attempt to meet this need. By bringing together the voices of nearly 50 prominent Muslims from around the world, it aims to present an accurate, comprehensive, and accessible account of Islamic doctrines, practices, and worldviews for a general reader at the senior high school and university undergraduate level. The subjects of the volumes—*Voices of Tradition; Voices of the Spirit; Voices of Life: Family, Home, and Society; Voices of Art, Beauty, and Science;* and *Voices of Change*—were selected to provide as wide a depiction as possible of Muslim experiences and ways of knowledge. Taken collectively, the chapters in these volumes provide bridges between formal religion and culture, the present and the past, tradition and change, and spiritual and outward action that can be crossed by readers, whether they are Muslims or non-Muslims, many times and in a variety of ways. What this set does *not* do is present a magisterial, authoritative vision of an "objectively real" Islam that is juxtaposed against a supposedly inauthentic diversity of individual voices. As the Egyptian-American legal scholar and culture critic Khaled Abou El Fadl has pointed out, whenever Islam is the subject of discourse, the authoritative quickly elides into the authoritarian, irrespective of whether the voice of authority is

Muslim or non-Muslim.[11] The editors of *Voices of Islam* seek to avoid the authoritarian by allowing every voice expressed in the five-volume set to be authoritative, both in terms of individual experience and in terms of the commonalities that Muslims share among themselves.

THE EDITORS

The general editor for *Voices of Islam* is Vincent J. Cornell, Asa Griggs Candler Professor of Middle East and Islamic Studies at Emory University in Atlanta, Georgia. When he was solicited by Praeger, an imprint of Greenwood Publishing, to formulate this project, he was director of the King Fahd Center for Middle East and Islamic Studies at the University of Arkansas. Dr. Cornell has been a Sunni Muslim for more than 30 years and is a noted scholar of Islamic thought and history. His most important book, *Realm of the Saint: Power and Authority in Moroccan Sufism* (1998), was described by a prepublication reviewer as "the most significant study of the Sufi tradition in Islam to have appeared in the last two decades." Besides publishing works on Sufism, Dr. Cornell has also written articles on Islamic law, Islamic theology, and moral and political philosophy. For the past five years, he has been a participant in the Archbishop of Canterbury's "Building Bridges" dialogue of Christian and Muslim theologians. In cooperation with the Jerusalem-based Elijah Interfaith Institute, he is presently co-convener of a group of Muslim scholars, of whom some are contributors to *Voices of Islam,* which is working toward a new theology of the religious other in Islam. Besides serving as general editor for *Voices of Islam,* Dr. Cornell is also the volume editor for Volume 1, *Voices of Tradition;* Volume 2, *Voices of the Spirit;* and Volume 4, *Voices of Art, Beauty, and Science.*

The associate editors for *Voices of Islam* are Omid Safi and Virginia Gray Henry-Blakemore. Omid Safi is Associate Professor of Religion at the University of North Carolina at Chapel Hill. Dr. Safi, the grandson of a noted Iranian Ayatollah, was born in the United States but raised in Iran and has been recognized as an important Muslim voice for moderation and diversity. He gained widespread praise for his edited first book, *Progressive Muslims: On Justice, Gender, and Pluralism* (2003), and was interviewed on CNN, National Public Radio, and other major media outlets. He recently published an important study of Sufi-state relations in premodern Iran, *The Politics of Knowledge in Premodern Islam* (2006). Dr. Safi is the volume editor for Volume 5, *Voices of Change,* which contains chapters by many of the authors represented in his earlier work, *Progressive Muslims.*

Virginia Gray Henry-Blakemore has been a practicing Sunni Muslim for almost 40 years. She is director of the interfaith publishing houses Fons Vitae and Quinta Essentia and cofounder and trustee of the Islamic Texts Society of Cambridge, England. Some of the most influential families in Saudi

Arabia, Egypt, and Jordan have supported her publishing projects. She is an accomplished lecturer in art history, world religions, and filmmaking and is a founding member of the Thomas Merton Center Foundation. Henry-Blakemore received her BA at Sarah Lawrence College, studied at the American University in Cairo and Al-Azhar University, earned her MA in Education at the University of Michigan, and served as a research fellow at Cambridge University from 1983 to 1990. She is the volume editor for Volume 3, *Voices of Life: Family, Home, and Society.*

THE AUTHORS

As stated earlier, *Voices of Islam* seeks to meet the need for Muslims to bear witness to their own traditions by bringing together a diverse collection of Muslim voices from different regions and from different scholarly and professional backgrounds. The voices that speak to the readers about Islam in this set come from Asia, Africa, Europe, and North America, and include men and women, academics, community and religious leaders, teachers, activists, and business leaders. Some authors were born Muslims and others embraced Islam at various points in their lives. A variety of doctrinal, legal, and cultural positions are also represented, including modernists, traditionalists, legalists, Sunnis, Shiites, Sufis, and "progressive Muslims." The editors of the set took care to represent as many Muslim points of view as possible, including those that they may disagree with. Although each chapter in the set was designed to provide basic information for the general reader on a particular topic, the authors were encouraged to express their individual voices of opinion and experience whenever possible.

In theoretical terms, *Voices of Islam* treads a fine line between what Paul Veyne has called "specificity" and "singularity." As both an introduction to Islam and as an expression of Islamic diversity, this set combines historical and commentarial approaches, as well as poetic and narrative accounts of individual experiences. Because of the wide range of subjects that are covered, individualized accounts (the "singular") make up much of the narrative of *Voices of Islam,* but the intent of the work is not to express individuality per se. Rather, the goal is to help the reader understand the varieties of Islamic experience (the "specific") more deeply by finding within their specificity a certain kind of generality.[12]

For Veyne, "specificity" is another way of expressing typicality or the ideal type, a sociological concept that has been a useful tool for investigating complex systems of social organization, thought, or belief. However, the problem with typification is that it may lead to oversimplification, and oversimplification is the handmaiden of the stereotype. Typification can lead to oversimplification because the concept of typicality belongs to a structure of general knowledge that obscures the view of the singular and the different. Thus, presenting the voices of only preselected "typical Muslims" or "representative Muslims" in a work such as *Voices of Islam* would only aggravate the tendency of many Muslims and non-Muslims to define Islam in a single, essentialized way. When done from without, this can lead to a form of stereotyping that may exacerbate, rather than alleviate, the tendency to see Muslims in ways that they do not see themselves. When done from within, it can lead to a dogmatic fundamentalism (whether liberal or conservative does not matter) that excludes the voices of difference from "real" Islam and fosters a totalitarian approach to religion. Such an emphasis on the legitimacy of representation by Muslims themselves would merely reinforce the ideal of sameness that Arendt decried and enable the overdetermination of the "typical" Muslim from without. For this reason, *Voices of Islam* seeks to strike a balance between specificity and singularity. Not only the chapters in these volumes but also the backgrounds and personal orientations of their authors express Islam as a lived diversity and as a source of multiple wellsprings of knowledge. Through the use of individual voices, this work seeks to save the "singular" from the "typical" by employing the "specific."

Dipesh Chakrabarty, a major figure in the field of Subaltern Studies, notes: "Singularity is a matter of viewing. It comes into being as that which resists our attempt to see something as a particular instance of a general idea or category."[13] For Chakrabarty, the singular is a necessary antidote to the typical because it "defies the generalizing impulse of the sociological imagination."[14] Because the tendency to overdetermine and objectify Islam is central to the continued lack of understanding of Islam by non-Muslims, it is necessary to defy the generalizing impulse by demonstrating that the unity of Islam is not a unity of sameness, but of diversity. Highlighting the singularity of individual Islamic practices and doctrines becomes a means of liberating Islam from the totalizing vision of both religious fundamentalism (Muslim and non-Muslim alike) and secular essentialism. While Islam in theory may be a unity, in both thought and practice this "unity" is in reality a galaxy whose millions of singular stars exist within a universe of multiple perspectives. This is not just a sociological fact, but a theological point as well. For centuries, Muslim theologians have asserted that the Transcendent Unity of God is a mystery that defies the normal rules of logic. To human beings, unity usually implies either singularity or sameness, but with respect to God, Unity is beyond number or comparison.

In historiographical terms, a work that seeks to describe Islam through the voices of individual Muslims is an example of "minority history." However, by allowing the voices of specificity and singularity to enter into a trialogue that includes each other as well as the reader, *Voices of Islam* is also an example of "subaltern history." For Chakrabarty, subaltern narratives "are marginalized not because of any conscious intentions but because they represent moments or points at which the archive that the historian mines develops a degree of intractability with respect to the aims of professional history."[15] Subaltern narratives do not only belong to socially subordinate or minority groups, but they also belong to underrepresented groups in Western scholarship, even if these groups comprise a billion people as Muslims do. Subaltern narratives resist typification because the realities that they represent do not correspond to the stereotypical. As such, they need to be studied on their own terms. The history of Islam in thought and practice is the product of constant dialogues between the present and the past, internal and external discourses, culture and ideology, and tradition and change. To describe Islam as anything less would be to reduce it to a limited set of descriptive and conceptual categories that can only rob Islam of its diversity and its historical and intellectual depth. The best way to retain a sense of this diversity and depth is to allow Muslim voices to relate their own narratives of Islam's past and present.

NOTES

1. Carl W. Ernst, *Following Muhammad: Rethinking Islam in the Contemporary World* (Chapel Hill and London: University of North Carolina Press, 2003), xvii.

2. *Time,* June 7, 2004, 10.

3. Hannah Arendt, *The Origins of Totalitarianism,* rev. ed. (San Diego, New York, and London: Harvest Harcourt, 1976), 54.

4. Ibid., 55.

5. Guillermo Gomez-Peña, "The New World (B)order," *Third Text* 21 (Winter 1992–1993): 74, quoted in Homi K. Bhabha, *The Location of Culture* (London and New York: Routledge Classics, 2004), 313.

6. Bhabha, *The Location of Culture,* 13.

7. Ibid., 14–15.

8. Frantz Fanon, *Black Skin, White Masks* (London, U.K.: Pluto, 1986), 116. The original French term for this condition is *surdéterminé*. See idem, *Peau noire masques blancs* (Paris: Éditions du Seuil, 1952), 128.

9. Ibid., 112.

10. Wilfred Cantwell Smith, *The Meaning and End of Religion* (Minneapolis, Minnesota: The University of Minnesota Press, 1991), 7.

11. Khaled Abou El Fadl, *Speaking in God's Name: Islamic Law, Authority, and Women* (Oxford, U.K.: Oneworld Publications, 2001), 9–85.

12. Paul Veyne, *Writing History: Essay on Epistemology,* trans. Mina Moore-Rinvolucri (Middletown, Connecticut: Wesleyan University Press, 1984), 56.

13. Dipesh Chakrabarty, *Provincializing Europe: Postcolonial Thought and Historical Difference* (Princeton and Oxford: Princeton University Press, 2000), 82.

14. Ibid., 83.

15. Ibid., 101.

INTRODUCTION: DAILY LIFE IN ISLAM

———————————————— • ————————————————

Virginia Gray Henry-Blakemore

One always hears Muslims say, "Islam is a way of life." What does this mean? If we entered a Christian home in Louisville, Kentucky, and spent a day with a family, what would we learn about Christianity? Spending a day in a home in Cairo, Egypt, will surely teach us something important about Islam because so much of daily life occurs within the framework and practice of Islam. The chapters in this volume provide the reader with a taste of what is meant by the statement, "Islam is a way of life."

At dawn one hears from the nearest minaret the *adhan,* the call to prayer broadcast by microphone over the surrounding neighborhood: *Allahu akbar! Allahu akbar!*

> God is most great! God is most great!
> God is most great! God is most great!
> I testify that there is no god but God.
> I testify that there is no god but God.
> I testify that Muhammad is the Messenger of God.
> I testify that Muhammad is the Messenger of God.
> Come to prayer! Come to prayer!
> Come to success! Come to success!
> God is most great! God is most great!
> There is no god but God!

As the birds begin to chirp and the mourning doves begin to coo, the members of the family make their way to the washroom to perform their ablutions (*wudu'*) before prayer. This purification is a conscious preparation made in advance in the act of standing before God. At dawn, the ablutions bring one fully into wakefulness, washing away the traces of sleepiness; during the daytime they serve as a transition between the mundane activities of the world and prayer. One makes *wudu'* in order to stand cleansed before God, but *wudu'* is not merely a physical washing. Externally, *wudu'* is the washing of the extremities, which would normally get dirty or dusty from being out in the world: hands (right hand first), mouth, nose, face, arms (right arm first), head, ears, neck, and feet (in this order). However, there are many ways for us to become "dusty" when out in the world. Our hearts can become dusty too.

The following story is often told to Muslim children to familiarize them with the deeper meaning of ablutions in Islam:

> A well-known Muslim scholar was about to go to bed one night when he heard a knock on the door. On his front porch was an old man in ragged clothing and with a torn blanket over his shoulders. The scholar inquired, "Can I help you with anything?"
>
> The old man said, "I'd like for you to teach me to do *wudu'*."
>
> Shocked and a bit annoyed, the scholar said, "What? In all these years has no one taught you to perform the daily ablutions?"
>
> "Yes, my father taught them to me when I was a boy, but you are a wise man and I would like to learn from you."
>
> So the scholar quickly began explaining the motions of the *wudu'*. But the old man persisted, "Please, I would like for you to show me."
>
> The scholar thought, "Can this old man not even understand simple language? Oh, I'll go ahead and show him just to get this over with." So the scholar welcomed the old man in, took him to the sink and began going through the motions quickly, explaining each one.
>
> Afterward, the old man said, "Now I will do the *wudu'* to make sure that I have understood correctly." But the old man proceeded to get everything wrong!
>
> The scholar exclaimed, "No! No! That's all incorrect! Were you not watching? Did you not understand?"
>
> The old man said simply, "I guess you were not able to teach me how to do *wudu'* properly," and he left.
>
> Bewildered but curious, the scholar asked his doorman if he knew the old man. His doorman said "Yes, of course! That is the great saint of our city, well-known all across the Muslim world!"
>
> Shocked and ashamed, the scholar rushed out and went to the house where the saint was known to live. He knocked on the door. When the saint opened it, the scholar knelt at his feet and said, "Please forgive me. Please, sir, teach me to do *wudu'*."
>
> The saint said the following, "There is no need to ask my forgiveness. But there is something you should understand. When you were trying to teach me about *wudu'*, you were talking all the time. That is wrong. When you do *wudu'*, you should concentrate on the ablution alone. You should be praying to Allah to forgive you whatever sins you have committed. You were not doing *wudu'*, you were just washing yourself. *Wudu'* must be done with concentration and repentance. Remember that."[1]

The saint then proceeded to explain that as one washes one's hands, one prays, "Oh God, forgive me for the thoughtless and wrong deeds that I have committed and let what I do from now on be pleasing in Thy sight." As one rinses out the mouth, he implores, "Forgive me for all that I have said that has been low and heedless and may everything I say from now on be permeated with goodness and love." When one wipes the ears, one asks of the Lord, "Please let me only listen to what is blessed and prevent me from opening myself to the hearing of faults and unmerciful chatter!" When wiping the top of one's head, the worshipper should request that God purify his own thoughts and intention so that he may better serve His Creator with humility. As the feet are cleaned, the believer mindfully concentrates on where his feet take him and prays, "Oh Lord, let all of my movements take me nearer to Thy Divine Presence and not in the direction which distances my soul from You."

The ablution in Islam is performed with the intention of asking for forgiveness and renewal—of becoming clean for prayer, when we draw near to God. If you were preparing to spend time with a very important person for whom you had much respect, you would shower and make yourself as presentable as possible. If we take such care for people in this realm, we must surely do the same for God; a physical and mental washing is the very minimum we can do. The following story told by a friend of mine illustrates the importance of preparing with care for the meeting with God:

> A teenage daughter and her friend were going out to meet some friends at a café, but wanted to perform the midday prayer beforehand because they would be out for the greater part of the afternoon. They quickly made their ablutions, and to save time, they threw towels over their heads instead of going upstairs to get their head scarves, as they were only praying among themselves in their own home. They then went into the living room, where the mother was also about to pray.
>
> The mother saw the towels on their heads and asked, with a disapproving eye, "What is this?"
>
> The daughter replied, "Oh mother, we had to be downtown five minutes ago! We're in our own home! Does it really matter?"
>
> The mother replied, "Imagine you were going to meet the Queen of England, would you walk into the palace and right up to her throne to greet her looking like that? No, you would be ashamed. You would take hours to prepare and you would dress up in your very best. This is not the Queen of England you are about to meet. It is God. The King of Kings, the very meaning and source of kinghood and queenhood!"

The point of this story is not that Muslims should spend hours preparing for prayer, but rather to stress the importance of the consideration and care one takes before approaching the Creator and Sustainer of the Universe.

Visitors to the Muslim world are struck by the five prayers that Muslims perform each day and how much prayers are respected by everyone in the society. When a person is being praised it is more common to hear, "He never misses his prayers," than "He is the CEO of this or that company." Often, one will hear, "Well, if we're going to play tennis at the club at four o'clock, we could do the afternoon prayers at a place beforehand, and then be finished in time to do the sunset prayers at such-and-such a place afterward." It is wonderful to see an entire day organized around prayer. It is quite a surprise to be in a busy office and notice that the secretary suddenly stands up from her typing and lays out her prayer rug next to her desk and proceeds to pray. At prayer times, hallways in office buildings stand in for mosques. Prayer is part of the normal flow of daily life.

Muslims often mention how good it is that the five canonical prayers interrupt the daily routine, allowing one to step away from the day's problems and enter into a time and space where one can breathe freely and get in touch, at least for a few minutes, with the sweetness of Ultimate Reality. If a person is talking with a friend about last night's dinner party, for example, and he hears the *adhan,* the call to prayer, immediately he becomes aware of the contrast between the burdensome reality in which he remains and the sacred, freeing space to which he is being called, between the narrowness of the secular world and the expansiveness of the Sacred. When a person is undergoing personal difficulties he may hold, for a while, the position of the prostration (*sajda*) where the forehead touches the ground and one is the most low before God the Most High. At such times, a Muslim has ample opportunity to recognize the reality of human dependence on Divine Mercy.

But, what of the time between the prayers? Does the rest of our life become secular and separate from the atmosphere of prayer? Of course, we may forget the beauty we experience in prayer, but ultimately, the five prayers are reminders of how we should live always, throughout the day and night. Our suffering comes from our distance from God, and our distance truly lies in our forgetfulness. The famous Muslim scholar Abu Hamid al-Ghazali wrote that we should live our lives as if, in one week, the King were coming to stay as a guest in our house. How would we keep house if we knew that the King was coming? And how would we "keep house" if the King was coming to visit the house of our heart? In Islam, the believer must do her best to live impeccably on all levels, always with God in mind.

One way in which this mindfulness becomes apparent is through language. Another thing that strikes the Western visitor to the Muslim world is the frequency with which God is mentioned in ordinary conversations. If you seem a bit agitated, someone may turn to you and quietly counsel, "God is with the one who is patient." If you undergo a trying experience, someone may state, "Put your trust in God." If you are worried about the success of an endeavor, someone may chime in, "God is Powerful over all things." Whenever you admire a possession or a child that belongs to another person, you must be sure to state *Ma sha' Allah* (This is what God has willed) in order to prevent the appearance envy or covetousness. One hears *In sha' Allah* (God willing) all the time in the Muslim world, since one would not dare presume that one's hopes or plans will automatically turn out as one expects; they will only happen if it is the will of God.

The phrase that one hears most often—sometimes in every sentence—is *al-Hamdulillah* (Praise be to God). The reason for this is as follows. As

Muslims, we must be thankful to God for all God gives us in our lives, including both blessings and trials. Instances of success and failure are like course adjustments that always bring us closer to the Center. If we treat all that occurs in our lives as gifts from God, as opportunities for spiritual realization, and accept them with gratitude, we can witness our life as part of an ongoing process of drawing closer to the Creator. It is deeply moving to be present when someone who has just lost a child or has received dreadful news says, *al-Hamdulillah,* praising God with all his heart. The following folk tale illustrates the seriousness with which this attitude of thankfulness is taken in Islam:

> A merchant of Cadiz went to the dock one day to receive his merchandise, which was scheduled to arrive that morning from Tunis. Upon his arrival he was told, "The boat with all of your cargo was shipwrecked and everything was lost." The merchant looked down in the direction of his heart, then looked back up at the man and said, "*al-Hamdulillah.*"
>
> A week later, the merchant received a knock at the door. When he opened it, he saw the man from the dock at his doorstep. He said, "Sir, I was mistaken! It was another boat that shipwrecked last week! The boat with all of your cargo landed safely this morning. Nothing was lost."
>
> The merchant again looked down toward his heart, and then looked back up at the man and said, "*al-Hamdulillah.*"
>
> The man asked, "Why do you always look down first and then say *al-Hamdulillah?*"
>
> The merchant replied, "In order to make sure that there is no change in my heart—whether I have lost everything or lost nothing—that I am truly grateful to God for whatever He decides to give me in this life."

The attitude of Muslims all over the world toward the treatment of the elderly is enviable. In the Islamic world, there are no old people's homes. The strain of caring for one's parents in this most difficult time of their lives is considered an honor and a blessing, and an opportunity for spiritual growth. God asks that we not only pray for our parents but also act toward them with limitless compassion, remembering that when we were helpless children they preferred us to themselves. Mothers are particularly honored: the Prophet Muhammad taught, "Paradise lies beneath the feet of the mothers." When they reach old age, Muslim parents are treated mercifully, with kindness and selflessness.

In Islam, serving one's parents is a duty second only to prayer, and it is the right of the parents to expect it. It is considered despicable to express frustration when, through no fault of their own, the old become difficult to manage. The Qur'an says: "Your Lord has commanded that you worship none but Him, and be kind to parents. If they reach old age with you, do not say 'Uff!' to them or chide them, but speak to them with honor and kindness. Treat them with humility and say, 'My Lord! Have mercy on them for they cared for me when I was little'" (Qur'an 17:23–24).

This volume contains many excellent chapters that will help clarify the nature of personal, family, and commercial life in the Muslim community. In "The Fabric of Muslim Daily Life," Susan L. Douglass investigates what living a day-to-day life as a Muslim really means. She also looks at other societies that do not function within a God-centered framework and discusses the challenges that Muslims face living in such societies. In her chapter, the reader follows a Muslim from the time of arising at dawn through the sacred rhythm and cycle of the day's devotions and activities. Matters discussed include Islamic dress—with considerable discussion of the issue of women's covering—hygiene, permissible food and fasting, public and private activity, family and marital relationships, and the natural world in the view of Islam.

In "Islam, Culture, and Women in a Bangladesh Village," Sarwar Alam separates the reality of Islamic social life from its scriptural ideals and portrays some of the struggles that Muslim women face in the South Asian country of Bangladesh. By presenting the results of original research that he conducted in Bangladesh in 2005, Sarwar demonstrates the influence of adapted perceptions and customary patterns on the way that the scriptures of Islam are understood on the ground. He provides important information on many aspects of social life, including marriage and divorce, inheritance, *parda* (called *purdah* in other South Asian countries), purity and pollution, and the important role of the *shalish,* the village council, in restricting the political and social roles of women in Bangladesh's rural communities. In this chapter, rural women of Bangladesh speak with their own voices through excerpts of hundreds of hours of recordings that Sarwar made during his research. In different ways, they express a sentiment that Sarwar uses to conclude his chapter: "What God gives, a man can take away."

In the chapter "Marriage in Islam," Nargis Virani provides some of the scriptural and legal background for the domestic relations discussed by Sarwar Alam in the previous chapter. Virani discusses the terminological meaning of marriage in Islam, the nonsacramental nature of the marriage contract, the form and stipulations of the contract, and preferred and forbidden marriage partners. She also discusses the Twelver Shiite practice of temporary marriage (*mut'a*), which differs considerably from the permanent marriages contracted by both Sunnis and Shiites. Perhaps the most intriguing part of her chapter is the final section "The Personal Voice: Growing Up in a Polygynous Household," in which she discusses her own experience of growing up in a household where her father had two wives, and her difficulties in expressing what it means to have "two mothers" to immigration authorities and others in the West.

In "The Spiritual Significance of Marriage in Islam," Jane Fatima Casewit expands upon the points made by Virani and discusses the role that Islamic marriage can play in the development and purification of the soul. The purification of the soul is the underlying purpose of Islamic legal prescriptions and is a major goal of the Islamic way of life. If the dissolution of the ego is needed for the attainment of humility and perfect service to God, then marriage provides a perfect opportunity for practicing self-sacrifice, loving mercy, and generosity. Starting from the Qur'anic verse, "And of everything [God] created a pair" (Qur'an 51:49), Casewit explains how the complementarity of man and woman in marriage mirrors the divinely ordained duality that can be found in many aspects of existence. She ends her chapter by discussing marriage and motherhood, bringing up the divine tradition: "I am God and I am the Merciful. I created the womb and I gave it a name derived from My own name. If someone cuts off the womb, I will cut him off, but if someone joins the womb, I will join him to Me."

In "Respect for the Mother in Islam," Aliah Schleifer—may God's mercy shine upon her in the next world—continues the discussion of motherhood in Islam that is started by Casewit. This chapter and the one by Schleifer that follows it, "Pregnancy and Childbirth in Islam," are surveys of motherhood, pregnancy, and childbirth as presented by the most important sources of Islamic teachings and regulations: the Qur'an, Hadith, and Islamic jurisprudence. Schleifer also provides discussions from selected works of the classical tradition of Qur'anic exegesis in Islam. In "The Birth of Aliya Maryam," Seemi Bushra Ghazi describes movingly and poetically her own experience of childbirth as a Muslim woman of South Asian origin. Her evocation of the Virgin Mary during her periods of pregnancy and childbirth is particularly beautiful. It is also touching to learn what it means to a Muslim woman to have lost children that were born before their time.

In Islam, whenever Muslims suffer the trial of illness, they are taught to see this experience as a great blessing and an opportunity for the purification of the soul. Virginia Gray Henry-Blakemore in "Even at Night the Sun is There: Illness as a Blessing from God" describes how her understanding of this outlook carried her through a painful and frightening experience of paralysis. In "Caring for the Ill in Islam," Kristin Zahra Sands tells the poignant story of what it means spiritually to care for a child who struggles with spina bifida and epilepsy. Through her study of the great Islamic saints and mystics, she presents us with multiple levels of giving and caring. The final stage of utterly selfless giving—which is the aim for every person of faith—recalls the example brought to humanity by all of the prophets of the Judeo-Christian-Islamic religious tradition. If we are able to give of ourselves in such a complete and perfect way by truly caring for each other, we will experience the presence of God infusing our very being.

Of all human experiences, life and death are the most important ones that are shared by all people, regardless of religion or origin. In "Death and Burial in Islam," Rkia Elaroui Cornell describes the attitudes and rituals associated with death and dying. As a way of introducing her discussion, she takes the reader along for the ride as she prepares to wash and wrap for burial the body of a young Muslim bride who had suddenly died in Los Angeles, California. In her chapter, she discusses how Muslims deal with death, including suicides and murders, how Islamic tradition describes the experience of death, the nature of the soul and its ascent after death, the reality of the Hereafter, the terrors of the graveyard (especially fascinating are the Moroccan legends of the She-Mule of the Graveyard and "Ali Wants His Hand Back"), the preparation of the body for burial, and the Islamic burial service. In "Reflections on Death and Loss," Imam Feisal Abdul Rauf reflects on the death of his father, a noted Imam and Islamic scholar in the United States, and the tragedy of the earthquake and tsunami of December 2004, which took over 100,000 Muslim lives.

The final two chapters in this volume address personal and social life through the prism of Islamic ethics. Kenneth Lee Honerkamp's "Sufi Foundations of the Ethics of Social Life in Islam " starts with the maxim, "Sufism is ethical conduct. Whoever surpasses you in ethical conduct, surpasses you in Sufism." He goes on to show how the Sufis combined an ethical *via activa* with their spiritual *via contemplativa*. In doing so, they followed the teachings of the Qur'an, the Prophet Muhammad, and early Muslim leaders (*al-Salaf al-Salih*), who continually stressed the complementarity of knowledge and action and the inner and outer dimensions of existence and human responsibility. Particularly important to this tradition were the teachings of the Sufi saint-exemplar, Abu 'Abd al-Rahman al-Sulami (d. 1021 CE), who developed in his followers a deep awareness of the moral consequences of their behavior. Honerkamp heavily draws upon the writings of this tenth-century Sufi to make his point. He provides the reader with a fresh perspective on how and why the teachings of the saint-exemplars of Islamic spirituality continue to resonate within the lives of contemporary Muslims and why these teachings remain as relevant today as they were centuries ago.

Abdulkader Thomas also stresses the interrelationship between ethics and spirituality in the chapter, "Islam and Business." We must not forget the material and mercantile sides of daily life in Islam, which may also be viewed in terms of God's will and justice. Thomas demonstrates to the reader how a concern for the eternal life of the soul is key to understanding the Islamic ethics of business transactions, including banking and investment. If a person takes seriously the role of steward of God's creation and believes that all wealth is a trust given to humanity by God, the businessperson has deep reasons for realizing what Thomas speaks of as a "win–win" situation in commercial affairs. Of particular ethical importance to this endeavor are the avoidance of unlawful profits (*riba*) and various forms of deception (*gharar*) in the practice of business.

For those who know the Islamic world well, what is perhaps so deeply touching about their experiences in this region is the absence of a strictly secular perspective, and the warmth and sweetness of people that literally *live* Islam in their daily lives. These are people who submit to God's Divine will with peace of heart and joy of spirit. The chapters in this volume, along with the exceptional poems by the American Muslim poet Daniel Abdal-Hayy

Moore, provide the reader who has never lived in the Muslim world an opportunity to feel this warmth and taste this sweetness for himself or herself.

NOTE

1.   Janet Ardavan, *Growing Up in Islam* (Essex, United Kingdom: Longman, 1990), 15.

1

THE FABRIC OF MUSLIM DAILY LIFE

•

Susan L. Douglass

It is common to speak of Islam as a "way of life." This means that Islam is more than merely a religion or a set of rituals. Islam is a blueprint for life. Its architect is the Creator and its contractor, Muhammad the final Messenger of God, built a house according to that blueprint and lived in it on earth, as did God's previous Messengers from Jesus to Adam. According to the teachings of the Prophets, religion is not a summer home that may be opened for an occasional visit, to be closed and ignored at other times. Being a Muslim means being a person who constantly strives to submit and draw near to the One God, *Allah. Muslim,* the term for a follower of Islam, thus does not denote a fixed or secured status, nor is it merely a cultural identity to be distinguished from other identities. Rather, it is a process. Submitting to God (*Islam*) means making the effort (*ijtihad,* from the same Arabic root as *jihad*) to have knowledge of God, to follow the guidance humankind has been given throughout human history, and to realize it in every aspect of life. Religion belongs to God, not to human agency. In short, Islam is something one does; it is not something that one possesses. As the Qur'an reminds us:

> It is not righteousness that you turn your faces toward East or West. But it is righteousness to believe in Allah and the Last Day and the Angels and the Book and the Messengers; to spend of your substance out of love for Him, for your kin, for orphans, for the needy, for the wayfarer, for those who ask, and for the ransom of slaves; to be steadfast in prayer and practice regular charity; to fulfill the contracts which you have made; to be firm and patient in suffering and adversity and throughout all periods of panic. Such are the People of Truth, the God-Fearing.

> (Qur'an 2:177)

THE NEED FOR A GOD-CENTERED LIFE

Regardless of a person's wealth, poverty, prominence, or involvement in society, everyone lives within a personal and intimate sphere that can be called "daily life." Daily life is the fabric in which we wrap ourselves. It is also the surface on which we tread, as we move back and forth from private to public spheres. It is the scene where we perceive time as passing heavily or lightly. This time is spent in the presence of the humble self and with people who are most familiar, engaged in the ordinary process of meeting life's needs on a simple or a grand scale. Daily life is also the field on which we live a God-conscious life. It is the main testing ground for such a life, the distinguishing area between sincerity and outward trappings. Either the principles that inform the Shari'a, the Law of Islam, find their implementation in daily life or they remain underutilized ideals.

The God-conscious life is not a prison, nor should it be thought of as an extreme way of life. Many people today have become accustomed to thinking of religion as just one part of life, a segment that may be viewed as desirable or undesirable, bounded by a perception that religion is a limited engagement. A widespread view of moderation in religion is that the "Religion" indicator light on our personal dashboard should not remain on all the time. Remaining on all the time means that our commitment to religion is excessive or extreme. This separation of religion from daily life was an outgrowth of the struggle in the Christian West to overcome the power and authority of religious institutions, which were perceived as a drag on scientific and social progress. The struggle between religion and science is far from over today. However, the clear victory for science in fields such as astronomy, geology, and physics has led to a backpedaling by historically transformed and weakened religious institutions and has led to the compartmentalization of religious belief. Efforts by ethicists to maintain the links between science and religion have been hampered by this compartmentalization. In the political and social realms, the battles over religious tolerance, human rights, and participatory government have widened the rift between religious and secular authority. The continuing perception that religion is an outmoded cultural artifact and a cause for conflict has given credence to the idea that secularization is a desirable goal for human society. Globally, religion has a bad name. With the rising power of nation-states, the ideas of modernization, secularization, and imperialism have become components of a political project whose object seems to be the elimination of religion as a meaningful part of life. Other than the former communist societies' internal efforts against religion, nowhere has this antireligious project been aimed with more potency than against the religion of Islam.

The contemporary discourse about religion is full of contradictions. It remains unclear what secularization is supposed to achieve, or how the religious bathwater is to be thrown away, leaving a healthy secular baby. Often, a person is considered a fundamentalist if she appears to practice her religion at all, especially if she dresses differently or refuses to participate in certain social activities and forms of entertainment, such as drinking alcohol and gambling. It is a common notion that the exercise of free will is restricted by having a comprehensive set of rules to live by, or a demanding set of rituals to perform. Some people are convinced that most rules and rituals are artificial and that individuals should not have to rely on such programming in their daily lives. In addition, many argue that religious ways of life are out of date and are counterproductive or even destructive to human welfare and progress.

Before rejecting the argument for the validity of a God-centered framework for life based on submission to God and the authority of revelation, one should consider the alternative. Today's society demands a great deal from the individual soul. Exposure to electronic media entails significant and pervasive psychological demands. Consider the following familiar vignette: an average adult in a developed country wakes up to a clock radio or a mechanical alarm. The abrupt transition from the bed to the outside world might be postponed a little until she enters the kitchen, the car, or the workplace, but it comes all too soon. At the first moment of consciousness after the quiet of sleep, the environment created by different forms of media takes over, broadcasting the latest news and traffic, reciting the names of the villains and heroes of the moment, and filling the mind with concerns, fears, hopes, and problems. Many people feel duty bound to partake in the news on television, radio, the Internet, or in print. Very few people can ignore it altogether, and some "news junkies" consume news in vast quantities. Hearing these reports, one is forced to respond, to take positions, and to assess oneself in comparison with the proffered ideals, values, and calls for action. There are calls to mind one's health and well-being, to advocate various causes, to measure one's children against expected achievements, and to assess the family in comparison with the societal ideal held up as an example. Standards of financial success are presented for personal comparison. In recent decades, calls to prepare for the financial burdens of the future have become pervasive, and the dire consequences of not doing so are frequently hammered home. Even persons of means are threatened by the idea that they are making the wrong preparations or that they might be missing an investment opportunity. Finally, images of sickness, war, poverty, and natural and human-caused disasters confront us with the needs of their unfortunate victims and remind us of the inability to relieve suffering, however much we may want to help.

Upon getting out of bed, the requirements of the day begin to flood into the consciousness. Hygiene rituals focus on appearance in comparison with others. We desire to be perceived as attractive and successful persons in a manner consistent with socially conditioned images: chiseled body, white teeth, antiseptic breath, fragrance, coiffure, makeup, and clothing. Dissatisfaction with one's appearance is a proven source of self-alienation among both men and women. At the breakfast table, even our foods send out messages on their packaging that demand value judgments and self-assessment. Is the packaged food vitamin enriched, fat- or cholesterol-free, free of preservatives, and liked by kids or moms? Almost everything a person consumes or applies to her body announces itself from the shelf with advertising messages, often accompanied by images of human bodily perfection. Colorful type flashes messages about price, value, health, or danger.

Most of the day is punctuated with messages blaring from radio or television, messaging gadgets, or cell phones, constantly subjecting the mind to a cacophony of conflicting ideas, commands, and exhortations. Individuals are confronted throughout the day with a multitude of situations that call for ethical or moral judgments requiring immediate responses. Individual proclivities, the ability to reflect and reason, the level of awareness of the issues involved, and the individual's moral upbringing all help determine the nature of one's responses. Multiplied by the days of the year, the passing decades, and phases of life, the sum total of these demands on the conscious and unconscious mind amounts to a pervasive, externally generated regimen. Combined with the responsibilities of caring for self and family and earning a living, this form of life surely deserves to be called a "Rat Race."

By contrast, a God-centered life cultivates a spiritual consciousness and reaches beyond the world of physical experiences toward the unseen. The most important aspect of any act, according to Islamic teachings, is the intention behind it. This is called *niyya* in Arabic. The Prophet Muhammad is reported to have said, "The reward of deeds depends upon one's intention; every person will get a reward according to what he has intended."[1] Spiritual discipline entails guidance about things one should and should not do, but it is also accompanied by an invitation to engage the faculty of reason, a constructive reminder and source of recentering, regeneration and renewed purpose. A God-centered life in Islam is not an inward-looking, monastic life, but one that reminds the believer of the central purpose of this life and places the demands of the external society in perspective by comparing its demands with the limitless power and presence of God. This consciousness is a source of strength, not of weakness.

A disciplined life in Islam offers an approach to handling the rigors of life, and especially for resisting its manipulations and ordering one's priorities and responses. It is a means of supporting the comprehensive incorporation of Islamic teachings into all aspects of life, from the ordinary to the most far-reaching. Such a discipline does not preclude participation in the modern regimen as described above. In fact, Islamic teachings do not require or prefer an isolated, monastic life away from society, nor a communalistic existence within religious enclaves. Muslims can and do enjoy living in both majority Muslim countries and in countries where they live as minorities. Wherever they live, Muslims find ways to maintain a way of life that is intertwined with Islam. This is the purpose of Islamic self-discipline. Islam is flexible, so Muslims can adapt to life anywhere on the globe. This fact has led Islam to become a cosmopolitan, global religion. The popular notion that Muslims would rather live separately, in a veiled, mysterious, and impenetrable isolation, is entirely false.

The formal act of accepting Islam is simple. In the presence of two witnesses, a person simply recites the *Shahada,* the Testimony of faith. The Arabic formula of the Shahada is *La ilaha illa Allah wa Muhammadun Rasulullah* (There is no god but God and Muhammad is the Messenger of God). This statement connotes the idea of a God that is as near as one's jugular vein but is also transcendent and requires no physical image. The second part of the Shahada places the Prophet Muhammad in the context of the sacred history of humanity. He is the last of a long and broad river of God's Messengers since Adam, all sent to guide and instruct human beings. Acceptance of Islam brings immediate changes in the daily life of the individual, just as the spread of Islam to a locality introduces institutions that make such changes permanent.

Five acts of worship are obligatory for every Muslim above the age of puberty who is sane and in possession of the physical or material means to carry them out. These acts of worship, called the Five Pillars of Islam, form the universal foundation of Islamic culture and civilization. The fact that these five practices are performed by all Muslims explains the unity within the diversity of Muslims around the world. Apart from the Shahada, these practices are Prayer, Charity, Fasting, and Pilgrimage. Each of these pillars of Islam has both a spiritual and a worldly significance, and each impresses itself in different ways upon the individual and the community. Each pillar also brings forth cultural expressions and institutions that are reflected in multiple dimensions of human life.

ISLAM: A PATTERN FOR DAILY LIFE

Human relationships may be imagined as a web or a matrix in three dimensions, in which individuals are located in interlocking webs that intersect with the webs of other people. These relations can be mapped within a single lifetime or onto succeeding generations. A hallmark of Islamic teachings is the way in which they allow people to view themselves and others in terms of the responsibilities and expectations appropriate to the multiple relationships in which they participate. Taken as a whole, this matrix describes a web of relations extending from God and the self to the family, the community, the world, and the universe.

The main responsibility of the Muslim is to the Creator. This relationship is described in Islamic teachings as one of gratitude and indebtedness. The Qur'an describes the central obligation of each person to believe and to worship, but the relationship is reciprocal, as the covenant of God grants mercy and everlasting life to the one who fulfills it. Giving oneself to God is described as a goodly exchange whose reward is unimaginable. The concept of homage and indebtedness to the Creator has three implications. First, such homage may be granted to no person or created being, but only to

God. This is the central idea of *tawhid*, the concept of the oneness of God in Islam. Second, this relationship means that we do not have the right to act according to whim, nor are we supposed to wrong our souls, which is how the Qur'an describes sin. We are creatures of God to whom life and physical existence has been entrusted. This means we may neither abuse nor take our own lives nor those of others with abandon. In Islam, suicide is the most heinous act after associating other deities with God.

Third, Islam requires worship, obedience, and submission to God. The purpose of worship is to renew and purify the self and the soul, and it is a path to achieving peace through submission. The teachings of the Qur'an and the Sunna outline the duties and specific rites of worship. These rites are both physical and spiritual on the one hand and worldly and otherworldly on the other. The collective expression of worship joins believers together and acts as a bridge to the universal community of souls. Beyond obligatory worship, individual striving increases the capacity to draw near to God. However, worship must not be taken to excessive lengths; and other rights and duties maintain the balance between these dimensions.

Prayer and Supplication

A Muslim is obliged to awaken at dawn for the morning (*fajr*) prayer at the sound of the call to prayer, the *adhan*, which echoes from the mosques in any village, town, or city in the Muslim world. Apart from mosques, the *adhan* is called in any place where Muslims gather for prayer. It may be called by an elder such as the head of a household, by a boy of sufficient knowledge, or by a woman or a girl among other women. The times for calling the prayer may be determined by the observation of the sun and shadows or calculated with sophisticated mathematical and astronomical instruments. Today, prayer charts based on astronomical calculations are published for urban locations, and personal electronic devices are programmed to broadcast the call to prayer at the proper times anywhere in the world.

Upon waking in the morning, it is considered good to pronounce a short invocation, such as "Praise be to God who gives us life after He has caused us to die, and unto Him is the return," which is one of many prayers and supplications taught by the Prophet Muhammad.[2] After rising, a Muslim performs the ritual washing or ablution (*wudu'*) that is required before each prayer. This washing must be performed with a pure source of water. If pure water cannot be found, it is permissible to strike the hands on pure earth, sand, or dust, shake them off, and then symbolically cleanse the hands and face. According to a tradition of the Prophet Muhammad, "When a servant of Allah washes his face for ablution, every sin he contemplated with his eyes will be washed away from his face along with the water, or with the last drop of water. When he washes his hands, every sin they have wrought will be effaced from his hands with the water, or with the last drop of water. When he washes his feet, every sin towards which his feet have walked will be washed away with the water, or with the last drop of water, with the result that he emerges pure from all sins."[3]

When a person proceeds to the place of prayer in the home or at the mosque, she may find that others may already have begun to perform the voluntary units of prayer. Then everyone performs the morning or *Fajr* prayer, followed by supplications. After the prayer, in the quiet of the morning, many Muslims read the Qur'an until sunrise. The habit of rising for the prayer at dawn encourages Muslims to begin their day's activities early and many find this quiet time very productive.

Prayer in Islam is a simple act that engages body and mind and consists of a cycle of movement and recitation called a *rak'a*. It is performed identically by men, women, and children. The recitation of the prayer is in Arabic, so that the Qur'anic passages are repeated in the language in which they were revealed. The desire of Muslims to

The Muslim Call to Prayer

1. *Allahu akbar* Allah is Great (said four times).
2. *Ashhadu an la ilaha illa Allah* I bear witness that there is no god but God (said two times).
3. *Ashhadu anna Muhammadan Rasul Allah* I bear witness that Muhammad is the Messenger of God (said two times).
4. *Hayya 'ala-s-Sala* Hurry to prayer (said two times).
5. *Hayya 'ala-l-Falah* Hurry to success (said two times).
6. *Allahu akbar* Allah is Great (said two times).
7. *La ilaha illa Allah* There is no god but God.

For the morning *(fajr)* prayer, the following phrase is inserted after Part 5 above: *As-salatu khayrun min an-nawm* Prayer is better than sleep (said two times).

learn Arabic stems from this obligation to pray in Arabic, but it also extends to the desire to acquire access to the original language of Islamic learning.

Standing, the Muslim begins the prayer with a recitation similar to the call to prayer, and then recites the opening chapter of the Qur'an, *al-Fatiha,* followed by at least three other verses of the Qur'an. Bowing from the waist, in an act called *ruku',* the Muslim recites praises to God, and then stands again, kneels with forehead, hands, knees, and toes touching the ground, in a posture called *sajda* or *sujud.* This term is often mistranslated as "prostration," which literally means lying face down rather than kneeling. The Arabic word for mosque, *masjid,* is related to *sujud* and means "place of performing *sujud.*"

The Muslim Ablution (*wudu'*)

1. Form the intent of performing ablution for the purpose of worship and purification by saying *Bismillah ar-Rahman ar-Rahim* In the Name of God the Beneficent, the Merciful (said one time).

2. Wash the hands up to the wrists, three times.

3. Rinse out the mouth with water, three times.

4. Clean the nostrils by sniffing up a small amount of water and then blowing it out away from the basin of clean water, three times.

5. Wash the face three times with both hands, from the top of the forehead to the bottom of the chin and from ear to ear.

6. Wash the right arm three times up to the far end of the elbow, and then repeat with the left arm.

7. Wipe the head once with the wet right hand.

8. Wipe the inner sides of the ears one time with the forefingers and the outer sides one time with the thumbs.

9. Wash the feet up to the ankles three times, beginning with the right foot.

The rhythm of the daily life of Muslims is set by the five obligatory prayers, which measure out the times of day and night in universally understood increments. Appointments between Muslims are often set according to the times of the daily prayers. In Muslim countries, businesses close down briefly at these times. The times for prayer were generally stated in the Qur'an and were fixed more exactly by the Prophet Muhammad, which he related as the direct teaching of the Angel Gabriel. Although it is best to perform the prayers at their appointed times, a certain amount of flexibility is allowed to account for the needs of daily life. The dawn (*fajr*) prayer is performed at the first light of dawn up to the beginning of sunrise. The noon (*zuhr*) prayer is called just after noon but can be performed up to mid-afternoon. At that time, the afternoon (*asr*) prayer is called. It may be performed up to the beginning of sunset, although Muslims are instructed not to delay it. The sunset (*maghrib*) prayer takes place immediately after sunset. Finally, the evening (*isha'*) prayer, the last obligatory prayer of the day, is called between the end of twilight and the passing of the first third of the night. In general, it may be performed any time before midnight. In addition to the obligatory prayers, voluntary prayers may also be performed as established by Prophet Muhammad. Among these are prayers during the small hours of the night. Muhammad taught his followers to pray at night but cautioned them not to be excessive in worship, to the neglect of obligations toward family and community.

ISLAM AND THE FULFILLMENT OF BASIC NEEDS

Islamic principles and guidelines cover the way in which Muslims fulfill basic requirements of clothing, food, and shelter. These involve duties and obligations for the individual person and other family members, who cooperate to meet basic needs in a reciprocal relationship. God has measured out provision for His creatures in the form of material things, which are acquired through labor and economic exchanges. Islamic legal rulings that cover permissible and impermissible acts for Muslims often involve guidance on the consumption or avoidance of material goods. The acceptance of what is *halal,* or permitted, and the avoidance of what is *haram,* forbidden or discouraged, sets the tone for a healthy and sound way of life. A constant part of daily life is seeking God's blessing in the provision of material things, through acknowledgment that each person has power only through the power of God and through submission to what God reveals about the best manner of fulfilling the needs of daily life.

Hygiene and Clothing

Out of the duty toward God that derives from the gift of life comes the duty to care for the physical body and the mind. The rights given by God in Islam begin with dignity, which pertains to life, and reason, which pertains to the mind. The integrity of the relationship between God and the human being—the broader concept of religion (*din*) in Islam—is also inviolate. Cleanliness supports purity of body and mind, and the daily rituals of washing, bathing, grooming, and dressing are performed with the intention and invocation of blessings from God.

The preservation of health grows out of the obligation to care for the body and the mind. Central to this obligation is the avoidance of excess in food and drink and the avoidance of substances that harm the body or the mind. Self-mutilation as part of religious rites or in response to grief is also forbidden. While patience in suffering is enjoined upon Muslims, putting oneself in needless danger is a violation of God's trust in the human being. Mutilating the body through scarring, tattoos, or any such cultural practices are forbidden despite their long heritage. In Islam, knowledge of God's commands and common sense in carrying them out are the final arbiters of culture. Emulating the example of the Prophet in personal cleanliness includes frequent bathing, caring for the hair, and making one's appearance clean and pleasant. Other matters of personal hygiene recommended by prophetic example are keeping the nails and hair trimmed. Weekly baths before Friday prayers, bathing after sexual relations and menstrual periods, and washing the private parts with water after using the toilet are universally recognized Islamic requirements for personal hygiene. The Prophet Muhammad frequently cleaned his teeth, using the fibrous twig of the Acacia tree that was peeled or chewed to make a brushlike ending. These natural toothbrushes, called *miswak* or *siwak,* are still widely used by Muslims. According to a hadith, Allah's Messenger said, "If I had not found it hard for my followers or the people, I would have ordered them to clean their teeth with *siwak* before every prayer."[4]

The Prophet Muhammad's example extended to the etiquette of personal care for hygienic, aesthetic, and spiritual reasons. For example, using the right hand for eating, drinking, putting on clothing, and receiving and giving gifts was enjoined for both hygienic and spiritual reasons. For example, dressing and washing begin with the right side of the body; stepping into a mosque is done with the right foot out of respect for the sacredness of the place; however, stepping out of a mosque and into a bathroom is done with the left foot because with such actions one enters into a space that is profane. A Muslim should not reveal herself to others while using the toilet, nor should she face in the direction of prayer. Special prayers and supplications for many occasions of daily life remind the Muslim to perform each act with full intent and a God-conscious frame of mind.

Islamic Principles of Dress

Dress in Islam is governed by the principle of modesty. However, the degree of modesty required varies according to the situation in which the individual finds oneself. In private, a Muslim is supposed to observe humility and modesty even when alone. Between husband and wife, there are no requirements for covering the body, nor is there any discouragement of taking pleasure in physical beauty in this intimate setting. On the contrary, each partner is enjoined to provide comfort and pleasure for the other, as a gift of God and as a reinforcement of the marital bond. In the home, Muslims are required to dress modestly but casually in the presence of extended family members such as parents or in-laws, and around those whom one may not marry, including children. Siblings, whether of the same or different gender, cover themselves out of modesty and respect for one another's sensibilities as well.

Men must cover themselves between the waist and the knee in all circumstances except with their wives. The Prophet Muhammad's example of dress was to be covered in a dignified manner when not performing strenuous labor, and this example has been followed by Muslim men throughout history. The idea of flaunting one's physique through provocative clothing is as foreign to the Islamic tradition for men as it is for women. Over time, a style of public dress for men that emphasizes both modesty and dignity developed, in which a loose shirt and pants are worn at a minimum, often with an overgarment such as a cloak or coat. Head coverings also became standard for public attire. The dignified image of the mature male who wears a long garment or shirt and trousers, covered by a tailored robe, cloak, or coat, and often topped by a long scarf or shawl, is one that resonates across cultures in graduation ceremonies, doctor's attire, clerical vestments, and judicial robes. Such an image is not specific to Islam, but rather reflects universally the dignity of the spiritual and intellectual powers of the human being.

When a woman who has reached puberty appears in public, the body is to be covered to a greater degree than in any other situation where she appears. A Muslim woman is required to protect her modesty in the presence of persons outside the family whom she is eligible to marry, by covering all of the body except the face and hands. Women's garments are supposed to conceal the figure by being opaque, and by a form that is loose and does not accentuate the figure. In the modern period, a style of dress involving multiple layers of clothing has become typical of Muslim women's dress.

To understand the principle of Islamic dress, whether for men or women, it is useful to consider the Western business suit. The appearance and function of this costume closely corresponds to the concept of public dress for women and men in Islam. The business suit confers modesty by conforming almost exactly to the requirements for Muslim women's public appearance: it covers all but the head and the hands, and does so in a way that is sober, often with dark, uniform color, and a shape that conceals more than it reveals. It speaks of uniformity and conformity far more than does modern Muslim clothing, with its variety of shapes, colors, and styles. The modern business suit, like Muslim clothing, is intended to level the differences among people, dignify the wearer, and place one in a professional, purposeful light before strangers. Interestingly, images of summit meetings of world leaders or business leaders reveal that the cultural norm of the business suit does not include the female attendees at such events. Among the dark-suited men who look as uniform as penguins, the occasional woman stands out by wearing a short-skirted suit in a bright color, her hair carefully coiffed. The best way to think of the difference between Muslim and Western norms of dress is as follows: In Western culture, the norm of understated dress that completely covers the body is applied to the male, whereas in Islam, it is applied to the female. In nature, does it matter which gender of bird has the plumage, and which has the neutral feathers?

The foregoing discussion does not include more extreme forms of cover that are traditionally worn in some Muslim regions and among certain classes of women. Some women prefer to cover their faces with the veil (*niqab*) because they want to emulate the Prophet Muhammad's wives, or because they have chosen to conceal themselves from men's gazes in public. Costumes like the *burqa* or the *chador,* or elaborate face veils simply carry the concept of modesty further than basic coverage. They are more limiting to free movement and access to significant activities and technologies of modern life, such as riding escalators, driving automobiles, and boarding public transportation. Women themselves perpetuate these types of dress through everyday decisions to wear them, although there have been extreme cases of civil enforcement by reactionary regimes. Less restrictive forms of Muslim women's dress have developed out of the choices exercised by Muslim women who work, study, and insist on the right to live active lives. In many Muslim countries and increasingly on the Internet, lines of fashion are sold to meet these needs and tastes. In Western countries, selective shopping allows Muslim women to clothe themselves according to Islamic traditions of modesty by purchasing pieces off the racks of mainstream department stores.

A gathering of Muslim women reveals the entire range of practice in dress. Some wear the *niqab* face veil, gloves, and capacious, multilayered, neutral-colored gowns, revealing nothing of their physical appearance in public. Others wear long skirts, light coats, jackets, long shirts or pants, and scarves. Some wear most or all of the former, but choose not to cover their heads, or choose to dress in a way that does not distinguish them as Muslim women in a crowd. On the far end of the spectrum from the *niqab* is the Muslim woman who embraces Western fashion and chooses to wear as revealing a costume—or nearly so—as current fashion and her taste dictate. The way a Muslim woman dresses is her personal choice.

The cultural politics of Muslim women's head covering (today called *hijab*) offers a remarkable case study in cultural and gender politics. While some governments of Muslim countries force women to wear the head covering by law, others forbid it in certain contexts. Both male and female Muslims often base their judgments about a woman's piety or morality upon the presence or the absence of the head covering. Some Muslim women view rejection of the head covering as a laudable decision and as an expression of personal freedom. Many academic commentators on Islam have explained the head covering as a political and even anti-Western or antimodern statement, rather than as a personal, religious statement. For this reason, lawmakers in France have banned the wearing of head coverings in government schools. One might imagine that the widespread Western concern for human rights would discount such arbitrary attributions of motive as a basis for state policy, but apparently such a threshold of religious tolerance is too high to allow for expressions of personal piety in French schools. Thus, we have the farcical spectacle of non-Muslim Western parliamentarians arguing in their august bodies about the Qur'anic foundations of Islamic law on the subject of women's dress. At the very least, the controversy over this simple practice of piety should arouse the suspicion of critical observers. The contested ground involves power politics on both sides: on the one side, self-appointed arbiters of Westernization insist that women should show their hair, while on the other side, self-appointed arbiters of Muslim *female*

modesty insist that women should conceal it. In both cases, the bodies of
Muslim women are used by others—usually men—as an ideological battle-
ground.

The Qur'anic verses most commonly cited as the basis for the practice
of modesty by both genders—and specifically for the women's practice of
covering their heads in public—is the following:

> Tell the believing men to lower their gaze and be modest. That is purer for them.
> Lo! God is Aware of what they do. And tell the believing women to lower their
> gaze and be modest, and to display of their adornment only that which is appar-
> ent, and to draw their veils (*khumurihinna*) over their bosoms (*juyubihinna*),
> and not to reveal their adornment.... Turn unto God together, O believers, in
> order that you may succeed.

(Qur'an 24:30–31)

The literal meaning of the term *khumurihinna* (singular *khimar*) is "their
coverings," but it is translated here as "their veils," which refers to a specific
type of covering for the face. In other words, it is an acquired cultural and
regional meaning associated with an article of clothing. The object of the
covering required in the verse is *juyubihinna*, literally, "their bosoms or
breasts." Nowhere in the verse is the term "their faces" (the Arabic would
be *wujuhihinna*) used, although the Prophet Muhammad's wives are said
to have concealed their faces in public. At a minimum, scholars have interpreted this verse as commanding that women should not go bare-breasted
in public, a practice that was followed in some ancient cultures. At a
maximum, this verse has been used as evidence that women must conceal
their faces from public view.

Without engaging in too much interpretation, one can discuss this matter
at the level of fabrics and practical considerations. It is possible to draw a fabric used for covering the head over the face in order to cover the chest, or a
strip of fabric can be wrapped around the head, neck, chest, and shoulders,
leaving the face or even the head free. Practically speaking, one would not
achieve the objective of covering both the chest and the face unless the fabrics
were both dark and sheer, a requirement that in the sixth century CE could
only have meant fine silk or linen fabric, an expensive luxury. A heavy fabric
over the face would render the wearer blind, and a sheer fabric might be
too transparent to exclude the view from without. Precedent in the time of
the Prophet Muhammad seems to indicate some latitude for choice in the
matter of covering the face. Centuries of regional and historical custom in
Islamic dress have resulted in a staggering array of sheer, opaque, perforated,
masked, wrapped, tied, pinned, layered, sculpted, draped, embellished, and
unembellished fabrics to carry out the intended meaning of this verse. Both
Western academics and some Islamic activists have tended to overlook this
diversity of practice by referring uniformly to "veiling" or "the veil." Such

scholars and political leaders have helped to make the veil a metaphor for Muslim women—and for Islam itself—by objectifying Muslim women in the process.

A particularly interesting twist in this contemporary dispute can be traced to another Qur'anic verse upon which the practice of wearing a modest, enveloping public dress is based:

> O Prophet! Tell your wives and your daughters and the women of the believers to draw their cloaks around them [when they go out of the house]. That will be better, that so they may be recognized and not annoyed. Allah is ever Forgiving, Merciful.

> (Qur'an 33:59)

No doubt, opaque clothing that visually masks the body sends a different message than clothing that reveals and enhances its form. Thus, the mere functionality of women's Islamic dress goes beyond the issue of conformity to cultural norms. Conformity to local cultural norms does, however, determine whether the person wearing such clothing is recognized as a Muslim: depending on the circumstances, it may make a woman more or less vulnerable to being bothered, annoyed, or even singled out for persecution. Muslim women in distinctively Islamic dress are instantly identifiable to others. A woman who wraps on a scarf a certain way in a non-Muslim country instantly becomes a minority representative who may well be tasked with explaining a host of doctrinal and cultural matters related to Islam. She had better be prepared to do so. The same is true of the woman who wears "Islamic" dress in a Muslim country where fashion is a matter of cultural politics. Depending on whether the woman is in Cairo, Egypt, or Cairo, Illinois, the role she is required to play may vary, but it will be predictable just the same.

A Muslim man, by contrast, can wear clothing that completely camouflages and neutralizes his religious identity. A Muslim man can escape both the recognition and the consequences that may result from revealing his identity in public. The practice of wearing the *hijab*, therefore, puts the Muslim woman directly on the front lines of the wars of cultural identity and in the forefront of Muslim evangelism (*da'wa*), whether she wants to be there or not. In countries such as Turkey, France, Germany, or Tunisia, wearing Islamic head covering in the wrong context may have legal or civil consequences of a serious nature. In Saudi Arabia, the lack of a head covering may have legal consequences, and in Western countries, it may result in lot of conversations in the supermarket checkout line or in the need to develop a flameproof exterior against public stares. A minority of Muslim men living in Western countries eschew local cultural norms in favor of traditional Muslim dress, such as ankle-length shirts and overgarments, and caps or turbans on their heads. Such men share the public experiences of their

Muslim sisters. In short, the controversy surrounding Muslim dress often creates postmodern situations that turn tradition and status quo thinking on its head. Without forcing any specific conclusions, there are certainly many lessons to be gleaned within the range of possible discourses on the topic.

Permissible Foods

When Muslims eat, they start with a blessing of *Bismillah* (an abbreviated form of "In the name of God, the Beneficent, the Merciful"), and an additional prayer of blessing. When taking food, Muslims also pronounce one of several possible invocations, such as: "Oh God, bless us in that which You have provided for us, and shield us from the fire." When the meal is complete, Muslims close with, "Praise be to God, who fed us and gave us drink, and made us Muslims."

The concepts of *halal* (permitted) and *haram* (forbidden) foods provide common guidelines for a diversity of diets and cuisines among Muslims. A verse of the Qur'an outlines the few prohibitions that Muslims have to observe: "[God] has only forbidden you carrion and blood and the flesh of swine and anything over which a name other than that of Allah has been invoked. But if one is forced [to eat forbidden foods] by necessity and without willful disobedience nor transgressing due limits, then Allah is Oft-Forgiving Most Merciful" (Qur'an 16:115). This verse forbids four categories of meats—the flesh of an animal that has died naturally, food made with blood, pork, and the flesh of an animal that has been consecrated to a god other than Allah—with the important exception that these may be eaten by Muslims in case of desperate hunger. The Qur'an also mentions the rites that must be observed to make consumption of animals permissible. "To every people did We appoint rites that they might celebrate the name of God over the sustenance He gave them from animals; but your god is one God: submit then your wills to Him and give the good news to those who humble themselves" (Qur'an 22:34). The ritual sacrifices that mark Islamic celebrations such as 'Id al-Fitr (the Feast of Fast-breaking after Ramadan) and 'Id al-Adha (the Feast of Sacrifice that marks the end of the Hajj pilgrimage) are very similar to the regular slaughtering for food, except in their special intent and the type of animal required for these special occasions. Sacrifice in Islam always involves distribution of the meat among family, friends, and the needy. As the Qur'an says, "It is neither their meat nor their blood that reaches Allah: it is your piety that reaches Him" (Qur'an 22:37).

The rites for slaughtering an animal for food require the person performing the act to pronounce the name of God in the formula, *Bismillah ar-Rahman ar-Rahim, Allahu akbar* (In the name of God, the Beneficent and the Merciful, God is Great!). The killing must be done quickly with a long, extremely sharp knife, slitting the jugular vein, the carotid artery, the windpipe, and the esophagus but not decapitating the animal. This rule is very similar to that followed by Kosher butchers in Judaism. Because animals slaughtered in the typical industrial method are often stunned with an electric bolt to the head, for some Muslims this would mean that such animals had died before slaughter, thus rendering them forbidden. Debates have been conducted about the relative humaneness of killing by the industrial method versus the traditional Kosher or Halal methods of slitting the throat with a very sharp knife. Islamic law requires humane treatment up to the moment of death. The animal is not to be harshly restrained, nor hoisted up by chains, nor is the animal to see the knife. Skillful slaughter brings about a quick and relatively painless death. According to studies of the correctly performed Halal method of slaughter, the animal registers little pain and dies quickly, but the heart continues to pump blood out of the body, which purifies the meat from potential disease.[5] Muslims are not allowed to eat blood in any form, except for what remains in the meat after draining. The list of animals that Muslims may eat includes all domestic birds, cattle, sheep, goats, camels, all types of deer, and rabbits. Fish and seafood such as mollusks need not be ritually slaughtered. The kinds of animals that are forbidden to Muslims include any animal that has already been killed or strangled, the pig and all of its food by-products (including rendered bones and cartilage that produce gelatin), carnivorous animals and birds of prey, rodents, reptiles, all insects except locusts, and mules or donkeys.[6] All other foods are permissible, unless a forbidden substance has been processed with it, or if it has been fermented to produce alcoholic content.

Muslims are encouraged in the Qur'an to "Eat of the things that Allah has provided for you, lawful and good: but fear Allah in whom you believe" (Qur'an 2:172). The word that is used in this verse for good and lawful foods is *tayyibat*, "beneficial provisions." Many permissible and beneficial foods are mentioned in the Qur'an, including fruits, vegetables, herbs, grains, milk, honey, and Halal meats as described above. With today's industrially prepared foods, eating what is lawful requires effort, education, and research to avoid questionable products. Food additives such as gelatin, vitamins derived from animal products, and animal fats used in processing make many food items questionable, along with the fact that industrial processing, packaging, and transport may introduce forbidden substances into otherwise permissible foods. The recent emphasis on avoiding cholesterol has been a boon for Muslims in the United States because products that once contained lard now proudly proclaim only vegetable fats. New labeling laws also help Muslims select permissible foods. Preparing young Muslim children for visits to the candy store or the cereal aisle gives many youngsters their first lesson in internalizing Islamic values.

Muslims are specifically permitted to eat meat slaughtered by Jews and Christians. This provision fosters social mingling because it makes it easier for Muslims to intimately socialize with the People of the Book. However, Muslims may not eat meat over which an invocation to any deity other than Allah has been made. This rule prevents some South Asian Muslims from eating at vegetarian restaurants owned by Hindus. It does not apply to Christians and Jews, however, since God in these religions is the same as the God of Islam. A religion that requires dietary isolation among people who worship the same God would prevent sharing among neighbors and visits among all sorts of associates. This would create great difficulties for people who convert to Islam, since the Islamic requirement to keep good relations with their birth families would conflict with their inability to eat with them. Among religiously heterogeneous neighbors in Muslim regions, the sharing of food among neighbors of different faiths is common, and it is frequently mentioned in literature. Not all Muslims in Western societies take full advantage of this permission, however, or seem to understand it fully.

The well-known Islamic prohibition against wine extends to all fermented alcoholic beverages that might be made from dates or grains (such as beer and distilled spirits). Addressing the Prophet Muhammad and the questions raised by his followers, the Qur'an states, "They ask you concerning wine and gambling. Say: 'In them is great sin and some profit for men; but the sin is greater than the profit.' They ask you how much they are to spend. Say: 'What is beyond your needs.' Thus does Allah make clear to you His Signs in order that ye may consider" (Qur'an 2:219). Another verse states, "Satan seeks only to cast among you enmity and hatred by means of strong drink and games of chance and to turn you from the remembrance of Allah and from worship. Will you then not abstain?" (Qur'an 5:91) Both verses justify the prohibition against drinking and gambling by describing the harm involved in them, even while acknowledging that they contain a certain benefit. Muslim scholars have interpreted the prohibition against wine as extending to any intoxicating substance, including drugs that cloud the mind and inhibit self-control.

The question of tobacco and smoking is more complex. No matter how widespread the addiction to tobacco and smoking may be among Muslims, few claim that it is beneficial, and multiple arguments exist for its prohibition or avoidance. It is costly and falls into the category of wasting money, since it has no nutritional or medicinal benefit. Its health risks are certain, with the risk of lung cancer, heart attack, and emphysema among smokers, including the known risk of secondhand smoke that endangers others. In general, Muslims have a responsibility to care for their own health, making it forbidden to harm the body in any way. This forms a strong argument against tobacco, in addition to the loss of self-control that accompanies any addiction.

Fasting

During the ninth lunar month of Ramadan, all adult Muslims of sound mind and body are obliged to fast for a period of 29 or 30 days. During Ramadan, the day begins with a predawn meal known as *suhur*. This might consist of a few dates and some water or it might even be a complete meal. After performing the dawn prayer, many Muslims conduct their day as usual; however, for some, daily life shifts toward the evening during Ramadan. The *iftar* meal that breaks the fast at sunset might be simple or elaborate, the former being the Prophetic example, whereas the latter is a widespread cultural practice.

The Qur'an describes fasting as an act of worship, a physical and spiritual self-discipline that was enjoined on all Prophets and pious people from time immemorial. To fast means to abstain from food and drink, sexual contact, conflict, arguments, and unkind language or acts. A traveler may break the fast and make up days later, as do menstruating women. People who are ill or whose condition would make fasting a health risk, including women who are pregnant or nursing, may compensate by preparing food for others or donating money (obligatory on Muslims who cannot fast). Children often participate in the fast but are not required to fast until reaching puberty. The Prophet Muhammad taught that while he himself fasted for long periods outside of Ramadan, other Muslims should not fast more than every other day during other months of the year. The Prophet preferred Mondays and Thursdays for voluntary fasting, and forbade fasting on Friday, the day of the communal *Jumu'a* prayer.

Ramadan is a time of increased fellowship among family members, neighbors, and friends, who share meals on many nights, attend prayer services in the evening, and increase charitable giving. Hosts compete for the merit of giving the *iftar* meal to their guests. At sunset, the Prophet Muhammad's example was to break the fast by eating a few dates and water. The sunset (*maghrib*) prayer follows the breaking of the fast, and a substantial meal is served afterward. The streets of Muslim cities come to life after *iftar*, as people visit each other in homes and mosques. Increased concentration on worship accompanies the physical rigor of fasting. Over the course of the month of Ramadan, the entire Qur'an is recited during lengthy prayers called *Tarawih*.

DAILY ACTIVITIES AT HOME AND IN PUBLIC

Every Muslim is responsible for how she spends her time. The Qur'an describes time as both a gift and a test but also as a mystery. The Prophet Muhammad related that God said, "The sons of Adam inveigh against Time, but I am Time. In My hand are the night and the day."[7] How each person puts her time on earth to use is part of the test of life. Time is for fulfilling basic needs but not to excess. Time for worship should be observed precisely, but one who worships excessively and neglects other responsibilities has misspent her time. The amount of resolve required to maintain a purposeful life in Islam is supported and eased by the concept of intention. Intention provides the criteria for short- and long-term decisions about allocating time. Islamic teachings encourage believers to avoid idleness and to not be deceived by the trappings of this life. Islamic teachings also encourage the believers to shun extreme asceticism and practice moderation in all things. Every Muslim is supposed to support her basic needs, carry out the duties owed to God, and care for those to whom she is responsible. Time is well spent in the pursuit of justice, according to individual talents. Prioritizing one's time helps a person escape the noise of things clamoring for attention and helps one make conscious choices not to give in to illegitimate demands, such as imitating what "everyone" is doing. Islam, like Christianity, demands a "purpose-driven life."

A Prayer for Daily Life

Muslims invoke blessings and greetings upon one another during the day and acknowledge God in framing each intention to do something, whether upon taking care of bodily functions, preparing for prayer, or asking for guidance. The purpose of these supplications is to purify the intention to act, to establish an appropriate frame of mind, and to attain God-consciousness.

The Prophet Muhammad taught many supplications (singular, *du'a*) during his lifetime, and his followers transmitted them to succeeding generations. These prayers may be compared to a set of keys, each designed to unlock a certain door. A good example of such a prayer is a supplication that is often made before deciding on a matter, a prayer that is called *istikhara*. The *istikhara* prayer is made after one of the formal daily prayers. After making her prayer, the worshipper performs two additional cycles of prayer (*raka'at*) and says: "Oh, Allah, I seek your favor through your knowledge and seek ability from you through your power and beg you for your infinite bounty. For you have power and I have none, you have knowledge but I know not, and you are the Knower of the Unseen. Oh Allah, if you know that this matter is good for me in my religion, for my livelihood, and for the consequences of my affairs, then ordain it for me. But if you know that this matter is evil for me in my religion, for my livelihood, and for the consequences of my affairs, then turn it away from me and turn me away from it, and choose what is good for me wherever it may be and make me pleased with it." After making this prayer, the worshipper states the difficulty or the need that she wants to be fulfilled.[8]

The words of this prayer first acknowledge the limitations of human knowledge and one's ability to influence the future, and then acknowledge the all-knowing and all-powerful nature of God. Second, the individual restates the criteria for any sound decision: in other words, that the matter be beneficial to preserving faith and life and that the matter may enhance the person's future situation. This part of the supplication gives a person a certain mental distance on the matter, so that she may avoid becoming obsessed with a desire or a course of action. Finally, the supplicant prays for God's guidance and submits to it in spirit. It might be sufficient if one was to simply consign any decision to fate, but this supplication goes further. It recognizes the need not only to resign oneself to possible rejection but also to be at peace with God's decision, and not to resent it. Thus, the supplicant asks God to "turn it away from me and turn me away from it...choose what is good for me, and make me pleased with it." It is often as important psychologically to be able to move on with life after a difficult decision as it may have been to make the decision itself. Many Muslims have expressed gratitude for the wisdom contained in this supplication, which has stood them in good stead throughout life. It provides a good example of the supplications that the Prophet Muhammad taught as part of his message to the believers.

Life at Home

In the matrix of human relations, family members form the first threads of the web surrounding the individual, and families are the nodes that, when joined together, make up the community. Islam raised human relations above the level of clan, tribe, ethnicity, and race, giving priority to piety and belief. Family relations, both of blood and of marriage, remain each person's responsibility.

Responsibility toward parents is most often mentioned in Islamic teachings. To honor parents—especially the mother—is a lasting duty that the Qur'an cites as a bedrock principle. Muslims are to speak kindly and respectfully to parents and care for them in need or old age. Obedience to parents ends when it conflicts with belief in God and the duties it entails, but beyond these specific instances, Muslims are enjoined to keep good relations with parents, whether they are Muslim or not.

Kin are an extension of the parents, who share the same lineage, and deserve kindness and aid before others. Responsibility toward siblings is defined by the shared womb and is second in importance only to responsibility toward one's parents in importance. Blood relatives claim priority over unrelated persons, according to the degree of closeness. This aspect of human relations provides a set of expectations and responsibilities toward immediate and extended families that includes every individual. Orphans are mentioned in the Qur'an as persons particularly deserving of care by both individuals and the community. This emphasizes the importance of the family bond as a functional network that includes everyone in a welfare safety net and that is explicitly extended to those unfortunate persons without kin. Islam does not recognize an adoption process that obliterates family identity or conceals true genealogy, but it does extend the benefits of adoption in terms of material and spiritual well-being, including welcoming such individuals into the household.

Marital Relations

Islamic marriage is the conclusion of an agreement between the man and the woman. Family members play an important supporting role in the selection of spouses, particularly because premarital relations among prospective mates are very limited in traditional Muslim societies. The legitimacy of the marriage contract requires the full, though sometimes silent, consent of the bride and gives the couple the right to cohabit and produce legitimate offspring. The groom provides a bride-gift, which is the property of the bride for her to save, spend, or invest as she chooses. Rights and responsibilities concerning material and spiritual support, authority and obedience, love and compassion, enmity and reconciliation are sufficiently complex as to belie any pat, unconditional explanations. Beyond the normative statements about marriage in the Qur'an, its stories of historical men and women and descriptions of events in the Prophet Muhammad's lifetime add dimension to the portrait of marital relations and gender issues.

Debates over the precise meanings of terms in the Qur'an have been used to support a view of the husband as the dominant or instrumental marriage partner, by virtue of his financial support or inherent qualities, or his ability to wield the final word or any other instrument over his wife. Scholars disagree about these points, however, and debates swirl endlessly on the subject. In the Qur'an, husbands and wives are both described as sources of compassion and mercy, as garments to one another, and as two beings of like nature. The Qur'an also warns that spouses may become enemies of each other's ultimate success, or helpers in attaining it. When married couples contemplate separation, the Qur'an demands that they seek an amicable decision to either continue the marriage or terminate the bond. Tyranny in marriage is destructive; thus, the rights of the husband bring forth similar rights for the woman, rights being reciprocal responsibilities. When discussing the roles of men and women in Islam, it is not enough to focus upon one verse or the other as the definitive position of the Qur'an. Instead, the verses of the Qur'an must be taken as a whole and within the overall context of individual relations with God, with the self, in the family, and in marriage.

With regard to the woman's social position in terms of work and her responsibilities to care for the home and children, the Qur'an prescribes no set role. Spouses can agree on obtaining help in nursing babies where both agree. Legal rulings by Muslim scholars do not lay down a quid pro quo in which a man's responsibility to provide food, shelter, and clothing for his wife is exchanged for the wife's responsibility to clean house, cook, and raise the children. The Qur'an grants women the right to their earnings, which implies the right to carry out economic activities that would result in such earnings. Similarly, any wealth the wife possesses may be contributed to the household or held for herself or her children. As the Qur'an says, "And in no wise covet those things in which Allah has bestowed his gifts more freely on some of you than on others: to men is allotted what they earn and to women what they earn: but ask Allah of His bounty: for Allah has full knowledge of all things" (Qur'an 4:32).

In our times, it is important to set aside the modern notion of the nuclear family and the related concept of wage labor in order to more broadly view men's and women's roles in supporting the family and participating in society outside of the home. The idea that a woman's place is in a two-bedroom apartment or suburban detached single-family dwelling, without access to extended family, other adults, or educational opportunities for herself or her children, is not a normal situation in which to raise a family. Living in cities or as minorities in non-Muslim countries, Muslim families raising children by themselves need to create their own community structures and surrogate extended families. Women's work is needed in these nascent communities to help build institutions, educate children and other family members, provide services and friendships for youth, and build other family support services. This work of institution building and defending the community against internal or external stresses is not the province of men only, but of both partners. Whether as volunteers or as paid workers, women's participation in these community-building activities is a form of work outside the home, but it can also be viewed as a direct extension of child raising and household support. Unfortunately, uncritical views of the nuclear family as the norm in modern society have left women and children—and for that matter men as well—more isolated than a broader rethinking of the definitions of family, work, home, and child rearing in an Islamic context might yield.

Public Life

Stepping outside the home, a Muslim enters into the realm of public life. Islam does not require or encourage seclusion but invites individuals to use their talents to seek the common good and social justice. This is a central idea of the term *jihad*, which does not necessarily have anything to do with warfare or violence, nor is it limited to the personal struggle to overcome temptation or sin.[9] The idea behind jihad, which includes all types of struggle for justice, is expressed in the following verse of the Qur'an: "The believers, both men and women, are protectors one of another. They enjoin what is just and forbid what is evil. They observe regular prayers, practice regular charity, and obey Allah and His Messenger. On them will Allah pour His mercy, for Allah is Exalted in Power and Wise" (Qur'an 9:71).

Entering the public sphere is always a challenge, but it is a challenge that the Prophet Muhammad felt was preferable to monasticism or withdrawal, out of either an excess of bitterness or fear of corruption. When Muslims begin work or travel, they often make a brief supplication that acknowledges the role of the Creator in every action and seek God's protection and guidance in whatever they do.[10] A common supplication for leaving the house is pronounced silently or aloud: "In the name of Allah, I believe in Allah, I rely on Allah. That which Allah wills takes place. There is neither power nor strength but in Allah."[11]

The Public Responsibilities of a Muslim

The place of the individual in the matrix of self, family, and marriage is lived out within the larger framework of the community, which includes those persons with whom every individual comes into contact in the course of daily or periodic occupations. The principles that govern individual and collective responsibilities in these relationships comprise the standards of Islamic ethics. Living a moral life requires the individual to understand and prioritize the demands of any given situation to find the most satisfactory response, to enjoin what is good, and to avoid harm.

Guests deserve utmost generosity and are required to be gracious and unobtrusive in return. Neighbors are to be treated with kindness and respect, and the Muslim is required to foster friendly relations and care if one's neighbors are in need. There is no room for thoughtlessness or the insistence that individual responsibilities end at the property line. Keeping the home and the streets clean of filth is required of Muslims. Removing a dangerous object or obstacle from the road is considered an act of charity, as is a kind word or a smile. Common byways, resources such as air and water, and even visual space involve rights of the neighbor that should not be violated. The concept of the neighbor may be readily extended to any person with whom one comes into temporary proximity, such as on public transportation or in a queue, sharing workspace, or similar situations. Within such a concept, the idea of annoying a stranger or an acquaintance, much less of ignoring a person in an emergency or in obvious hardship, would be unethical in Islam.

Economic Relations

Economic relations with others, regardless of whether the others are seen or unseen, fall into the category of public behavior. Islamic teachings give scrupulous attention to fair and honest dealings concerning economic transactions. Islamic legal traditions elaborate detailed guidelines for buying and selling; for entering into, recording, and fulfilling contracts; and for relations between the employer and the employee. A common example of this concern is the tradition that a person who is hired to do work must be paid before his sweat has dried. In return for this consideration, labor and production are to be performed with integrity and excellence. Economic exploitation based on neglect, deception, or greater financial might is prohibited, including individual or institutional attempts to use financial strength to reduce people to indebtedness. Both debtors and lenders are warned against placing themselves or one another into disadvantageous and spiritually impoverishing relationships because of money.

The central concept of property in Islam is that everything is given to us by God as a provision for this life and that ultimately everything belongs to God. Private property must be honored, but people hold their wealth as a trust from the Creator. The desire for wealth, often associated with envy, greed, and avarice, can only be held in check by generosity. *Zakat,* the annual Alms Tax of Islam, amounts to annual obligatory giving, whereas *Sadaqa* is voluntary charity that may be given at any time, and takes many different forms. Charity may involve money, services, in-kind goods, and even a simple act of kindness or aid. Charity is not the privilege of the wealthy alone but is a responsibility for everyone.

The term *Zakat* carries the meanings of "purification" and "growth," implying that personal wealth is purified by giving and that its growth is predicated upon sharing. All adults who are sane, free, and financially able have to give a small portion of their wealth each year. This money may be disbursed by individuals, or given to a common fund in the absence of a recognized authoritative body. These funds are to support specific groups of people who are mentioned in the Qur'an: "Alms are only for the poor and the needy, those who collect [alms], those whose hearts are to be reconciled, to free captives and the debtors, for the cause of Allah, and (for) the wayfarers; this is a duty imposed by Allah. Allah is the Knower, the Wise" (Qur'an 9:60). The obligation to practice charity is firmly established in the Qur'an, the Sunna, and the consensus of the companions of the Prophet Muhammad and the Muslim scholars.

The condition for paying *Zakat* is the accumulation of a certain amount of money beyond basic needs. In Arabic, this condition is called *nisab*. If one does not reach the required level of wealth within a year, no *Zakat* is due. The amount of the *nisab* varies for currency, precious metals, or other forms of wealth such as natural resources, land, or livestock. The wealth must have been held in the owner's control for a full lunar year, after which 2.5 percent of the accrued wealth is owed as *Zakat*. Any outstanding debts are deducted from the *nisab*, and any additional earnings or losses are figured as well. Each Muslim is responsible for calculating the amount of *Zakat* that she owes.

The Local Community and the Global Umma

The mosque (*masjid*) is at the center of Muslim community life. It is also a platform for Muslims' interaction with other communities and a place of spiritual renewal, learning, mutual support, and collective organization and decision making. Performing the prayer in the company of others is preferred over praying alone. Muslim men are encouraged to perform their prayers at the mosque and are obliged to attend the Friday communal prayer (*al-Salat al-Jumu'a*). Women are permitted to pray at the mosque and attend Friday prayers but are not obliged to do so. In some Muslim countries, custom discourages or excludes females from entering the mosque, but there is no clear basis for this practice in Islamic law.

The minimum requirement for a place of prayer is a clean spot on the earth or a piece of fabric sufficient for a single person to carry out the prayer movements. This is the origin of the prayer rug, which has no further sacred significance in Islam, although such rugs are an important facet of Muslim textile arts. A place of prayer may be a room oriented toward the Ka'ba in Mecca, a borrowed room in a public building, a converted building, or a large and elaborately decorated purpose-built structure. Mosques can be found in a marvelous array of architectural forms and decorations, including recent examples that combine modern and traditional features.

Men's and women's spaces for prayer are sometimes separated by physical barriers such as walls, curtains, low partitions, or special sections such as a balcony. The construction of adequate spaces for women in new mosques, especially in the West, is a contested aspect of building design. Women's spaces are often too small, too isolated to hear or participate effectively, and lacking in sufficient space for children, who most often pray alongside the women. The fact that mosque construction has not kept pace with Muslim population growth in many Western countries compounds this problem. Today, such factors often conspire to make attending the mosque for prayers an uncomfortable and sometimes spiritually unfulfilling experience for women. However, Muslim women have begun to speak out about such problems, and the planning bodies of local Muslim communities are now beginning to address issues of unequal access. Some women have stopped coming to the mosque entirely, while others work hard to improve accommodations in existing spaces and future construction, and to argue for the positions they favor concerning use of these spaces by both genders.

As a center of religious and cultural life, the mosque or local Islamic center takes on many functions. Traditionally, the mosque served as a school, as a place where the homeless or a traveler could sleep and receive charity, and as a sanctuary. In minority Muslim communities today, the mosque may include spaces where lessons in the Qur'an and other types of education are given to adults and children. Such education may include courses on the basic duties of a Muslim, Arabic language, or other topics. Lectures and even social and medical services are often provided in Islamic centers, and business affairs as well as community outreach services are conducted within its precincts. Funerals, marriages, and other contractual arrangements, as well as arbitration and counseling, might take place within a mosque or Islamic center.

Cultural, Temporal, and Generational Challenges

The Muslim community is among the most culturally, ethnically, and geographically diverse religious communities in the world. Today, Muslims live in nearly every country in the world. Thirty-six countries have a Muslim population greater than 66 percent, while an additional 10 countries have between 36 and 65 percent. Islam is increasingly a South Asian and Southeast Asian phenomenon, with half of all Muslims living east of Lahore, Pakistan. Over one-third of Muslims are minorities in non-Muslim countries, and the Muslim minority of India is the largest Muslim population in the world—roughly the same size as the largest Muslim nation of Indonesia. Several European countries now have significant Muslim populations, including Germany, France, the United Kingdom, and the Netherlands, mainly because of postcolonial immigration and labor shortages in Europe.[12]

As Islam spread into Asia, Africa, and Europe, Muslims came to represent a dazzling array of cultures that nonetheless retained uniform doctrines and practices, which were embodied in the Five Pillars of Islam. A process of doctrinal winnowing took place, as knowledgeable converts became aware that customs contradicting Islamic law—such as infanticide, bride price, and alcohol-related rituals—were unacceptable to Muslims, although pre-Islamic customs have persisted to some extent. Beyond such prohibitions, however, cultural variations in Islamic practice were tolerated, and cultural forms such as food customs, dress, sports, artistic expressions, architecture, and commercial practices continued to shape people's lives. The spread of Islam was not a melting pot or even a mosaic, but rather, to use the metaphor of the American Muslim scholar Umar Faruq Abdullah, "a clear river flowing over a varied cultural bedrock."[13]

Historically, many cultural practices entered Muslim daily life and radiated out from the bearers of Islam to new regions. This phenomenon may be explained by the gradual spread of Islam among local populations, even in regions that came under Muslim rule in the sixth and seventh centuries CE. Despite the stereotypical view of conversion to Islam by force, there were in general no sudden mass conversions to Islam, and many regions experienced centuries of exposure to Muslim culture before a majority of their populations accepted Islam. A second explanation for the variety of Muslim cultures relates to the tolerant attitude toward other religions and toward culture in general that is enshrined in Islamic law. "People of the Book," who were mostly Jews and Christians, were accorded freedom of worship and even the right to live under their own religious laws. In practice, this condition often extended to other groups as well, although individual rulers carried out contrary and even brutal policies at times. Unlike the form of tolerance that depends upon the whim of individual rulers, the Qur'anic mandate "Let there be no compulsion in religion" (Qur'an 2:256) enshrined the principle of religious tolerance in Islamic law. This principle was further reinforced by the practices of the Prophet Muhammad during his lifetime.

Islamic dietary and marital laws facilitated the mingling of religious groups and permitted close social and economic interaction. The practice of Islam in distant places did not require the construction of hermetically sealed enclaves. A spirit of curiosity and openness to knowledge, ideas, and the products of different cultures is attested by the vast expansion of trade and urbanization in Muslim history. This exposure to the wider world and the economic influence it fostered made developing Muslim cultures porous entities that absorbed influences from the cultures around them. The mingling of cultures in the modern era of globalization continues this trend. However, today, it unfolds in an environment of political decline among Muslims who are under the threat of an engulfing wave of cultural dominance by Western forms. As Abdullah notes in the article, "Islam and the Cultural Imperative," the tolerance of earlier times has been supplanted in some Muslims by the perception that a single cultural model must be shored up by rigid imitation if Islam is to survive. For example, among immigrants and converts to Islam in the United States, this cultural ambivalence affects issues such as youth education and the participation of Muslims in civil society. The process of "re-centering Islam"—a term used by Richard W. Bulliet in describing Muslim cultural development—is far from complete, whether among Muslims in Western countries or among Muslims in majority Muslim countries.[14]

The Pilgrimage

The Hajj is the fifth pillar of Islam, a once in a lifetime journey of pilgrimage to Mecca during the Hajj season. It is not a part of daily life but is a special occasion for those who fulfill this obligation. Integral to daily life, however, is the *desire* to perform Hajj, a Muslim's consciousness of not having fulfilled this duty, or a longing to repeat the experience. Hajj represents the constantly renewed consciousness of a larger geographic space that contains the entire Muslim community, and it is reinforced with every prayer performed facing the Ka'ba in Mecca. The existence of this universalistic pillar of the religion prevented Islam from becoming a religion of separateness. To the contrary, every Muslim renews her outward orientation through praying for and imagining the Hajj journey, and each actual journey to distant Mecca reinforces the unity and connectedness of the Umma. The Hajj reinforces universal Islamic practices; carries knowledge, ideas, and technologies far and wide; maintains communication and travel infrastructures; and maintains a vision of unity that persists to the present day. The past 50 years have seen a tremendous increase in the number of participants in the Hajj, especially in the number of women who perform Hajj.

MUSLIMS AS CITIZENS OF NATIONS AND OF THE WORLD

Relations between and among nations and their citizenry exist at a different order of magnitude than those among individuals, but they belong to a realm of collective responsibility that touches everyone. National and international relations impinge on daily life through their impact on local populations and influence awareness in a media-saturated and globalized world such as ours. As voters, taxpayers, and participants in decisions great and small, individual citizens bear the responsibility to inform themselves and to work toward justice. The expression "think globally, act locally" sheds light on the impact of such issues on daily life. Making the effort to work for justice and avoid harm to the greatest degree possible is preferable in Islam to remaining ignorant and unaware. In the words of the Qur'an, "On no soul does Allah place a burden greater than it can bear. It gets every good that it earns and it suffers every ill that it earns" (Qur'an 2:286).

The daily life of Muslims is shaped by a variety of factors beyond geographic or cultural diversity. The Palestinian *Intifadas,* the Afghan and Gulf Wars, and the American Muslim community's feeling of crisis and doubt following the atrocities of September 11, 2001, have all had an impact on the daily life of Muslims in the United States. Centuries earlier, the long-term effects of the Crusades, the Spanish Reconquista, and the expulsion of Muslims from Spain created watersheds in attitudes that must have been similar, although these events may not have impinged as rapidly on the consciousness of Muslims as today's media dictates. The historian Steven Runciman, writing about the Crusades while witnessing World War II in Britain, described these effects: "Even more harmful was the effect of the Holy War on the spirit of Islam.... The savage intolerance shown by the Crusaders was answered by growing intolerance amongst the Muslims."[15] Although the Crusades happened generations ago, the expectation that the collective body of Muslims must have "gotten over it" by now presupposes that more constructive relations have erased such memories. What came later, however, were just as bad, if not worse. Attitudes about the cultural and racial superiority of the West have been woven deeply into global education and communications. The very term "civilization" was contested in its application to other cultures and races, and the study of history in the education systems of modern nation-states became a platform for promoting Western civilization as being synonymous with world civilization. Were such attitudes the possession of only a few educated elites, they would have had less of an impact. However, universal education in the West has made such attitudes more pervasive, a situation in which ignorance of Islam has flowed back and forth between mass education and mass media in an endless loop.

It is not surprising that bitterness has followed two centuries of Western colonization and domination over Muslim regions, dividing them into nations according to the desires of outside powers. Frustration has only increased among educated as well as uneducated Muslims because of the continuing disputes over countries and their resources, and by the portrayal of Muslims as "anti-Western," a term assumed too often to be synonymous with reactionary political tendencies and antimodern ideas. In Europe, the atmosphere in the half-century since World War II has been marked by turbulence as colonialism declined and Muslim immigration increased. For African American Muslims in the United States, the additional insult of slavery's legacy is another factor. Muslims are affected by such developments in their view of themselves, in their choices of how to rear their children, in their choices of education and living space, and in the choices to socialize or live in relative isolation from their neighbors.

There is another side to this story, however. The past century has also seen Muslims' daily presence in the West for the first time in the history of both civilizations. Non-Muslim neighbors, schoolmates, colleagues at work, and families of individuals who have converted to Islam all are beginning to experience Muslim culture on a more intimate basis. In the United Kingdom, Canada, and the United States in particular, Muslim culture is no longer as distant and exotic as it once was, as each culture samples from the other. A sense of exhilaration and optimism has resulted from this encounter on both sides, even against a backdrop of negative imagery in many sectors of the mass media. Muslims are witnessed engaging in daily prayer in the workplace and at school, observing the Ramadan fast, giving charity, and living according to Islamic precepts. To the dismay of many Muslims, their coreligionists are now seen to suffer from domestic violence and family dysfunction like people in any other community, and social service providers now serve Muslim communities along with those of the majority. Religious and secular charities, political organizations, and professional groups have witnessed Muslims' generosity and civic values. During the past decade, major newspapers, national news magazines, and television networks have increased their coverage of local Muslim affairs, in contrast to earlier coverage of Islam as mainly a foreign policy story. The increase in positive portrayals of Muslims in print, in educational materials, and online has been countered somewhat by the efforts of groups who think it is in their interest to discourage Muslims' input in education about Islam in schools and the media and to challenge positive coverage of Islam. Despite such moves, however, public school systems in the United States have written religious accommodation policies that now allow Muslim students to perform their daily prayers, wear distinctive Islamic dress, and enjoy release time to celebrate their religious holidays.

How one lives, whether as a member of a minority or a majority, in a small Muslim community or a large one, and how one is perceived by one's neighbors profoundly affect daily life and the education of a new generation of Muslims. Acceptance by neighbors, schoolmates, and colleagues helps determine how Muslims dress, how they name their children, and whether they are comfortable living among the larger population or clustered in ethnic or religious enclaves. Muslims are entering professional careers in all occupations and making their impact on the cultures of the nations where they live.

Relations with the Natural World

At the outward reaches of the matrix of a Muslim's responsibility is the individual's relation to the earth and ultimately to the universe. To Muslims, God revealed the outlines of natural laws and the mysteries of creation. He celebrates them in revelations that have stimulated many generations of thinkers and scientists. God teaches that the natural order was provided for His creatures. Stewardship of the environment, both the natural environment and that built by humans, is a commonly invoked concept in the Abrahamic religions, and it finds expression in Islamic sources in ways that affect individual decisions and daily acts. The creation of the human being as the vicegerent of God (*khalifat Allah*) on earth implies a degree of mastery conferred upon humankind but also of awesome duty. Together with the gifts of language and knowledge, this concept frames the responsibility of the human being toward the environment. An important verse in the Qur'an describes the paradoxical nature of the human condition, which is simultaneously honored but fraught with danger: "Lo! We offered the trust unto the heavens and the earth and the mountains, but they shrank from bearing it and were afraid of it; but the human being assumed it. Lo! He has proven to be a tyrant and a fool" (Qur'an 33:72). However, this indictment of humankind does not negate the promise of humanity in Surat al-Rahman (The All-Merciful):

Al-Rahman!
He it is who taught the Qur'an.
He it is who created man.
He it is who taught him to understand.
The sun and the moon follow courses exactly planned.
The plants and the trees bow in adoration.
He raised high the firmament and set up the weighing-pan
So that you will not exceed the mean.
Establish measure with justice and cheat not in the balance,
For it is He Who spread out the earth for all creatures.

(Qur'an 55:1–10)

Another translation of verses 7–9 in the above passage captures a different nuance: "And the sky He hath uplifted; and He hath set the measure, that ye exceed not the measure, so observe the measure strictly, and do not fall short thereof." Surely such lofty language surrounding the Qur'anic verses about balance and justice cannot refer merely to the accurate weighing of vegetables in the marketplace! Clearly, the verses that follow these later on in the Sura encompass what is in the earth and beyond. "Oh company of jinn and men, if you have the power to penetrate the regions of the heavens and the earth, then penetrate (them)! You will never penetrate them save with (Our) permission!" (Qur'an 55:33). Modern environmental science has shown us that nature is balanced in highly complex and unsuspected ways and that human activity in a spirit of conquest has upset the balance of nature. The integration of economic and political spheres in modern life has moved the responsibility for the stewardship of the earth into every household. Thus, decisions about what products to use and to avoid, how to dispose of trash, and how ordinary daily actions affect the environment are within individual purview, however small the immediate impact. As a community, Muslims have lagged behind in such environmental awareness, but the tools of understanding the environment and the consequences for individual and collective responsibility are present in the sacred texts of Islam. Both high-level scholarship and popular consciousness-raising on this subject are finally underway within the Muslim community.

THE RETURN OF THE DAY

Returning home each day, a Muslim greets the inhabitants of the house and expresses thanks for her safe return. After taking food accompanied by a blessing, she performs the sunset and evening prayers. Reading the Qur'an, she contemplates God's forgiveness and seeks guidance for the day's problems and her plans for the future. When she retires for bed, she performs an invocation first made by the Prophet more than 1400 years ago: "In Your name, Oh God, I die and I live." When she wakes up, she says, as did the Prophet, "All Praise is due to God, Who makes us live after He makes us die and unto Him is the Resurrection."[16]

Sound relations with oneself, the family, the community, the world, and the environment are described in Islamic teachings as instrumental in achieving the very purpose of life. The Qur'an describes this mutual responsibility in the following verses:

> The believers, both men and women, are protectors one of another. They enjoin what is right and forbid what is evil. They observe regular prayers, practice regular charity, and obey Allah and His Messenger. On them will Allah pour His mercy, for Allah is exalted in power and Wise.

> (Qur'an 9:71)

> Let there arise out of you a band of people inviting to all that is good, enjoining what is right and forbidding what is wrong. They are the ones to attain felicity.

> (Qur'an 3:104)

Achievement of the overriding purpose of life outlined in these verses presupposes a level of social and gender equality, freedom of speech and thought, and access to education, whether between spouses or siblings, kin or neighbors, or community members at large. For an individual, carrying out this purpose requires that the indicator light of God-consciousness be always "on." For the community, it means that collective responsibility must be borne for fulfilling this purpose. This is the true meaning of the phrase, "Islam is a way of life," which some modern thinkers seem to find so mysterious and excessive. It makes mockery of a concept that has often been touted as a goal of Western governmental policies toward Muslims, namely that they should become secularized and that Islam should become a mere accessory, a bland but perhaps mildly interesting cultural identity. If the principles of Islam are linked to daily life in essential and convincing ways, then it is difficult to see how one could conceive of separating the Islamic faith from the daily life of Muslims. Such an option would leave daily life without purpose or substance in the absence of the spiritual goals that daily life in Islam is meant to support.

NOTES

1. *Sahih al-Bukhari*, Hadith 1.51, cited from *The Alim*, software.

2. See, for example, "Morning and Evening *Du'a*," http://www.geocities.com/mutmainaa/dua1/morn_and_evening.html. *Du'a* is the Arabic word for a prayer of supplication.

3. *Sahih Muslim,* hadith 475, cited from *The Alim,* software.

4. *Sahih al-Bukhari,* hadith 2.12, cited from *The Alim,* software.

5. See, for example, http://pages.britishlibrary.net/smb/halal.htm.

6. See, for example, the guidelines of the Canadian Council of Muslim Theologians, Toronto, Canada. These Halal guidelines can be found at the web site, http://www.jucanada.org/halalguidelines.htm.

7. Ezzedin Ibrahim and Denys Johnson-Davies, *Forty Hadith Qudsi* (Beirut: The Holy Koran Publishing House, 1980), Hadith Qudsi 4, 48.

8. See for example, Yusuf Islam, *Prayers of the Last Prophet* (London, U.K.: Mountain of Light, 1998), 18, and many other sources with similar texts.

9. Sherman A. Jackson, "Jihad and the Modern World," *The Journal of Islamic Law and Culture,* 7 (Spring/Summer 2002): 1.

10. The most common supplication for travel is cited in Yusuf Islam, *Prayers of the Last Prophet*, 18. It includes part of the Qur'an and is as follows: "God is the greatest, God is the greatest, God is the greatest. How perfect is He, the One who has placed this [transport] at our service, for we ourselves would not have been capable of this. To our Lord is our final destiny. O God, we ask You for piety and blessing in this journey of ours, and we ask You for deeds which please You. O God, ease our journey and let us cover its distance quickly. O God, You are the companion on the journey and the Trustee of the family. O God, I take refuge with You from the difficulties of travel, from having a change of heart and being in a bad predicament, and I take refuge in You from an ill-fated outcome in wealth and family."

11. See for example, http://www.duas.org/routine.htm.

12. See for example, the map of Muslim populations from *The Islam Project,* 2003, http://www.theislamproject.org/education/Africa_Mideast_etc.html.

13. Umar Faruq Abdullah, *Islam and the Cultural Imperative, a Nawawi Foundation Paper* (Chicago, Illinois: The Nawawi Foundation, 2004). http://www.nawawi.org/courses/index_reading_room.html.

14. Richard W. Bulliet, *Islam: the View from the Edge* (New York: Columbia University Press, 1994), 185–207.

15. Steven Runciman, *A History of the Crusades, Volume III* (London, U.K.: Cambridge University Press, 1951), 472.

16. *Sahih al-Bukhari,* hadith 8.336.

SELECTED BIBLIOGRAPHY

Abd al 'Ati, Hammudah. *The Family Structure in Islam.* Indianapolis, IN: American Trust Publications, 1977.

———. *Islam in Focus.* Beltsville, MD: Amana Publications, 1998.

Ahmed, Akbar S. *Islam Today: A Short Introduction to the Muslim World.* London, U.K.: I.B. Taurus, 1999.

Ali, Abdullah Yusuf, trans. *The Meaning of the Holy Qur'an.* Brentwood, MD: Amana Corporation, 1993.

Bulliet, Richard W. *The Case for Islamo-Christian Civilization.* New York: Columbia University Press, 2004.

Douglass, Susan L., ed., *World Eras: Rise and Spread of Islam, 622-1500.* Farmington Hills, MI: Gale Group, 2002.

Esposito John L., ed., *The Oxford Encyclopedia of the Modern Islamic World.* New York : Oxford University Press, 1995.

————. *Islam: The Straight Path.* New York: Oxford University Press, 1988.

Ibrahim, Ezzedin, and Denys Johnson-Davies, eds. and transl. *An-Nawawi's Forty Hadith: an Anthology of the Sayings of the Prophet Muhammad.* Cambridge, U.K. : Islamic Texts Society, 1997.

————. *Forty Hadith Qudsi.* Beirut: Dar al-Koran al-Kareem, 1980.

Jackson, Sherman A. "Jihad and the Modern World," *The Journal of Islamic Law and Culture,* 7:1 (Spring/Summer 2002).

Naqvi, Syed N. Haider. *Ethics and Economics: An Islamic Synthesis.* Leicester, U.K.: The Islamic Foundation, 1981.

Nasr, Sayyid Hossein. *Man and Nature: The Spiritual Crisis of Modern Man.* London, U.K.: George Allen and Unwin Ltd., 1986.

————. *Islam, Islamic Secularism and the Environmental Crisis.* Chicago, Illinois: Kazi Publications, 1993. Audiotape.

Pickthall, Muhammad M. trans. *The Meaning of the Glorious Qur'an.* New York: Muslim World League, 1977.

Robinson, Francis. *Atlas of the Islamic World Since 1500.* New York: Facts on File, Inc., 1982.

Runciman, Steven. *A History of the Crusades, Volume III.* London, U.K.: Cambridge University Press, 1951.

Shah, Shahid N. *The Alim Islamic Software, Release 4.5–6.0* ISL Software, Inc., 1986–1996.

Smart, Ninian, and Heritage, Ailsa, eds. *Atlas of the World's Religions.* New York: Oxford University Press, 1999.

The Islam Project at www.theIslamProject.org.

Von Denffer, Ahmad. *Ein Tag Mit Dem Propheten* [One day with the Prophet]. Leicester: The Islamic Foundation, 1981.

2

ISLAM, CULTURE, AND WOMEN IN A BANGLADESH VILLAGE

•

Sarwar Alam

Whatever way it is defined, power is a factor that influences the lives of all people. In studying power and powerlessness in Appalachia, John Gaventa observed that the feeling of powerlessness comes about as a response to the perceived experience of defeat.[1] He found that belief systems that justify powerlessness as a natural condition are created by social and economic factors that lead one to think that a person does not have the power to affect one's course of life. This study complements Gaventa's findings by examining the perceptions of power and powerlessness among village women in Bangladesh. Power has different meanings for Bangladeshi men and women in many aspects of life, including decision making in the family or community, employment, health care, and education. Such differences in the understanding of power often stem from religion because power-laden issues such as inheritance, marriage and divorce, custody of children, and social mobility are governed, at least in part, by religious laws and customs. Hence, it is natural to conclude that religion would have an important influence on the perceptions of power and powerlessness among Muslim women in the rural communities of Bangladesh.

Experience shows that the statuses of men and women are not the same in many Muslim societies. This impression is reinforced by data such as the sex ratio of the population, maternal mortality rates at childbirth, and the different rates of adult literacy between men and women. In Bangladesh, the male–female ratio is 104:100, and 87 percent of the country's population is Muslim.[2] Bangladesh is also an agrarian country; 76.61 percent of its population live in rural areas and 51.3 percent of the civilian labor force are engaged in agriculture.[3] Although agriculture is the dominant sector of the economy, the government traditionally gives priority to urban development, which is reflected in the resource allocations of the central government's annual development programs. The unequal allocation of resources creates unequal development patterns between urban and rural areas and between men and women in the country as a whole.

In addition, the rise of religious politics in recent decades has adversely affected the position of women. From the very inception of Bangladesh in 1971, the government has taken constitutional, legislative, and administrative initiatives to address inequalities between men and women. Such initiatives have included the establishment of equal rights for every citizen irrespective of gender, ethnicity, or faith; quotas for women in Parliament as well as in local government bodies; a family law ordinance, the Child Marriage Restraint Act, the Prohibition of Dowry Act, and the Violence Against Women and Children Act; tuition waivers and stipends for female students up to grade 12; and quotas for women in all public sector jobs.[4] Despite these governmental initiatives, however, disparities between the male and female populations of Bangladesh still exist, especially in the rural areas. For example, the adult literacy rate of urban and rural males is 77.1 and 57.3 percent, respectively, whereas the adult literacy rate for urban and rural females is 59.7 and 37.8 percent, respectively.[5] Life expectancy at birth is more equally distributed; it is 72.9 years for a male and 72.7 years for a female in the urban areas, but 67.1 years for a male and 66.2 years for a female in the rural areas. The maternal mortality rate per 1,000 live births is 2.7 in the urban areas, whereas it is 4.2 in the rural areas.[6] Disparity is also visible between males and females in the political arena. For example, out of 300 general Members of Parliament in Bangladesh, only seven are women.[7]

In discussing the roots of gender inequality, Amartya K. Sen has drawn attention to factors such as adapted perceptions, customary patterns, and social arrangements.[8] Some researchers have argued that gender inequality is related to intrahousehold decision-making processes that determine resource allocations for education, training, health, and nutrition.[9] Feminist theorists have discussed the issue of inequality and the subordination of women in terms of sexuality and the sexual division of labor resulting from social change, colonialism, dependency, and modernization.[10] Some researchers argue that women's issues are subsumed in the nationalist discourse without acknowledging women's sufferings and contributions, and the prevalence of inequalities between males and females.[11]

What are the causes of the inequalities between men and women in Bangladesh? It seems that there is no easy answer to this question. One cause might be the consequence of unequal power relations between men and women in most aspects of their lives. Others might include culture, the psychological acceptance of unequal relations by both males and females, or the physical and biological distinctiveness of females. Religion might also contribute to the unequal power relations that result in the subordination of women in the family and in the community. Such inequalities deprive women of an equal share in society and deny them the opportunity to participate in intrahousehold as well as community decision making.

How do rural women in Bangladesh perceive the limits of their power? Do they relate their perception of power or powerlessness to Islam? Do rural women in Bangladesh see themselves as an oppressed group? Do they have grievances against males? To date, few researchers have studied women's perceptions of the influence of Islam upon their lives. In 2005, I studied women's perceptions of power and powerlessness in a rural community in Bangladesh and investigated the influence of religion upon their perceptions. I asked, how do Muslim women of rural Bangladesh perceive Islam as a factor influencing their ability to make decisions in their families and in their communities? As part of my study, I paid special attention to issues such as marriage, divorce, inheritance, and *purdah* (*parda* in Bangla, the language of Bangladesh), which influence rural women's participation in society. Findings from the ethnographic study and in-depth interviews discussed below suggest that deeply held beliefs, rooted in both the teachings and the culture of Islam, influence the perceptions of power and powerlessness among rural women in Bangladesh.

SITE AND PARTICIPANT SELECTION

Because the subjects of my study were rural Muslim women, I selected a site for my research based on three criteria: homogeneity of the local population, my command of the local dialect, and my ease of access to local community members and leaders. I decided to collect data from my native rural village in the subdistrict of Purbadhala in the Netrakona district. The village is homogenous in terms of religion (100 percent Muslim) and ethnic origin, I speak the same dialect of Bangla as the villagers do, and I have access to the leaders and members of that community. In fact, I spent my boyhood in this village. Many of my relatives and friends still live in that community, and I assumed that they would help me in gaining access to the people that I wanted to interview. The Purbadhala subdistrict is located approximately 100 miles north of the capital city of Dhaka, and approximately 15 miles northwest of the Netrakona district headquarters. The total population of the village I studied is 1,288.[12]

I studied the lifestyles of the women of the village, the influence of religion on their day-to-day lives, the extent of their personal relations, the religious rites that they practiced, the extent of their physical mobility, and the power relations in the family and in the community. During my fieldwork, I conducted in-depth interviews as well as informal conversations. This latter style of interview was necessary because nonliterate people in Bangladesh, and especially women, often feel uncomfortable with the prospect of structured formal interviews, tape-recorded conversations, and signing consent forms.[13]

I spent the period from January 2005 to July 2005 conducting fieldwork. I selected informants who were information-rich and to whom I had relatively easy access. In all, I interviewed a randomly selected sample of 53 people, of whom 34 were women and 19 were men. In selecting the informants for the interviews, I noted the status and socioeconomic background of each person. It was my assumption that the information gathered from this cross section and background of informants would make the data more reliable (Table 2.1).

METHODOLOGY

In my research, I employed qualitative methods such as participant observation, informal conversations, in-depth interviews, and document collection. The theoretical aim of the study was to investigate the social construction of religious meaning among village women in Bangladesh. However, like other qualitative researchers, I was concerned with process as well as with meaning: that is, how does religion help people make sense of their lives, experiences, and structures of the world?[14] A qualitative researcher deals with the socially constructed nature of reality, the intimate relationship between the researcher and his subject, and the situational constraints that shape one's inquiry. To put it another way, qualitative research is concerned with how social experiences provide meaning in people's lives.[15] As Catherine Marshall and Gretchen B. Rossman have observed, a qualitative researcher is like a detective.[16] Thus, by becoming a participant observer, I tried to play the role of a detective in order to discover the religious roots of the social construction of meaning among rural women in Bangladesh.

As indicated above I interviewed 53 people of the village, out of whom 34 were females and 19 were males. Among the female respondents, only 9 had either a high school education or above, and 12 were nonliterate. Among the male respondents, five had either a high-school education or above, and six

Table 2.1: Demographic Characteristics of Female Respondents

Category	Number	Mean age (yrs)	Status
Housewife	18	47.3	Dependent on husband
Housewife/Singer	1	38	Self-dependent
Widow	2	61.5	Head of family
Widow	2	64	Self-dependent
Widow	2	73.5	Dependent on son
Divorcee	1	45	Self-dependent/Head of family
Student	7	16.1	Dependent on fathers
Teacher	1	27	Self-dependent
Total	34		

were nonliterate. The respondents were randomly selected and represented each neighborhood of the village. In addition, I interviewed two government officials (a Joint Secretary and a Senior Assistant Secretary) from the Ministry of Women's and Children's Affairs.

While interviewing the female respondents, I was often assisted by one of my female cousins, a married graduate student majoring in Sociology. She carried out five interviews by herself. Interviews with the female respondents mostly took place in the daytime in open places that were visible to others but separate from the home. Interviews with male respondents mostly took place during the evening when they returned home from work. These interviews were conducted in more secluded places than were the women's interviews, although the crowded situation of many households sometimes made privacy difficult. In most cases, while conducting interviews, we insisted that the respondents focus on the relevant issues, but we intervened directly only when it was necessary to keep the respondents on track.

STAGES OF DATA COLLECTION

The first stage of my data collection was gaining entry into the social life of the village. My boyhood experiences and connections allowed me to survey the community and select the range of people I wanted to talk to and interview. Here, personal connections and prior acquaintances were an advantage in selection as well as observation. In addition, I tried to make sure that my presence would not affect the behavior patterns of people whom I wanted to observe. I tried to accomplish this goal by living with them and by creating a bond of friendship with them. Getting entry to the village was a challenge at first. My last long-term visit to the village was in 1994. However, my family's reputation and my status as a public servant helped me a great deal in being accepted in the community. The villagers showed real interest in my project when I told them that after the completion of my Ph.D. degree, and by dint of this research work, the name of the village would be stored forever in the body of scientific knowledge about Bangladesh.

In the second stage of my research, I began my observations by attending community meetings. I attended family and community gatherings for 24 weeks to observe interactions, language, the formation of groups, routines, rituals, and nonverbal communication. During this period, I conducted interviews and collected documents. I kept field notes and journal entries for each informant and wrote down my thoughts, queries, and confusions. I took particular note of the relevance of events that I encountered with respect to research problems and the overall theoretical framework. The third stage of my data collection was triangulation. After returning from the field, I compared observation notes with in-depth interview records and documents.

THE SETTING

The village that I studied in the subdistrict of Purbadhala has 1,288 inhabitants, of which 684 are males and 604 are females. The total number of households is 264, of which 20 are headed by women. The village consists of four neighborhoods (*paras*): *Pub* (East), *Pashchim* (West), *Dakkhin* (South), and *Chawlk* (Middle). It has one registered elementary school (grades 1–5), one *maktab* (an unregistered nongovernmental and locally managed religious school), and two mosques. The overall adult literacy rate of the village is 60.13 percent.[17] Among the adults in the village, only 14 (11 males and 3 females) have a baccalaureate (the equivalent of three years of college in the United States) or a higher level of education. In addition, there are five *hafizes* (those who have memorized the Qur'an), of whom only one is female.

There are also five overlapping groups of *baul* or *marfati* (folk or mystic) singers in the village. One of these groups is led by a woman. A number of men spend their leisure time in *jalsas,* gatherings of singers and listeners to folk or mystic songs, either as singers or as listeners. Mystical *marfati jalsas* are divided along the lines of the followers of *pirs,* holy mystic teachers. A few people in the village follow the strict principles of Tablighi Jama'at, a conservative movement of Islamic reform founded in India, and spend their leisure time in prayer. Except for the female *baul* singer noted above, no women participate in communal religious activities outside of their homes.

Other groups of males are involved in politics. The two major political parties, the Awami League and the Bangladesh Nationalist Party, have followers and leaders in the village. Leaders of these parties have connections with influential urban politicians. They exercise power over community decision making, especially in selecting and electing local government representatives. Again, these are male domains; women do not have access to such political activities.

Other groups in the village are organized by microcredit providers, such as the Grameen Bank and BRAC (Bangladesh Rural Advancement Committee). There may be as many as six microcredit organizations working in the village at a given time. Such organizations ostensibly provide small-scale business loans to groups of poor women. However, in reality, the husbands or male family members of the borrowers control most of these funds. There are also other groups of people who borrow money from individual moneylenders or *mohajans.*

The villagers hold collective observances of two religious festival days celebrated by all Muslims (*Eid ul Fitr* at the end of Ramadan and *Eid ul-Adha* during the Hajj pilgrimage period), plus *Shab-i-Barat* (the fifteenth night of the Islamic month of Sha'ban) and *Shab-i-Qadar* (the twenty-seventh night of the Islamic month of Ramadan). They also observe the fast of Ramadan and the day of *'Ashura* (the tenth day of the Islamic month of Muharram) on an individual basis. National holidays such as Mother Language Day (February 21), Liberation Day (March 26), and Victory Day (December 16) have little or no impact upon the villagers. Instead, they participate in the *melas* (fairs) on the eve of *Pahela Baishakh* (the first day of the new year of the Bengali calendar) or in the *austamis* (fairs in remembrance of the Hindu God Lord Krishna). The latter festival of pre-Islamic origin continues to be popular despite the long history of Islam in Bangladesh. Community participation is also visible in *janajas* (funerals), *khatnas* (circumcisions), *mehmanies* (public feasts), *bi'e* (marriages), *miladunnabis* (rituals in honor of the Prophet's birth and death anniversaries), *akikas* (celebrations, and also public feasts for a child's birth), and *shalishes* or *bichars* (which are rural dispute-settlement bodies). Here again, community participation primarily means the participation of males.

The villagers maintain separate domains and spaces for males and females. In general, the division of labor is based on tradition, in which females—especially wives—are responsible for work inside the home, while males are expected to work outside the home. There are some exceptions where females work outside the home. This is especially the case for women who are extremely poor and work at a relative's or a neighbor's home. Spending time by oneself is not seen as desirable in village culture. People are expected to socialize with each other and frequent visits among neighbors, extended family members, or friends are much appreciated.

SOCIAL LIFE

Marriage

Marriage holds great importance within the village community (*samaj*). Marriage provides a woman with a sense of prestige and identity and ensures her social standing in the *samaj*. Marriage is heterosexual, a union between a man and a woman. There is evidence of homosexuality among some unmarried males in the village, but such relationships are private and isolated in nature and cease when one of the partners gets married. Although according to Hanafi jurisprudence every adult Muslim woman has the right to choose her own marriage partner, in reality it is either her father or her elder brother who chooses the spouse. The same is also true in determining the *mohr*, the dower. The payment of dowries is widely practiced in the village, despite the fact that it has been declared illegal by Bangladesh law. It may also be noted that polygamy is not practiced in the village, probably because of the strict bureaucratic requirements necessary to carry out this custom.[18] The bride and the groom never spend time with each other before marriage, for such practices are not appreciated by the *samaj*. The marriage market is male dominated, an observation that is consistent with previous findings.[19] Male dominance over marriage is also reflected in the word *bi'e*, the term used for a marriage ceremony in the Bangla language. *Bi'e* comes from the Arabic word *bay'a,* which designates an oath or a pact of allegiance. In a marriage, the wife makes an oath of allegiance to the husband similar to the oath of allegiance made by a subject to a ruler. The average age difference between a husband and his wife is 10 years. Marriage is often seen as a way of expanding a relationship or a power base between two families or *gusthis* (patrilineal descent groups). Jean Ellickson,[20] John P. Thorp,[21] and Geoffrey D. Wood[22] observed similar trends in their research. As Jitka Kotalova[23] and Santi Rozario[24] have noted, the fact that marriage provides a woman with a social identity as a wife and later as a mother is a major reason why it is thought that a woman should marry at least once in her lifetime. Both Muslim and Hindu women in Purbadhala subdistrict are dependent on their fathers before marriage and on their husbands after marriage. This is a major factor in how a rural women's identity in Bangladesh is subsumed into male-dominated lines of descent.

Divorce

The existing law of Bangladesh has made it difficult for a husband to marry a second wife. However, he still enjoys significant advantages in the case of divorce.[25] A husband can divorce his wife at will with 90 days prior notice by making an application to the Chairman of the local Union Council. If the right to initiate a divorce is not delegated to the wife in the original marriage contract, she requires the court's intervention to divorce her husband.[26] By initiating a divorce, a wife risks her share in her husband's property, her entitlement to recoup her dower, and the right to claim a maintenance allowance after the divorce. During my research, I found that the majority of villagers were aware of a woman's right to initiate a divorce in principle. However, they were not clear about how this right was to be applied. Some were confused about the difference between the provisions of the secular law and the Shari'a. According to Shari'a law, a husband can divorce his wife at will and he is not required to give notice to his wife through a mediating institution. In contrast, the right of a wife to divorce her husband is severely limited under the Shari'a, and she is required to proceed through the judicial system upon initiating divorce.[27] Not everybody is aware of such distinctions, and the nongovernment organizations operating in the village were not successful at making every woman aware of her legal rights in this regard.

In actual practice, the end of a marriage for a rural woman in Bangladesh results in the loss of emotional support, a loss of prestige, and economic ruin. This usually compels a woman to return to her parental home with shame and the prospect of becoming an economic burden on her family. During the period of my research in the village, I found no instance where a wife initiated a divorce against her husband. However, there were several cases where husbands divorced their wives but refused to provide the required maintenance allowance after the divorce.

Inheritance

The inheritance rules of the village are based on the Shari'a law of inheritance, where a daughter inherits half the amount of a son. A Muslim wife has a share in the property of her husband. When her husband dies, the widow inherits one-eighth of his property. If he dies childless, she inherits one-fourth. The rest of the property is passed on to the husband's closest relatives. If no son is born to a couple, daughters alone cannot inherit all of the property of their parents. In such a case, part of the property goes to the sons of the father's brother.[28] During my time in the village, I did not find any evidence of a woman claiming the portion of inheritance that was her right from her natal family. When asked about this departure from Shari'a law, some respondents said that they did not claim their inheritance rights because of love. Others said that deferring their inheritance helped assure the support of their family in case of divorce or widowhood. This is consistent with the findings of other researchers.[29] A wife must maintain some security against the possibility that she will be widowed or divorced. Should either of these misfortunes befall her, she has little recourse but to return to her childhood home. If she does not take the inheritance that is due to her under law, it is likely that her brothers will take her back with greater willingness and grace than would be the case if she had angered them by taking her share of the inheritance.

Parda

Women of the village were very concerned about *parda* (also known as *purdah*). This concept literally means "hiding one's face" but in practice, it refers to a set of rules and regulations that determines women's interactions in society. "Observing *parda* is an integral part of a Muslim woman's life," argued many of my informants. Others observed, "Those who do not observe *parda* are *besharam* (shameless)." There are different ways of observing *parda*, depending on the age and social status of women. Children and elderly women do not observe *parda* but women of marriageable age are supposed to observe the practice. However, *parda* does not have to be observed every time a woman leaves the home. For example, women who visit their next-door neighbors do not cover their faces with an additional garment. In general, women use an additional garment known as a *chadar* (similar to the Iranian *chador*) to cover the upper body and head while visiting neighborhoods within the village. When women visit a different village, such as when they visit their natal family members from another village, they use the traditional *burqa,* a long single garment that covers the head, instead of the *chadar.* Whatever the type of garment, *parda* plays a major role in determining the nature of women's interactions with others in the community and between communities. However, gone are the days, observed one female informant, when a man could hardly ever see a woman from outside her community. As an example of the virtues of the "golden days," she mentioned the story of the marriage night of the great Sufi saint *Bara Pir* Hazrat Abdul Quadir Zilani,[30] whose wife was supposed to be crippled and blind:

> *Bara Pir* married his wife without ever seeing her, as was the tradition in those golden days. On their very first night together, *Bara Pir Saheb* came out of his bedroom and found a beautiful woman in his bed. He went straight to his *shashur*(father-in-law) and asked him whether there was any mistake. His *shashur* smiled and told *Bara Pir,* "I described my daughter as crippled because she has never gone out of her home; she does not know how to go out. I described her as blind because she has not seen any male except me in her life. Go to her my child, that beautiful girl in your bedroom is very much your wife. Nobody made a mistake."

Some informants argued that to become *pardanashin,* observant of *parda,* is a matter of prestige for a Muslim woman because it marks a difference from the followers of other religions. *Parda* and the seclusion it entails play a major role in determining the cultural construction of work and the sexual division of labor in the rural communities of Bangladesh.[31] It is also a powerful means of social control in these communities.[32]

Purity and Pollution

The villagers also exhibited a strong sense of purity and pollution. This is particularly important with regard to the virginity of unmarried women, which, it is believed, helps sustain the honor of the *paribar* (family). Researchers have observed that keeping the bodies of nubile females intact is an asset for the family and is a form of symbolic capital that ensures honor and acceptance for a woman in the community. Purity also refers to a woman's self-control and virtue. The virginity of an unmarried woman proves that she is both restrained and virtuous. Rape pollutes a woman's body and renders her unmarriageable. Pollution also occurs because of sexual misconduct. Since both rape and sexual misconduct make a woman unfit for marriage, there is a tendency to "blame the victim" in cases of rape, which may lead to personal and family tragedies in extreme cases.

Pollution has another dimension as well, which is a product of women's biology, in that it is linked to women's menstrual periods. Women are perceived as impure during their menstrual periods, which marginalizes them religiously as well as socially. Although most schools of Shari'a law regard the blood of menstruation as no worse than that caused by a cut, it is seen differently in Bangladesh culture. The fact that a woman cannot pray or enter a mosque during menstruation means that women are impure by nature. Several of my informants argued that the punishment for eating *gandom,* the prohibited fruit tasted by Eve in the Garden of Eden, was her menstruation. Because of attitudes such as these, David Abecassis has concluded, "[Muslim women in Bangladesh] are cut off from the mainstream of society and from the most important processes of power and decision making, not just by *parda* but by the attitudes which lie behind it; they are cut off from God and from other men and women by pollution-related ideas and by religious practice."[33]

The Shalish

Disputes that cannot be settled within the family are brought before the *shalish* or *bichar,* a council led by village elders who are popularly known as *matbars.* While studying the concept of power in a rural district of Bangladesh, Thorp (1978) found that each residential brotherhood has a leader who is a major landowner as well as having the skill and knowledge in settling disputes in a *shalish* or a *bichar.* A chosen leader of the community may order this person to punish an offender from within the family group, or isolate a person or a family from the *samaj* as a punishment.[34] The *shalish* was created as an instrument to maintain social control and to concentrate power in the hands of influential villagers. Leadership in the *shalish* mostly depends on the possession of landed property, personal reputation, and connections with influential public officials.

The *shalish* imposes its will through threats to honor and the inducement of shame. Sometimes, it also dispenses judgments that result in divorce or corporal punishments. A meeting of the *shalish* can be convened by any male disputant, a village elder, or a religious leader. If a *shalish* is convened for settling a dispute related to inheritance, divorce, the observance of *parda,* or adultery, a religious leader presides over the session. This religious leader is usually the local *Imam,* who leads the congregational Friday prayers in the mosque. Sometimes, the *shalish* is headed by a *mufti* (Islamic jurist), who participates to judge the issue in dispute from the point of view of Islamic law. If the *shalish* is headed by such a person, he may pronounce a decree (*fatwa*) that might entail the beating, lashing, or even stoning to death of the alleged offender. Village women cannot sit as members of the *shalish.* When they appear as the accused or as victims, they usually defend themselves through their male relatives.[35] Ironically, a *fatwa* does not have any legal recognition in Bangladesh. In January 2001, the High Court Division of the Bangladesh Supreme Court declared *fatwas* illegal. In this judgment, Justice Golam Rabbani and Justice Najmun Ara Sultana, the first female high court judge in Bangladesh, observed that the legal system of Bangladesh empowers only the state courts to decide all questions relating to legal opinions, thus making a *fatwa* illegal. Although the government of Bangladesh challenged the ruling, the Appellate Division of the Supreme Court upheld the decision of the High Court. The case is still pending with the Appellate Division.[36]

During the period of my fieldwork, nobody recalled any *fatwa*-related incidents or disputes having occurred in the recent past. However, a number of incidents resulted in the convening of a *shalish*. One *shalish* was convened against the female folk singer of the village. She described this dispute, which occurred some years previously, in the following words:

> When I started a *jalsa* (a session of religious and folk singing) in the front yard of my house, and when I started participating in *jalsas* in other villages, our *matbars* organized a *shalish* against me because of my alleged shamelessness. They said that my behavior was causing harm to the honor of our village. They asked my husband to bring me before the *shalish*. We went there. They asked my husband many questions, and later directed my husband to divorce me. But my husband played a trick. He told the *matbars* of the *shalish* that he would follow their directive, but that he needed some time because we have small children. Then we fled, first my husband and then I. I spent so many days in *parabash* (exile)! I returned home, and so did my husband, when everything cooled down.

PERCEPTIONS OF POWER

Men and women are perceived as separate beings in rural Bangladesh, and each of them has a separate domain for decision making. A woman is not supposed to interfere in men's affairs, and a man is not supposed to interfere in women's affairs. The female folk singer who organized a *jalsa* session in the account reproduced above transgressed such a boundary. Familial and social relationships are thought to be based on religious directives, although such "directives" often contradict the actual teachings of the Qur'an. Females in rural Bangladesh are seen as the shadows of their male counterparts within the institutional framework of the family (*paribar*). The identity of a woman as an independent, autonomous self is hardly recognized in this male-dominated society. According to one of my male informants:

> From the very beginning of creation, Allah created Adam as a male, not as a female. Therefore, males are Allah's preferred creatures. To ease the loneliness of Adam, Allah created *Hawa* (Eve) from Adam's left rib. Thus, Hawa is a part of Adam's body. Hawa's prayer was synonymous with providing pleasure to Adam. (Note: The Arabic root of *Hawa* is related to the word for passion.) Thus, Hawa's first priority was not to satisfy Allah but Adam. The same is true in the family. The wife's first priority is to make her husband happy, this is her prayer. She should wipe her husband's wet feet with her hair the way *Ma* (mother) Fatima (the daughter of the Prophet Muhammad) used to do for her

husband. It is better for a wife to offer her husband one *khili* of *paan* (betel leaf and nut) with a smile than to offer *nafal namaj* (supererogatory prayers) throughout the night.

Often, a woman's perception of the role and status of other females is even harsher than that of a male. A female informant characterized the ideal woman and wife in the following terms:

> The ideal woman is she who takes care of her husband, children, and in-laws. Taking care of her husband is everything for her (*shamir shebai tar shabkichu*). This is because the wife's heaven is located beneath the feet of her husband (*shamir paer niche strir behest*). She does everything she can to ensure happiness of her husband. The ideal wife is she who keeps a rope (*dori*) ready in case her husband wants to tie her up, and who keeps a cane (*bet*) ready in case her husband wants to beat her.

Although marriage provides a form of shelter for the wife, she holds a position in the family that is not equal to that of her husband. "It is [my husband] who brought me here. Allah made him superior to me, Allah made the husband superior from the day of creation. It is my sacred duty to obey him," said one of my female informants. Another female informant said, "It is [the husband's] family, [the husband's] children, and [the husband's] wife, so it is his responsibility to maintain the family." Another female informant said, "For me, power means the one who has wealth, the one who has power [over others]. One who has the ability to run a family is powerful." Another view expressed by a woman informant is as follows: "The male is superior (*purush boro*) because he gives everything to his wife during marriage. He ensures her *parda,* keeps her in honor, and provides for her food and clothes. If these are his responsibilities, then is he not superior? To me he is superior." Another informant noted, "The husband has the power because he has wealth, land, and money. He can go anywhere; it does not matter whether it is day or night, evening or morning, hot summer or cold winter. But I cannot do so. It is Allah who gave this power to husbands."

The majority of informants held that power (*khamata*) is the ability of a person or a group to act autonomously. Sources of *khamata* might be wealth, education, or political connections, but overall, the real source of all power is Allah (*sakal khamatar malik Allah*). It is Allah who makes one person powerful and another person powerless. Among men and women, the men are blessed with power by Allah. A major reason for this blessing is the division of labor, which is viewed as a natural, unchangeable condition, in which men provide food and wealth for the family and the women take care of the home. As one female informant explained:

> Power came from Allah. He gave this to us to cultivate land so that we could survive. Allah asked us to do this, to cultivate in order to survive. Allah gave this power to males. Allah said, "I am sending you to the earth to cultivate it. You will earn according to your ability." Thus, the male is the owner of the family

(*shonsharer malik*). He is the guardian. I am also an owner, but a minor one; he is the major owner. It is natural that he enjoys more power because he is a man; it is also natural that I enjoy less power because I am a woman.

The statuses of men and women and their perceptions of power in the rural Muslim communities of Bangladesh were first described and analyzed by Thorp nearly 30 years ago. The subjects of his study, like my informants, perceived that men and women are descendants of Adam, who was created by Allah out of the earth in order that man might possess the earth and be its master (*malik*). Because of this, the person who possesses land is most like Adam and thus is a perfect individual. Thorp maintained that rural people in Bangladesh believed that Allah created *Hawa*, Adam's wife, from Adam's body as an autonomous creature, although she is dependent on her husband. Because Hawa was created from Adam, a male *malik* considers his wife part of himself. A husband and a wife are equal partners in the reproductive process, and a wife might become *adhikari*, "masterful," by inheriting lands. However, Thorp observed, "A wife is not her husband's equal in the political or economic fields, or in the field of public religious activity. However, she is considered to have equal authority (*saman adhikar*) in intra-family affairs."[37] As a "junior partner" with her husband in ownership—to use the metaphor employed by one of my female informants above—the most important external power that is theoretically possessed by the wife is her ability to sell or mortgage her land. Thorp, whose position on women's power and autonomy in rural Bangladesh is more optimistic than my own, comments:

> Women are capable of assuming and carrying out the responsibilities of *maliks* [owners] because they share the same fundamental constitution as their husbands. The dominant element in their constitution, like that of their husbands, is earth, with the strength and skill (*sakti/khamata*) it contains. Their creation is dependent upon receiving part of a bone from their husbands, but with it they receive the basic capacity and talent (*khamata*) that distinguished Adam from all the things whose names he learned and from the angels as well.[38]

Despite Thorp's optimistic view of the theoretically equal nature of men and women in rural Bangladesh, my research reveals that a woman may have the right to inherit land and dower, and to manage properties and household affairs, but that such rights are ascribed primarily within the purview of her male-dominated household. Even in religion, women's social space is starkly separated from that of men. A woman's identity is ascribed as a daughter, a wife, a sister, or a mother, but not as an *Imam*, a religious teacher, or even a religious singer. One also finds that religious leaders and local landowners, who for the most part are men, act together in the determination of family and community affairs through institutions such as the *shalish*. Such institutions are powerful supports for the assumption of male power and dominance. Above all, it is the ownership and autonomous disposition of land that gives a *malik* mastery over the family and eventually over the community. Religion provides the moral justification for such mastery by influencing prevailing notions of right or wrong, good or bad, or proper or improper.

Marriage in Islam is a civil union between a man and a woman. Marriage has three salient characteristics: (1) a contract, (2) consent of the groom and bride, and (3) payment of *mohr* (dower) by the groom to the bride. An Islamic marriage is not a sacrament; rather, it is a civil contract between a man and a woman that creates a relationship between them.[39] If any one of the partners breaches the contract, the marriage could be dissolved. In the culture of Bangladesh, marriage is regarded as a union of two individuals as well as of two families, legalizing intercourse and the procreation of children. According to Hanafi jurisprudence, the free consent of the man and the woman is obligatory to make this union legal. Payment of the *mohr* (dower) to the wife by the husband is an integral part of a marriage, and this payment is an obligation for the husband. For a married woman, the right to receive and keep the *mohr* is a source of self-esteem. Shahla Haeri holds that Islamic marriage is a contract that involves a sort of ownership by a man over a woman's reproductive organs in exchange for the dower that a man pays to a woman.[40] Kecia Ali has argued, according to early Islamic jurisprudence, "Marriage is a bilateral transaction that establishes unilateral control" by the husband over the wife's reproductive capabilities.[41] "In marriage, the dower is exchanged for control (authority, ownership: *milk*) over the wife or, more particularly, over her sexual organ."[42] Thus, the belief in Bangladesh that a man has majority ownership over the marriage partnership is consistent with the reasoning of Islamic jurisprudence. However, from the participant observation and interviews I conducted in 2005, it appears that Muslim women in rural Bangladesh are either not conscious or not fully aware of their right to a contract, their right to free consent to the marriage, and also about their right to dispose of their own property within a marriage.

In rural Bangladesh, the notion of a woman's agency is centered on her reproductive capacity. A woman receives recognition as a full individual only after her first pregnancy. She receives another level of recognition if she bears a male child. It is believed that women are responsible for conceiving male or female children. Restrictions that are imposed upon the woman by social customs or religious beliefs are taken for granted. She expands her agency by taking on responsibilities in her family within these socially recognized parameters. On the other hand, husbands are expected to provide adequate income and protection. One of my female informants argued, "No woman wants to work outside her family. It is men's duty to keep their women inside, within *parda*. What a woman wants is husband (*shami*), family (*shongshar*), and children (*chelemeye*)."

Regarding the wife's place among her husband's family, another female informant said,

Because I came to a man's home I have to obey him. He did not come to my home; rather, he brought me to his home; hence, he is superior, so I have to obey him. First comes the husband, then come other worldly matters. I have worked very hard, but I have never considered leaving my husband and marrying somebody else to avoid these hardships. I told myself, "Well, this is the only marriage I will have. I will die one day, so let me pass through this life." One cannot throw away her husband. After all, he is the husband. One cannot leave her husband if she has faith in religion. I am following the religion. Let me pass this life in my husband's home.

In rural Bangladesh, Islam determines the boundaries and spaces of interaction between males and females through the institution of *parda*. According to my informants, Allah predetermined the spaces of social interaction for both males and females. However, from Rozario's (1992) research in another rural community of Bangladesh, we find that Hindus and Christians also observe *parda*. *Parda* is thus part of Bengali culture irrespective of religious orientation. *Parda* existed even before the advent of Islam in Bangladesh. The practice of *parda* differs among women on the basis of their economic condition, education, and religiosity. However, it is widely perceived that a woman's world is different from that of a man. In rural Bangladesh, a woman's world is supposed to consist of her family, irrespective of her level of education or wealth. Her legitimate goals are getting married, having children, and nurturing the family. The ability to accomplish these goals constitutes a sort of power, although it is limited in scope. Religion helps the woman become a better wife, a better mother, and a better member of the family. It gives her confidence in her role and a feeling of strength. On the other hand, education, wealth, and external support may help a woman gain a stronger position in the family and may even expand her influence beyond the family. For the rural women I interviewed, power means the ability to accomplish goals and influence others. According to one female respondent, males have the ability to influence others because "earning is the sole responsibility of the male. A female cannot earn, and thus males are powerful. This is also the directive of the religion. Religion also asks us to worship males."

The consensus of my informants was that within the village community, the wealthy and educated males have the power. From wealth comes education and personal connections with other wealthy people or political leaders. Only a very few people, those whom Allah prefers, can accumulate wealth. Women may also accumulate wealth through inheritance or through other means, but they do not play a role in community affairs. Although the Prime Minister of Bangladesh and the leader of the opposition party in Parliament have been women for more than a decade, the majority of the villagers believe that political office is not a proper occupation for a woman and that those who are elected to such positions will go to Hell.

CONCLUSION: ISLAM AND POWER IN RURAL BANGLADESH

Max Weber defined power (*Macht*) as the "probability that one actor within a social relationship will be in a position to carry out his own will despite resistance, regardless of the basis on which this probability rests."[43] Weber described power in relation to control, authority, and legitimacy. According to him, control is exercised by the command of the power holder as well as the loyalty and obedience of the group the power holder commands. In this regard, he held, "All conceivable qualities of a person and all conceivable combinations of circumstances may put him in a position to impose his will in a given situation." By virtue of obedience, this command receives the necessary authority, and thus legitimacy, which ultimately allows the power holder to use force or coercion in order to gain control over the group he commands.

In the rural communities of Bangladesh, males possess the authority and legitimacy of command, and "the basis on which this probability rests" is culture and religion. From the statements reproduced above, it can be seen that women's perceived agency and their sense of power and powerlessness, are contingent to a considerable degree on their perception of Islam. At the same time, their perception of Islam is greatly influenced by the prevailing cultural practices of their region and community. Whatever rights and privileges Islam provides for women are subsumed within the patriarchal culture of their village and region. Religion is seen as a major support for this culture. According to my informants, wealth, education, and connections to influential people are the main sources of power and these are contingent upon God's blessings. Female informants perceive that their identity is subject to the will of their husbands, who have access to wealth and education. Furthermore, because of their greater autonomy in society, they have greater opportunities to develop connections with influential people.

In short, the female informants that I interviewed perceive power as the ability to act in a way that influences another's behavior. This belief recalls Robert A. Dahl's definition of power. Dahl similarly contended that power is the ability to influence the behavior of others. In his chapter, "The Concept of Power," he describes power in the following terms: "A has power over B to the extent that he can get B to do something that B would not otherwise do."[44] Dahl argued that power also depends on *resources* or *bases* of power (opportunities, acts, or objects), *means* or *instruments* of power (threats or promises), the *range* or *scope* of power (B's response to A), and the *amount* or *extent* of power (the probability of power being exercised successfully in conjunction with the means and scope of power). In their response to Dahl, Peter Bachrach and Morton S. Baratz argued that power also has a second face, which they called "non-decision-making"—the attempt to prevent an issue from ever reaching the decision-making stage.[45] They noted that a person uses power not only to influence the behavior of another but also to exclude the other from participating in the decision-making process. This tactic of "non–decision making" depends on the mobilization of bias. The paradigm of bias was developed by Elmer Schattschneider, who argued, "All forms of organization have a bias in favor of the exploitation of some kinds of conflict and the suppression of others because organization is the mobilization of bias. Some issues are organized into politics while others are organized out."[46]

Bachrach and Baratz also held that the exclusionary aspect of power sustains a form of bias that favors the values, myths, rituals, and institutions of a dominant group relative to the others. They maintained that the exercise of autonomous decision making could be prevented by force, threat of sanctions, manipulating symbols, or creating new barriers to participation.[47]

Steven Lukes extended the approaches developed by Dahl, Bachrach, and Baratz and added what he called "power's third dimension." He held that a person exercises power over another not merely by direct action or by creating barriers to participation but also by "influencing, shaping, or determining his very wants."[48] He also maintained that powerless people "accept their role in the existing order of things, either because they can see or imagine no alternative to it, or because they see it as natural and unchangeable, or because they value it as divinely ordained and beneficial."[49] This might occur, he argued, by controlling another's thoughts or by affecting another's perceptions through social forces and institutional practices that affect individuals' decisions. Gaventa, in his study of power and powerlessness among Appalachian Valley people, showed how socialization as well as ideology influenced the behaviors of the majority. His findings, he argued, warrant "the study of social myths, language, and symbols, and how they are shaped or manipulated in power processes."[50]

The findings of Dahl, Bachrach, Baratz, Lukes, and Gaventa are borne out in the results of my ethnographic study of a rural village in Bangladesh. Males have power over females to the extent that they can get females to do things that they would not otherwise do. The men of rural villages in Bangladesh possess the *resources* of power (property, education, greater mobility) they wield the *instruments* of power (for example, by convening the *shalish* or *bichar* councils) and they exercise the "second face" of power by using such instruments to compel an attitude of "non–decision making" on the part of women. Institutions such as the *paribar* (family unit) and the *shalish/bichar* (ad hoc councils) are male-dominated, and thus may be used to exert the pressure of mobilization bias against females. In addition, the sanctions that are imposed by the *shalish/bichar* are a potent deterrent for any behavior that is considered undesirable.

Most important, rural women in Bangladesh take the dominance of men for granted. The basis of male dominance is rooted in the belief system of their community, which depends largely on religion. In his famous definition of religion as a cultural system, Clifford Geertz stated: "Religion is (1) a system of symbols which acts to (2) establish powerful, pervasive, and long-lasting moods and motivations in men by (3) formulating conceptions of a general order of existence and (4) clothing these conceptions with such an aura of factuality that (5) the moods and motivations seem uniquely realistic."[51] Geertz argued that religion is one of the essential elements of culture through which the dynamics of symbols are expressed.[52] The overlapping relation between religion and culture can be seen in the fact that cultural patterns "give meaning, i.e. objective conceptual form, to social and psychological reality both by shaping themselves to it and by shaping it to themselves."[53] In a similar manner, the Christian theologian Paul Tillich maintained, "Religion is the essence of culture and culture is the form of religion."[54] He further noted that all human experience occurs within a cultural milieu and that religion provides culture with form and content but also meaning, a process he called the "import of meaning."[55] For the women of rural Bangladesh, it appears that the institutions of a patriarchal culture whose roots were prior to Islam, combined with the institutions and practices of Islam to subsume the autonomous identity of woman by relegating them to a position of "non-decision-making." In this situation, the rural woman is taught to regard herself as the shadow of a man. What Allah gives to man, is given to woman only because she is part of a man, not a whole unto herself. Thus, to paraphrase a famous passage of the Bible, "What God gives, a man can take away."

NOTES

1. John Gaventa, *Power and Powerlessness: Quiescence and Rebellion in an Appalachian Valley* (Urbana and Chicago, Illinois: University of Illinois Press, 1980).

2. Bangladesh Bureau of Statistics, *Statistical Pocketbook of Bangladesh 2003* (Dhaka: Government Printing Press, 2005), 3, 424.

3. Ibid., 3, 149.

4. See, for example, Article 28 of the Constitution of Bangladesh; Ministry of Women and Children Affairs, *Narir Ainee Odhikar* (Legal Rights of Women) (Dhaka: Technical Assistance for Gender Facility and institutional Support for Implementation of the National Action Plan Project, 2000); and Ministry of Women and Children Affairs, *An Introduction to Development Projects* (Dhaka, 2004).

5. Bangladesh, Ministry of Planning, *Bangladesh Data Sheet 1999,* available at http://www.bbsgov.org.

6. *Statistical Pocket Book of Bangladesh 2003,* 136–137.

7.   In the Parliament election of 2001, only six female candidates won seats, and later another woman won in a by-election. Results of the original election are available at the Bangladesh Election Commission's website, http://www.ece.gov.bd/stat/Index/htm.

8.   Amartya K. Sen, "Women, Technology and Sexual Divisions," *Trade and Development—An UNCTAD Review* 6 (1985): 195–223; see also, idem, *Rationality and Freedom* (Cambridge, Massachusetts: Harvard University Press, 2002).

9.   World Bank, *Toward Gender Equality: The Role of Public Policy* (Washington, D.C.: The World Bank, 1995).

10.   For example, see Carolyn M. Elliot, "Theories of Development: An Assessment," in *Women and National Development: The Complexities of Change,* eds. B.X. Bunster et al. (Chicago/London: The University of Chicago Press, 1977), 1–8.

11.   For a detailed discussion of the place of women in nationalist discourses, see Ranajit Guha, ed., *A Subaltern Studies Reader, 1986–1995* (Minneapolis, Minnesota: University of Minnesota Press, 1997), Chandra's death, 34–62; and Dipesh Chakrabarty, *Provincializing Europe* (Princeton, New Jersey: Princeton University Press, 2000).

12.   Census conducted by the present author.

13.   See Jenneke Arens and Jos V. Beurden, *Jhagrapur: Poor Peasants and Women in a Village in Bangladesh* (Birmingham, U.K.: Third World Publications, 1977).

14.   See Sharon B. Merriam, *Case Study Research in Education: A Qualitative Approach* (San Francisco, California: Jossey-Bass, 1988).

15.   Norman K. Denzin and Yvonna S. Lincoln, "Introduction: The Discipline and Practice of Qualitative Research," in *Handbook of Qualitative Research, Second Edition,* eds. Norman K. Denzin and Yvonna S. Lincoln (Newbury Park, California: Sage Press, 2000) 1–28.

16.   Catherine Marshall and Gretchen B. Rossman, eds., *Designing Qualitative Research,* 3rd ed. (Thousand Oaks, California: Sage Publications, 1999).

17.   Census conducted by the present author. Statistically, an adult is a person who is 15 years of age or older.

18.   According to the Muslim Family Law Ordinance of 1961, polygamy is not illegal but difficult. Written permission of the first wife is necessary for the husband to have a second wife, which then must be justified and endorsed by the Chairman of the Union Council. It is thus easier for a husband to divorce his first wife than to gain her permission to marry a second wife.

19.   A. Miranda, "Nuptility in Bangladesh," *Journal of Social Studies,* no. 9 (1980): 58–98.

20.   Jean Ellickson, "A Believer among Believers: The Religious Beliefs, Practices, and Meanings in a Village in Bangladesh" (Ph.D. dissertation, Michigan State University, 1972).

21.   John P. Thorp, "Masters of Earth: Conceptions of Power among Muslims of Rural Bangladesh" (Ph.D. dissertation, University of Chicago, 1978).

22.   Geoffrey D. Wood, "Class Differentiation and Power in Bandakgram: The Minifundist Case," in *Exploitation and the Rural Poor: A Working Paper on the Rural*

Power Structure in Bangladesh, ed. M.A. Huq (Comilla, Bangladesh: Bangladesh Academy for Rural Development, 1976), 60–96.

23. Jitka Kotalova, *Belonging to Others: Cultural Construction of Womanhood Among Muslims in a Village in Bangladesh* (Uppsala, Sweden: Acta Universitatis Upsaliensis, 1993).

24. Santi Rozario, *Purity and Communal Boundaries: Women and Social Change in a Bangladeshi Village* (North Sydney, Australia: Allen & Unwin, 1994).

25. The Muslim Family Law Ordinance of 1961.

26. See for details, Saira R. Khan, *The Socio-Legal Status of Bangali Women in Bangladesh: Implications for Development* (Dhaka, Bangladesh: University Press, 2001).

27. For a detailed discussion and review of the laws of divorce in other Muslim countries, see Alamgir M. Serajuddin, *Shari'a Law and Society: Tradition and change in South Asia* (Oxford, U.K.: Oxford University Press, 2001).

28. See Khan, *Socio-Legal Status of Bangali Women;* see also, Taslima Monsoor, *From Patriarchy to Gender Equality: Family Law and Its Impact on Women in Bangladesh* (Dhaka, Bangladesh: University Press, 1999); and Tazeen Murshid, *The Sacred and the Secular: Bengal Muslim Discourses, 1871–1977* (Calcutta: Oxford University Press, 1995).

29. See Kirsten Westergaard, *State and Rural Society in Bangladesh*, Scandinavian Institute of Asian Studies Monograph Series no. 49 (London/Malmö, U.K./Sweden: Curzon Press, 1985).

30. Abdul Quadir Zilani, popularly known as *Bara* Pir, was a famous Sufi saint of twelfth-century Baghdad. Known to history as 'Abd al-Qadir al-Jilani (d. 1166 CE), he was the founder of the Qadiriyya Sufi order, one of the most widespread Sufi confraternities in the Muslim world.

31. For detailed information on the social effects of *parda,* see Sajeda Amin, "The Poverty-Purdah Trap in Rural Bangladesh: Implications for Women's Roles in the Family," Working Paper Series no. 75 (New York: Research Division, The Population Council, 1995).

32. Shelley Feldman, "Purdah and Changing Patterns of Social Control among Rural Women in Bangladesh," *Journal of Marriage and the Family,* 45 no. 4 (1983): 949–960.

33. David Abecassis, *Identity, Islam, and Human Development in Rural Bangladesh* (Dhaka, Bangladesh: University Press, 1990), 57.

34. See for further details Peter J. Bertocci, "Models of Solidarity, Structures of Power: The Politics of Community in Rural Bangladesh," in *Political Anthropology Yearbook 1,* ed., Myron J. Aronoff (New Brunswick, New Jersey: Transaction Books, 1990), 97–125; Rafiuddin Ahmed, ed. "Islam and the Social Construction of the Bangladesh Countryside," *Understanding the Bengal Muslims: Interpretative Essays* (New Delhi: Oxford University Press, 2001), 71–85.

35. See, for example, Taj I. Hashmi, *Women and Islam in Bangladesh: Beyond Subjugation and Tyranny* (New York: St. Martin's Press, 2000).

36. See the US State Department's website http://www.state.gov/g/drl/rls/irf/2005/51616.htm retrieved on March 29, 2005 and also Amnesty Internationals

website http://web.amnesty.org/library/index/ENGASA130012001?open& of=ENG-BGD retrieved on April 03, 2006.

37.   Thorp, "Masters of Earth," 68.

38.   Ibid., 74.

39.   On early Islamic jurisprudential opinions on marriage, see Kecia Ali, "Money, Sex, and Power: The contractual Nature of Marriage in Islamic Jurisprudence of the Formative Period" (Ph.D. dissertation, Duke University, 2002).

40.   Shahla Haeri, *Law of Desire: Temporary Marriage in Shi'i Iran* (New York: Syracuse University Press, 1989), 34.

41.   Ali, "Money, Sex, and Power," 475.

42.   Ibid., 354.

43.   Max Weber, *The Theory of Social and Economic Organization*, trans. M. Henderson and T. Parsons (New York: Oxford University Press, 1947), 152–153.

44.   Robert A. Dahl, "The Concept of Power," *Behavioral Science* 2 (July 1957): 202–203.

45.   Peter Bachrach and Morton S. Baratz, "Two Faces of Power," *American Political Science Review* 56 (December 1962): 947–952.

46.   Elmer E. Schattschneider, *The Semi-sovereign People* (New York: Holt, Rinehart and Winston, 1960), 71.

47.   Peter Bachrach and Morton S. Baratz, *Power and Poverty: Theory and Practice* (New York: Oxford University Press, 1970), 42–46.

48.   Steven Lukes, *Power: A Radical View* (London, U.K.: Macmillan, 1974), 23.

49.   Ibid., 24.

50.   Gaventa, *Power and Powerlessness,* 15.

51.   Clifford Geertz, "Religion as a Cultural System," in Anthropological Approaches to the Study of Religion, ed. M. Banton (London, U.K.: Tavistock, 1966), 1–46.

52.   Clifford Geertz, *The Interpretation of Cultures: Selected Essays* (New York: Basic Books 1973), 4.

53.   Geertz, "Religion as a Cultural System," 1966, 8.

54.   Paul Tillich, *Theology of Culture* (New York: Oxford University Press 1959), 42.

55.   Paul Tillich, *What is Religion?* (New York: Harper Torchbooks, 1969), 59.

3

MARRIAGE IN ISLAM

———————————— • ————————————

Nargis Virani

The Qur'an is the foundational and inspirational basis of all Islamic laws, albeit interpreted and adapted to the historical and contemporary circumstances and situations of various groups. Over the last century, some of the traditional rulings related to the person and the family were codified in a modern category known as Muslim Family Law. One or another version of Muslim Family Law is in force in most Muslim countries today. In other countries where Muslims do not form a majority, there may be a provision for the application of Muslim Family Law for its Muslim population. For example, enshrined in the Constitution of the Republic of India is the right of Indian Muslims to be governed by Muslim Family Law in their personal and religious affairs.

Over time, besides the Qur'an, other sources of law were developed and acknowledged. These played a highly significant role in the codification of Islamic Law in general, and family law in particular. Where the specificities of particular situations were not directly addressed in the Qur'an, or where the application of a specific verse of the Qur'an to a particular situation permitted several interpretations, Muslim jurists customarily turned to the Sunna, including the Hadith of the Prophet Muhammad. In addition, the jurists routinely resorted to *ijtihad* (personal, intellectual, and jurisprudential endeavor), which resulted in a system of reasoning and interpretation that developed important foundational principles over the course of several centuries of implementation. One such principle states that laws may change according to time, place, and circumstance. There is a clear recognition that previously unencountered situations demand the boundaries of Islamic law to be reexamined and, if necessary, expanded, albeit within the confines of Qur'anic regulations. Theoretically, this principle offers a reasonable degree of flexibility for the application of Islamic law at all times and for all communities. In practice, however, the *ijtihad* of jurists on all matters generally, and on marriage and divorce particularly, was often partial to their various environments. In addition, the male gender of almost all jurists until contemporary times, irrespective of the particular school of jurisprudence, resulted in the exclusion of the female perspective.

Nowadays, matters related to marriage and divorce fall under the rubric of Muslim Family Law. In the earlier periods of Islamic history, however, Muslim Family Law was not codified. Thus, each judge resorted to the Qur'an and Hadith when faced with a certain issue and performed his own *ijtihad*. Over time, different schools of legal thought became established. This resulted in diverse groups influenced by varied sectarian and theological persuasions, as well as different ruling powers, which selected the jurisprudence of a particular school as the basis of their legal system. This practice continues in our times. The major schools of Islamic law are the Maliki, Hanbali, Hanafi, Shafi'i, and Ja'fari (largely followed by the Twelver Shiites), named as such after their founder figures. An important point to note is that it is possible to encounter substantial jurisprudential variations between schools and among different scholars within each school.

THE CONTEXT OF MARRIAGE IN ISLAM

In Islam, marriage is an institution in which a man and a woman are joined in a physical, social, and legal relationship. The Qur'an lays down the foundations of the physical and social aspects of the institution of marriage and specifies some of the legal rules that govern them. It also stipulates clear rules for the dissolution of marriage in the unfortunate case that the marriage becomes unsustainable. Hence, both marriage and divorce are issues that are discussed extensively in the Qur'an.

The Qur'an conceives of marriage as a civil contract between a man and a woman. As such, it is governed by rules that define the relationship between two contracting parties. Marriage is the favored institution for a legitimate sexual relationship between a man and a woman. The Qur'an recognizes sexuality as a central feature of the natural world and consequently as an innate and vital dimension of human existence. Thus, even though it lays down certain rules that govern human sexuality (for example, within the confines of marriage), it authorizes sexual pleasure and does not only condone sex for the sake of procreation.

In premodern times, concubinage was a possible secondary institution whereby a man purchased a female slave and contracted a sexual relationship with her. Outside of the institutions of marriage and concubinage, however, the Qur'an views all other sexual relationships as illicit. Either explicitly or by implication, it condemns incest, adultery, fornication, prostitution, promiscuity, lewdness, and homosexuality. It also stipulates punishments for such infringements. Chastity is an essential virtue demanded of all Muslims, both men and women alike. Marriage is desirable for every member of the Muslim community, even for slaves. Celibacy is not regarded as a virtue. The Prophet

Muhammad is reported to have said, "There is no monasticism in Islam." He is also reported to have given the following advice to his followers: "Whoever is well-off, let him marry, for he who does not marry is not one of us." He also stated, "Oh assembly of young men! Whoever can afford to marry, let him do so, for it is more effective in lowering one's gaze and keepings one's privates chaste. Whoever cannot do this, should fast, for it has the effect of restraining lust."

Allowable sexual relations in the Qur'an are designated by the term *nikah*, which connotes both marriage and intercourse (Qur'an 2:221, 230, 232, 235, 237; 4:3, 6, 22, 25, 127; 24:3, 23, 33, 60; 28:27; 33:49, 50, 53). Marriage prevents sexual frustration and the temptation to sin (Qur'an 24:32). Married persons, in other words, those with a licit sexual partner, are called *muhsan* (masc.) or *muhsana* (fem.), "guarded" or "fortified." Illicit sex or contraventions of sexual conventions are called *fahisha* (Qur'an 3:135; 4:15, 19, 22, 25; 6:151; 7:28, 33, 80; 17:32; 24:19; 27:54; 29:28; 33:30; 42:37; 53:32; 65:1). The collective term *al-fahsha'* also appears in the Qur'an (Qur'an 2:169, 268; 7:28; 12:24; 16:90; 24:21; 29:45). The Qur'an refers to adultery or fornication as *zina* and to the adulterer as a *zani* (masc.) or *zaniya* (fem.) (Qur'an 17:32; 24:2, 3; 25:68; 60:12). The Qur'an is silent on other sexual infractions, including homosexuality (*liwata*), lesbianism (*sahq, sihaq*), bestiality, and masturbation (*istimna, nikah al-yad, jald 'umayra*).

Another obvious and practical reason to contract marriage is to ensure the flourishing of the community through reproduction. In practical terms, most of the laws of marriage and divorce in Islam are primarily concerned with safeguarding the rights and well-being of children (Qur'an 4:2; 7:189; 16:72; 17:24). In addition, Qur'anic rulings support and protect female members of the community such as widows, divorcees, and orphans, who may, for one reason or another, no longer have access to family support.

TERMS FOR MARRIAGE IN ISLAM

Among Muslims, the most commonly used term for marriage is *nikah*, which literally means "sexual intercourse." As a legal term, *nikah* denotes the situation resulting from a contract entered into by a Muslim man and a Muslim woman, which legitimizes cohabitation and sexual intercourse between the signers of the contract in the eyes of God and their co-religionists. Among many contemporary Muslims, the term *nikah* has acquired religious significance, particularly for those living under secular governments where court registration of the marriage contract is mandatory. A civil registration or marriage license is perceived as a secular and legal obligation as opposed to *nikah*, which is a religious obligation. The verb *nakaha,* "to marry," is used to denote either the man marrying the woman or the woman marrying the man.

Based on the Qur'anic term for a pair, *zawj,* each of the marriage partners is called *zawj* (fem. *zawja*), literally, "one of a pair" or "one of a couple." In Muslim countries where Arabic language and culture predominate, marriage is referred to as *zawaj,* literally, "pairing." More recently, the term *zawaj* has gained currency on cyberspace among non-Arabs as well. According to both tradition and Islamic law, a marriage is a public act, and thus it must be publicized. A feast or a celebration is usually held on such an occasion. The marriage celebration may be referred to as *'urs* (Arabic), *izdiwaj/'arusi* (Persian and Dari), *shaadi* (Urdu), or *dugun* (Turkish).

The Qur'an repeatedly cites the universe as evidence of God's existence and omnipotence. Naturally occurring pairs are an important part of the order of the universe: "He created the pair, male and female." (Qur'an 53:45). "We have created everything in pairs that you might reflect" (Qur'an 51:49). In accordance with God's command, Noah brought pairs of each species of animal onto the ark (Qur'an 11:49; 23:27). This universe of pairs extends to the human species as well: "Oh humankind! We have created you male and female, and have made you nations and tribes, that you may know one another" (Qur'an 49:13). "And God made [from a drop of sperm] the pair, the male and female" (Qur'an 75:39).

The Qur'an also notes a higher order of the male–female relationship beyond sexual fulfillment. The lasting consequences of marriage, the feelings of togetherness, companionship, love, tranquility, and peaceful and mutually supportive interdependence are underscored in several verses. "Among [God's] signs is that he created for you mates from yourselves so that you might find tranquility in them, and he put love and mercy between you. Therein are indeed signs for folk who reflect" (Qur'an 30:21). "[Women] are a garment for you and you are a garment for them. So lie down with them, and seek what God has prescribed for you" (Qur'an 2:187).

ELEMENTS OF THE ISLAMIC MARRIAGE CONTRACT

The Islamic marriage is founded on a contract that is rendered null and void when certain elements are absent. Shiite Muslims recognize two foundational elements to the marriage, Sunnis of the Hanafi and Maliki schools of jurisprudence recognize three elements, and Sunnis of the Shafi'i and Hanbali schools recognize four elements. All schools of Islamic thought agree that the first two elements of the marriage contract, namely, the Formula and Personal Status, are mandatory.

The Formula (Sigha)

A Muslim marriage is legalized by a contract (*'aqd*), which consists of a declaration (*ijab*) and an acceptance (*qubul*). The woman "declares" that she is entering into a marital relationship with the man, and he "accepts" her as his wife. Different law schools propose different terminology for both the declaration and the acceptance. However, all agree that both the declaration and the acceptance must be uttered in a single session. Except for the Hanbalis, none insist on the order in which the declaration and acceptance are uttered. If a person knows the Arabic language, he or she can pronounce the formula in Arabic, otherwise the person can use equivalent terms in his or her own language. A mute is permitted to use sign language.

Personal Status (Mahall)

The personal status of the man and the woman should be free from legal impediments to their marriage as specified by the particular law school that they follow. The Malikis also include freedom from physical defects that may be detrimental to the marriage. In addition, the specific identity of the persons contracting the marriage must be clearly stated. Generic statements, such as "One of my daughters or sons is marrying one of yours," uttered by the guardian are not acceptable. This nullifies the marriage contract.

Preferred Marriage Partners

Certain types of marriage partners are more preferred than others are, certain other types are strictly prohibited. For example, it is preferable for all Muslim men and women to marry their coreligionists. However, all of the Sunni legal schools agree that a man may marry a non-Muslim woman who is one of the "People of the Book" (*Ahl al-Kitab*). This includes Jews, Christians, and Sabeans (a sect that most Muslims believe no longer exists). Zoroastrians, certain types of Hindus, and Buddhists are accepted by some Muslims as "People of the Book" as well, but this is a matter of dispute. Shiite law only permits a temporary (*mut'a*) marriage, not a permanent marriage between a Muslim man and a woman from the "People of the Book" (Ar. *kitabiyya*).

All schools of Islamic thought agree that a Muslim woman should not marry a man who is not "sufficient" (*kafi*) for her. The Shiites restrict the concept of sufficiency (*kafa'a*) to religion only; in other words, the man must be a Muslim. Thus, a Muslim woman is forbidden to marry a non-Muslim man until he becomes a Muslim by reciting the *Shahada*, the Islamic testimony of faith, before two witnesses. In addition to the requirement that the groom must be a Muslim, all four Sunni law schools require, to varying degrees, the following factors as part of the determination of sufficiency: lineage, profession, free status (as opposed to slavery), piety, and property. In Sunni Islam, a woman may petition to divorce her husband if he cannot provide for his wife materially, in the way she was accustomed among her natal family.

Number of Marriage Partners

A Muslim woman is allowed to have only one husband at a time. However, the Qur'an specifies that a Muslim man may have as many as four wives at the same time, provided he could treat them equally. The Qur'an states: "If you fear that you cannot do justice to orphans, then marry from among women such as you like, two, three, or four. But if you fear you will not be fair, then one only; that is the safest course" (Qur'an 4:3). However, another verse of the Qur'an raises strong doubts as to the ability of the husband to meet the condition of equal treatment: "You will never be able to do justice among women, no matter how much you desire to do so" (Qur'an 4:129). For this reason, some modern scholars such as Fazlur Rahman (d. 1988) have concluded that, based on the dictates of the Qur'an, the established marital norm should be monogamy and not *polygyny*, in which a man has the right to marry more than one wife.

It seems that the Qur'anic permission to marry more than one woman may have been prompted by special historical circumstances in Medina at the time of the foundation of the first Islamic state. These circumstances may have included a surplus in the number of women with respect to men, the large number of widowed or separated wives because of battle losses and conversion to Islam from polytheism, and the unfair treatment of female wards by their guardians. One also imagines that for a man who physically "must" have more than one partner, polygyny safeguards his religion, his partner's piety, and the status of their children. Other circumstances may justify the practice of polygyny as well. For example, if the first wife is bedridden or disabled for life, she may accept a second wife into the household because she is physically unable to provide for her husband's needs. Furthermore, when one witnesses the frequency with which men of means leave their wives for younger women after the first wife has spent her youth establishing the family, one might imagine that polygyny is better than divorce. Instead of losing everything, including her social status, by being divorced by the husband, the first wife can look forward to the prospect of being maintained in her own home with dignity and can still claim her husband's attention half of the time.

Forbidden Marriages

Among the marriages that are forbidden in Islam, some are permanently forbidden and others are forbidden only temporarily. Marriages that are permanently forbidden are based primarily on rulings contained in verses 22–24 of *Surat al-Nisa'* (Sura 4, "The Women") of the Qur'an. Categories of people that Muslims are forbidden to marry under any circumstances are as follows:

1. Heathens and polytheists (Qur'an 2:221; 60:10)
2. Adulterers and fornicators
3. Close blood relatives

   a. Mother

   b. Stepmother

   c. Grandmothers of any generation

   d. Daughters and granddaughters of any generation

   e. Sisters (whether full, consanguine or uterine)

   f. Father's sisters (including paternal grandfather's sisters)

   g. Mother's sisters (including maternal grandmother's sisters)

   h. Brother's daughters

   i. Sister's daughters

   j. Son's wife

   k. Wife's mother

   l. Stepdaughter (The daughter by a former husband of a woman one has married if the marriage is consummated. However, if such a marriage was not consummated, there is no prohibition.)
4. "Milk" relatives (a foster relationship based on the sharing of breast milk)

   a. Foster mother

   b. Foster mother's sister

   c. Foster sister

Categories of persons for whom temporary marriage prohibitions apply include in-laws and former wives who are in various stages of divorce or separation. For example, a man cannot marry two sisters or an aunt and a niece at the same time. He may marry a sister or a niece, however, if the wife dies before her sister or if the aunt dies before her niece. When a woman's husband dies, she must not marry another husband until she has completed a waiting period (*'idda*) of four months and ten days. This rule is to ensure the paternity and inheritance rights of any child that might have been conceived before the husband's death.

When a man divorces his wife, he cannot remarry until after the *'idda* waiting period is completed. If he divorces his wife irrevocably, he cannot marry her again unless she has first married another man, who also divorces her irrevocably after consummating the marriage. In such a case, the former husband would also have to wait until his former wife's *'idda* period has been completed. As in Western societies, a married woman cannot marry another man unless she obtains a divorce or unless her husband dies. In both cases, however, she must wait for the fulfillment of the *'idda* period before remarrying.

Besides the irrevocable divorce, a man's marriage to his wife is invalidated in a few other cases as well. One of these cases is called *ila'* (forswearing). In such a case, the husband takes an oath in God's name not to have a sexual relationship with his wife, either forever or for a period exceeding four months. If the husband does this, a judge (*qadi*) has the right to annul the marriage. In the case of *li'an* (a repudiation or sworn accusation), the husband takes his wife before a judge and either accuses her of infidelity or denies being the father of their child. He must swear to this accusation four times in God's name. The wife may also swear in similar manner that she is innocent. After a *li'an* divorce, both parties are ineligible to have any further sexual contact with each other. *Li'an* divorces tend to occur when a husband suspects his wife of infidelity but cannot prove his claim objectively. Although the wife might suffer damage to her reputation in such a divorce, she is not considered guilty of infidelity and thus is not subject to the severe punishments that may be inflicted in a case of proven infidelity. Finally, in the first century of Islam, some women were repudiated by their husbands through a pre-Islamic practice known as *zihar*. In *zihar*, the husband forswears a sexual relationship with his wife by declaring her to be "like his mother" or like any other female relative that is forbidden to him. *Zihar* repudiations were forbidden in Islamic law and resulted in the annulment of the marriage.

Guardianship (Wilaya)

The schools of Islamic jurisprudence generally agree that a Muslim woman who has not previously been married needs a legal guardian (*wali*) to enter into a marriage. The regulations of guardianship also apply to boys who have not yet attained adulthood, and to mentally incompetent men. The guardian may be the father or the father's father (the position of the Hanafi, Shafi'i, and Ja'fari schools of jurisprudence). If the father is not present, the guardian may be an elder brother. The mother has no guardianship except in the Hanafi school, which allows her to conclude a marriage contract in the absence of the father. In addition, among the Hanafis, a woman of adult age may act in her own behalf. The legal schools disagree significantly as to the extent, nature, and duration of the guardian's authority. In the Maliki, Hanbali, and Shafi'i schools, the approval of the guardian is one of the conditions (*shart*) of concluding the marriage contract. Hence, in these three schools, if the girl or the woman is a virgin, she does not have the right to conclude a marriage contract without her guardian's participation irrespective of her age. This is justified on the ground that virgins lack experience with men and may be swayed by emotions in their decision to marry. She may act on her own behalf, however, if she has been married previously.

The other schools allow varying degrees of exception to the role of the guardian, and to the requirement of obtaining the consent of the female to be married, on the basis of her age and her virginity. In the Ja'fari and Hanafi schools, the guardian's permission is required only for a girl who has not yet attained adulthood, an incompetent or insane girl or woman, or a woman of advanced age. In both of these schools, a girl who has attained adulthood may marry whomever she wishes. However, the Hanafis give the guardian the right to annul the marriage contract of a young girl if, in his opinion, the condition of economic "sufficiency" (*kafa'a*) is not fulfilled. In Hanafi practice, a woman who has attained majority age can "marry down" in accordance with her own wishes. She may also petition a judge to act as her guardian and thus overrule the objection of her familial guardian if she deems such objections unfair. In actual practice, both the Hanafis and the Malikis have added cultural-based class and economic distinctions to the original piety-based articulation of the notion of "sufficiency." The Shiites, on the other hand, view a woman who has reached puberty, whether virgin or otherwise, as a full legal person coequal with her male counterpart. She is considered legally competent to make her own marriage decisions and even to conclude her own marriage contract, regardless of the father or guardian's approval, or of the social or economic status of the prospective spouse.

Witnesses (Shahid)

In Sunni Islam, a marriage contract is a public document. Thus, all Sunni schools require the presence of two male witnesses for the marital contract to be valid. The presence of one male and two females may also fulfill this requirement. The Shi'a do not require the presence of any witnesses as a condition of the marriage contract. Thus, a man and a woman may conclude a marital contract in private or in secret, if they wish to do so.

Bride Wealth (Mahr or Sadaq)

The *mahr* or *sadaq*, "dower," is an essential feature of the marriage contract. It is specified as a payment to the bride herself, and not to her father or guardian. The *mahr* is a gift of money or property that must be given by the prospective husband to legally validate the marriage. Theoretically, the amount of *mahr* is to be negotiated between the bride and the groom. In practice, however, the guardian frequently negotiates the *mahr,* often without the bride's input or knowledge. Such practices usually occur because of lack of knowledge about the proper Shari'a rules or because of established cultural traditions. Although it is technically not permissible under Islamic law for the guardian to negotiate the dower, sanctions against this practice are seldom applied.

The *mahr* may be given all at once or it may be divided into two parts; one to be paid before consummating the marriage (*mahr al-muqaddam*) and the other stipulated for future payment in the event of divorce or death (*mahr al-mu'ajjal* or *mu'akhkhar*). The amount of the *mahr* is individually determined and is customarily commensurate with the economic and social standing of the bride's family. It is henceforth considered the sole property of the bride. This stipulation is not to be confused with the practice prevalent in some parts of the world, in Muslim and non-Muslim societies alike, whereby the bride's family demands the "bride price" as the price for the woman they are giving away. The *Mahr* would thus be more accurately understood as "bride wealth," which is theoretically intended to establish the woman's financial independence.

In contemporary times, the *mahr* has assumed a more significant role for Muslim women who, due to greater access to education, have come to a better understanding of the theoretical significance of this practice. Many women, devout and religiously nonobservant alike, have come to view the *mahr* as a sort of "divine protection" afforded to Muslim women centuries before secular laws offered financial protection to all women, particularly in the Western world. Undoubtedly, better educational levels have empowered many Muslim women to actively participate in the negotiation of the *mahr* amount. In addition, a better sense of individual rights has conferred upon them the power to negotiate, to their advantage, other conditions within the marriage contract. Islamic jurisprudence had always left these conditions open for negotiation in principle, except that only a few women could avail themselves of the practice because of their social, economic, and educational levels, or of their guardian's open-mindedness and willingness to negotiate to their advantage.

MUT'A MARRIAGE: A TEMPORARY MARRIAGE CONTRACT

This form of marriage practice is limited in Islamic jurisprudence to the Twelver Shiites, the *Ithna 'ashariyya,* who comprise the majority of the Shi'a in contemporary Islam. Other Shiite groups, such as the Ismailis, considered this practice illegal. *Mut'a* marriage is sometimes described as "marriage of limited duration" (*al-nikah al-muwaqqat*) or "discontinued marriage" (*al-nikah al-munqati'*). Most often, it is understood as "temporary marriage."

The Arabic dictionaries define the term *mut'a* as "enjoyment, pleasure, delight." Thus, this marriage may also be understood as "marriage for the purpose of pleasure." Both Shiite and Sunni authorities agree upon the fact that this form of marriage was practiced in early Islam. However, they disagree as to the reasons why it was permitted. They also disagree about whether it was to be continued beyond a certain time and circumstance, or whether it was meant to be abolished when circumstances changed. The Sunnis believe that the permission to practice *mut'a* marriage was eventually abrogated. However, the Twelver Shi'a, based on reports from their early Imams, believe that it was to be continued.

Although it is not as widely practiced as the normal Muslim marriage, Twelver Shiite jurisprudential works discuss *mut'a* marriage with the same care and detail that they do for a "permanent marriage." Thus, the foundational elements of this type of marriage are similar to those of any other marriage: both types of marriage rely on a prescribed formula for marriage, both share concern for the physical and psychological health of the individuals contracting the marriage, and both require the negotiation of *mahr*, "bride wealth." The most important difference between the *mut'a* marriage and the normal Muslim marriage is that in a *mut'a* marriage the duration (*mudda*) of the marriage must be specified in the marriage contract. There is no lower limit to the duration of a *mut'a* marriage. However, the upper limit is 99 years. For this reason, the duration of the marriage must be stipulated so that there is no room for ambiguity. The stipulated duration must be strictly adhered to.

It is permissible to add other conditions to the *mut'a* contract so long as they are legitimate, such as the stipulation of particular meeting times, the number of sexual acts, and the expected time of the consummation of the temporary marriage. By consensus of the jurists, however, divorce is not allowed in a *mut'a* marriage. The two parties separate after the end of the stipulated period, once the other stipulations of the marriage contract have been fulfilled. There are no further rights or obligations on the part of either party beyond what is clearly specified in the contract. The *'idda*, "waiting period," before a woman can marry again is two menstrual cycles in a *mut'a* marriage. This is shorter than the waiting period of three menstrual cycles (usually equivalent to three months) that is required after the dissolution of a normal marriage. If the wife is pregnant at the time of separation, her waiting period is extended to the time it takes for her to give birth or to the end of her *'idda* period, whichever is longer. In all cases, whether in a permanent marriage or in a temporary marriage, the waiting period is mandated in order to safeguard the legitimacy and rights of the child that may be born after the separation of the wife from the husband. The husband is obligated to provide for the child irrespective of the nature of the marriage.

Within the rules of *mut'a* marriage, certain types of women are recommended for marriage, others are forbidden for a man to marry, and still others are considered reprehensible for the man contracting the temporary marriage. Some of these rules are as follows:

a.   It is preferable to contract a *mut'a* marriage with a free and chaste Muslim woman.

b.   It is permissible to contract a *mut'a* marriage with women from among the "People of the Book," but one may not contract such a marriage with a polytheist or with an enemy of the Household of the Prophet.[1]

c.   A man may not contract a *mut'a* marriage with the daughter of his permanent wife's sister or brother without his permanent wife's permission.

d.   A man may not contract a *mut'a* marriage with another person's slave without her master's permission and without his own permanent wife's permission.

e.   It is reprehensible, but not forbidden, to contract a *mut'a* marriage with a woman of loose morals. If a man were to contract a temporary marriage with such a woman, it is his duty to command her not to have a sexual relationship with any other person during the stipulated time of their marriage.

f.   It is reprehensible to contract a *mut'a* marriage with a virgin. This would cause hardship to her family because it would make her less desirable for a permanent marriage. If a temporary marriage contract were somehow concluded with a virgin, the man is not permitted to consummate the marriage without her father's permission. Such a condition is almost impossible to imagine in most Muslim societies.

The agreement between Shiite and Sunni authorities concerning the practice of *mut'a* marriage during the Prophet's lifetime confirms the original sanction of this practice. Both groups agree that 'Umar ibn al-Khattab, the second Caliph of Islam (r. 634–644 CE), ordered the practice to be discontinued. This confirms that the practice was continued after the Prophet Muhammad's death, at least through the Caliphate of Abu Bakr (r. 632–634 CE). The ensuing debate between Sunnis and Shiites about whether 'Umar had the authority to discontinue the practice of *mut'a*—and whether or not the Shiite Imams allowed the practice to continue—underscores the fact that, early on in Islamic history, there was a pliability of attitude with regard to the continuity or abrogation of certain practices in Islam.

MARRIAGE IN THE LAWS OF CONTEMPORARY MUSLIM COUNTRIES

The intrinsic capacity for evolution within Islamic law is illustrated by the contemporary efforts undertaken by Muslim states to revisit family law and enact legislation accommodating contemporary sensibilities. Most present-day Muslim countries have codified their family laws primarily on the basis of a particular school of Islamic jurisprudence, to which a majority of their population adheres. Sometimes, however, the laws of a particular country combine the jurisprudence of one school with that of other schools. Such combinations, when consistent and properly reasoned, are justified because of the Prophet Muhammad's famous statement that difference of opinion among his community is a source of divine mercy. The Qur'anic verse emphasizing that Islam is a religion of ease, not of complications and difficulties, further strengthens the approach of combining codes from different schools. The North African country of Tunisia leads the way among the Muslim nations that have enacted the most far-reaching reforms in family law. The Tunisian Code of Personal Status, enacted in 1956, not only provides for a minimum age of marriage for women (now 17), but has also abolished polygyny and has abrogated the right of a guardian to contract a marriage without the woman's consent. In effect, Tunisia, whose legal culture is based on Maliki jurisprudence, has abandoned the Maliki notion of guardianship altogether, at least as it pertains to marriage. The same is true of the requirement for "sufficiency" or "suitability" (*kafa'a*).

The Personal Status Code of Syria (1953) modifies the position of Hanafi jurisprudence by limiting the guardian's powers over the marriage of a daughter who has reached majority. The Moroccan Personal Status Code (1957) departs from the basic Maliki position by prohibiting the guardian from forcing marriage on a virgin ward who has attained majority. The Kingdom of Saudi Arabia and other Gulf states continue to follow an uncodified system of family law. According to this system, individual cases do not constitute binding precedent since the system relies on the independent juridical reasoning and application (*ijtihad*) of the judge. Thus, it is possible that different judgments will be rendered in similar cases. Some countries such as Syria, Jordan, and Morocco have attempted to control marriage contracts between very young girls and much older men by setting limits on the age difference between the spouses. For example, in Jordan an 18-year-old woman cannot be married to someone more than 20 years her senior. However, in rural areas, lack of accurate documentation registering the birth of either party may invalidate the positive effects of such legislation.

All traditional schools of law interpret the Qur'an as permitting polygyny as long as certain conditions of fairness are observed. As noted earlier, the Tunisian Code explicitly prohibits polygyny. However, even within a traditional framework, mechanisms exist to enable a woman to prevent or limit her prospective spouse from contracting multiple marriages. For example, in some schools of Islamic law, a woman may stipulate in her marriage contract that her husband may not take a second wife. However, the Shafi'i and Shiite schools of law reject this provision on the basis that a contract may not forbid what is allowed in the Qur'an. Turkey remains the major exception among Muslim nations in that it abolished Muslim Family Law altogether. In 1926, the family law aspects of traditional jurisprudence were replaced by the Swiss Civil Code, which remains to this day the basis of Turkish Civil Law.

A number of contemporary scholars of Islam have contended that in actual practice, modern legislation regarding marriage and divorce has contributed very little to alleviating gender inequalities in Muslim societies. Rather than modifying the Shari'a, in many cases modern legislation tends instead to codify it. For example, the requirement of court documentation for divorce cases assures the wife's right to be informed about her husband's petition for a divorce. In the past, in accordance with some interpretations of the law, she might not have been aware that her husband had divorced her. However, the mere fact of documentation does not restrict a husband's right to divorce his wife without grounds. In addition, it is possible that in the process of codifying Shari'a laws, modern legislation might also codify and strengthen traditional cultural attitudes that affirm men's power over women and provide additional justification for perpetuating unfair gender practices. For example, if it is assumed, according to traditional norms, that women must make themselves available to their husbands at all times, then working women, simply by pursuing a career or working because of economic necessity, may provide grounds for divorce. Even worse, their supposed economic independence, even if paid a low salary, may render them ineligible for maintenance during marriage or ineligible for child support after divorce.

Even though all Sunni legal schools continue to uphold the guardian's powers in contracting the marriage of a female ward, the realities of modern life have begun to supersede the traditional practice of arranged marriages in Muslim countries. Men and women now meet and choose each other through personal contact in universities, in the workplace, through mutual friends, or even on the Internet. Furthermore, modern legislation in most Muslim countries now forbids compulsion in marriage. This is not to say that parental guidance in the choice of a spouse will disappear completely. On the contrary, professional and well-educated Muslims continue to allow their parents to arrange marriages for them. Certain cultural norms persist, although these too are subject to modification. For example, a Lebanese friend of mine, when discussing contemporary marriage practices among Lebanese Muslims, noted that parents sometimes ignore the requirement of "sufficiency" or "suitability." Instead of having their daughters marry men of equal or higher social status, they prefer their daughters to marry "one notch down," as this supposedly guarantees the wife an upper hand in the marriage. Perhaps this practice came about to counter centuries of unfair gender-related practices. In any case, this example demonstrates that in Islam, as in other religious traditions, principles or practices that are supposedly required by the Law can be modified to suit the reality on the ground.

THE PERSONAL VOICE: GROWING UP IN A POLYGYNOUS HOUSEHOLD

I grew up within a polygynous household in India. My father's first wife was unable to have children beyond the first two daughters because of a permanent injury during her second childbirth. It was her deepest wish to "give" her husband a male offspring; this is a highly desirous goal in South Asian culture, irrespective of one's religious persuasion. My father's first wife blamed herself for bringing to an end any prospect for further continuation of my father's genealogical line. She found this an unbearable prospect and insisted that her husband remarry to give himself a chance to father a son.

Based on her personal testimony, which she often used to narrate to all of my siblings including myself, my father refused to consider her suggestion and never held her responsible for their situation. He was surprised that she would even suggest he remarry because that might endanger her own personal status vis-à-vis a second wife, who would rise in esteem were she to "produce" a son. An even more important hurdle was that, being Nizari Ismailis, my father and his first wife were governed by the rules related to marriage and divorce enjoined by the Ismaili Constitution, which the Imam of their time, Sir Sultan Mohammed Shah, Aga Khan III, had promulgated.[2] According to the Ismaili Constitution's interpretation of Muslim Family Law, monogamy was to be the norm practiced by all Ismailis irrespective of their economic or communal standing. However, there were exceptions to this rule that took into consideration issues such as the infertility of the wife. In such a case, an Ismaili man would have to petition the relevant Ismaili social institution for permission to marry a second wife and seek formal permission to do so from his first wife. In my father's case, this exception clearly did not apply; his first wife had already "produced" two daughters, so infertility was not a factor.

My father tried to mollify his first wife by reminding her that he could not justify a second wife under Ismaili rules. She was not about to give up, however. Despite the fact that she was illiterate and that her official signature was her thumb impression, she appeared before the entire Ismaili Council (a 20-member body) and appealed "her case"—not her husband's—for a second wife. She asserted that if she gave her husband permission to have a second wife, and if this were her honest desire, the Council was obligated to grant her husband permission to remarry. The Council members, considering her interests, reminded my father's first wife that she may have been acting emotionally at the time and that she may later regret her decision. She remained adamant, however, and assured the Council that even if her husband were to abandon her, she would never petition the Council again. Eventually, the Council allowed my father to have a second wife, but only after requiring him to set aside a substantial portion of his wealth for his first wife.

As it turned out, these assets assured her financial independence after my father's death.

My biological mother was much younger than both my father and his first wife. She was a very young widow from rural Gujarat whose first husband had died very young within months into their marriage, having contracted some fatal disease. She was chosen as a bride by my father's first wife, who went out of her way to convince my mother and her family that she would never treat her as "the other woman" but rather as a daughter. In any case, it would have been difficult for the young widow to find another husband of my father's standing in that region. They got married and she moved to Mumbai with my father. My father's household now consisted of both wives living under the same roof with the younger of his two daughters from the first marriage. Although such an arrangement is not unique, it is not a typical situation either, because Islamic law requires separate quarters for each wife. My father's eldest daughter, who was in fact older than his second wife, was already married at the time. She became pregnant a couple of months before my father's second wife, so my father became a grandfather and a father almost at the same time.

It must have been because of the first wife's deep prayers and intense wishes that the first child from the second wife turned out to be a boy—the only boy among five children that were born to my mother. The rest of us turned out to be girls! I was the second-to-last child to be born. My younger sister was born seven months after my father died. My mother was two months pregnant at the time of my father's sudden death from kidney and heart failure. We grew up calling my father's first wife *Maji*, a term generally used for a grandparent or an elderly person. She was *Maji* and our biological mother was *Mummy*. To this day, I find it incredible that the two wives shared their husband, living under the same roof, for approximately nine years! If that were not baffling enough, they both continued to live together for 30 years after my father's death, with the younger wife, my *Mummy*, passing away at age 60 in 1992, followed by my *Maji* passing away at age 91 in 1993.

After my father's death, my biological mother, my *Mummy*, attended to my father's business every day, despite the fact that she was from one of the smallest villages in Gujarat and had less than a fourth-grade education. She was motivated by the desire to secure her children's well-being by protecting their inheritance and source of livelihood from being gobbled up by family members and friends. Her other personal *jihad* (struggle for a good cause) was to ensure that her children got a decent education. On his accession to the Imamate in 1957, the Nizari Ismaili Imam, Aga Khan IV, made it clear to his community that he wished to continue the policy of the previous Imam by insisting on the education of all young Ismailis, especially girls. The previous Imam, his grandfather, had been unequivocal about the necessity for educating girls and stated, "Educate all your children well. However, if you have a son and a daughter but have the financial capacity to educate only one child, choose your daughter." The new Imam now wished that parents would doubly commit themselves to providing a high-quality education for their children. Thus, my mother fought hard to enroll us in the best schools, although she occasionally fell prey to scammers who would promise admission for a child in a nearby Catholic school for a certain amount of money. Once they received the money from her, they were never seen again.

As I look back on my early life, I now realize that my two mothers instinctively divided the task of raising their children. My *Mummy* went to work, struggled, and fought in the outside world, while my *Maji* stayed at home feeding us and spoiling us with the attention that my *Mummy* did not have time to give us. Was life always stress free and did all things go smoothly? Probably not, for I am sure that there were strong undercurrents of emotion and power struggles between the two women when their husband was alive, and even during the three decades they spent together without him. However, both women chose to continue living together and become a source of support for each other. The younger wife always addressed the older wife respectfully as *Ben*, "sister." For us children, the main inconvenience was being brought up in a home that could most aptly be described as a perpetual "open house." Relatives from rural and urban areas of India sent their daughters to marry under my *Mummy's* watchful eye. There were other relatives too; those living in the Ismaili diasporas of Malaysia, Burma, Tanzania, Kenya, and Uganda, regularly descended upon us to ensure that their children "kept in touch with their roots," continued to speak an Indian language, and married within the culture and the faith.

Growing up in that household, neither the children of the first wife nor the children of the second wife considered themselves as two separate families. I remember two distinct incidents in my life that demonstrate how deeply etched this reality was in my mind. Years later when I settled in Canada, I tried to bring both of my mothers and my half sister from India to live with me. The Canadian Immigration Board made it categorically clear to me that I could sponsor only my "biological" mother and my half sister, who were related to me by blood, but not my *Maji*. I was upset that they did not understand our family dynamics, that *Maji* was also my mother, and that it was inconceivable that she would have to stay behind on her own. In the end, I was forced to drop the whole idea. Another time, when I suffered from droopy eyelid syndrome, my first response to the doctor trying to determine whether my genetic background had caused this condition was to say, "Well, my Mum developed this condition in her seventies." Then I stopped myself in my tracks. This was *Maji*, who could not have transmitted this condition to me because she was not my biological mother!

My objective in sharing these deeply personal experiences with the reader is not to condone, let alone glorify, polygyny in any way. As a Muslim woman, even having grown up in a polygynous household with largely positive experiences, I would still find it intolerable for my spouse to consider having a second wife, even if we were living in a country that permitted polygyny. However, I think it is important to share the variety of possible experiences and dynamics that are often subsumed under the generally negative preconceptions of polygynous marriages in the West. While understanding the potential for abuse in polygynous marriages, I have also come to appreciate that multiple factors may lead to unconventional relationships or households and that such factors need to be studied in detail. Polygynous marriages should not be dismissed as mere oddities that are prevalent in "other" societies and cultures, while "our" society is considered completely free from such practices. The polygynous relationships among Mormon Fundamentalists who adhere to what is called "The Principle"—as depicted in the currently popular U.S. television mini-series *Big Love*—prove that experiences like mine are far from unknown in the West, even in the United States.

NOTES

1.   An "enemy of the Household of the Prophet" would today only include those few extremist Sunni Muslims who consider Shiite Muslims to be unbelievers or heretics. In the past, this term was used to designate supporters of the Umayyad dynasty of Caliphs, who denied the claim of the family of 'Ali and Fatima to the leadership of Islam.

2.   Ismailis are adherents of a branch of the Shiite Islam that considers Isma'il, the eldest son of the Shiite Imam Ja'far al-Sadiq (d. 765 CE), as the latter's successor. Doctrinally, they follow the guidance of a living guide, an Imam, who governs the Ismaili community by interpreting the sources of Islamic Law and applying them to his community's contemporary situation. The present Imam of the Nizari Ismailis is Karim Aga Khan, who claims direct descent from the Prophet and is the 49th in line of succession from Prophet Muhammad, through his daughter Fatima and cousin and son-in-law 'Ali.

SELECTED BIBLIOGRAPHY

Arabic Sources

Al-Jaziri, 'Abd al-Rahman. a*l-Fiqh 'ala al-madhahib al-arba'a*. Vol. 4. Beirut, 1969.

Al-Mughniya, Muhammad Jawad. *al-Fiqh 'ala al-madhahib al-khamsa* Beirut, 1960.

The Pillars of Islam: Da'a'im al-Islam of *al Qadi al-Nu'man*: Vol. II: Mu'amalat: *Laws Pertaining to Human Intercourse,* translated by Asaf A. A. Fyzee, revised and annotated by Ismail Kurban Husein Poonawala (New Delhi: Oxford University Press, 2004).

Sources in European Languages

Doumata, Eleanor Abdella. "Marriage and Divorce: Modern Practice." In *The Oxford Encyclopaedia of the Modern Islamic World*, Vol. 3 Editor in Chief, John L. Esposito, Oxford–New York: Oxford University Press, 1995.

Al-Hibri, Azizah. "Marriage and Divorce: Legal Foundations." In *The Oxford Encyclopaedia of the Modern Islamic World*, Vol. 3 Editor in Chief, John L. Esposito, Oxford–New York: Oxford University Press, 1995.

Murata, Sachiko. Temporary Marriage in Islamic Law. Ahlul Bayt Digital Islamic Library Project, http://www.al-islam.org/al-serat/muta.

Motzki, Harald. "Marriage and Divorce," in *Encyclopaedia of the Qur'an*, Vol. 4, edited by Jane Dammen McAuliffe, 276–281. Leiden/Boston, New York/ Massachusetts: E.J. Brill, 2004.

Stewart, Devin. "Sex and Sexuality," in *Encyclopaedia of the Qur'an*, Vol. 5, edited by Jane Dammen McAuliffe, 580–585. Leiden-Boston: E.J. Brill, 2004.

4

THE SPIRITUAL SIGNIFICANCE OF MARRIAGE IN ISLAM

———————————•———————————

Jane Fatima Casewit

INTRODUCTION: AN EGYPTIAN SCENARIO

Like many Egyptian couples, Wafa and Ali married relatively late in life. This is because the acute housing shortage in Cairo and rampant inflation renders material life very difficult for most Cairenes. Despite these setbacks, Wafa and Ali married, placed their trust in God for their future, and lived contentedly for many years in a very small flat in a poor, crowded neighborhood. As the years passed, it became clear that Wafa would not be able to bear children. Although, as pious Muslims, they submitted to this situation as God's will, both Wafa and Ali felt emptiness in their lives without children and the joys they bring.

After much prayer and consultation, they both agreed that Ali should take a second wife, so that there would eventually be children in the family. No longer a young man, Ali sought the advice of his relatives and neighbors. One neighbor had a daughter, Aziza, about 17 years old, who was beautiful but deaf from birth. Realizing that it would not be easy to find a husband for a deaf girl, and that it is not easy to find a wife for a man getting on in years, Wafa and Ali decided that Ali should marry Aziza. If she consented to this arrangement, it would suit all concerned, as well as being a charitable act.

The marriage took place and Wafa continued her job as an assistant in a local nursery school. Aziza initially took over most of the household tasks. After retiring from her job at the nursery school, Wafa became a sort of "older sister" to Aziza, looking after her and helping her to communicate with the outside world. The family anxiously looks forward to the arrival of Aziza's baby, especially Wafa, who always wanted a child of her own. As Wafa grows older and her health declines, Aziza will undoubtedly look after Wafa, showing the same trust and care as Wafa did for Aziza.

Should the above scenario be seen as a norm or as an exception? How can such polygynous marriages (marriages in which a man can have more than one wife) "work" for everyone concerned? Why would most Western couples and many modern Muslims be unable to accept such an arrangement? In attempting to approach these questions, this chapter outlines the spiritual significance of the institution of marriage in Islam. It examines its underlying, deeper significance by addressing the Muslim concept of marriage through the lenses of symbolism and metaphysics, as well the positive effect of stable marriages on society as a whole. The broader, general responsibilities and rights of both wife and husband are highlighted according to the rules of Islamic jurisprudence. The virtues necessary for sustaining a long-term relationship and the possibilities of extending the marital bonds to three persons are also examined. This chapter is not an analysis of current social ills in the Muslim world, nor do I intend to apologize for abuses committed in Muslim societies. Instead, I hope to present the fundamental spiritual principles upon which Islamic marriage is based.

In all civilizations, marriage celebrates and regulates the intricate relationship between husband and wife and the resulting procreation of children. The uniting of male and female in a conjugal bond is one of the most sacred and important institutions in all world cultures. The institution of marriage is granted the utmost importance in all religious traditions and societies, although the emphasis on its various aspects differs from one civilization to another. Both male and female reflect qualities of the Divine, and the most profound significance of the union of a man and a woman is that marriage mirrors the union of the human soul with the Divine spirit. This union of the soul with God is the highest human aspiration.

Yet, despite the deep spiritual implications of marriage, never before has this institution come under such a grave threat as it is undergoing today. People around the world are suffering the devastating effects of broken families on children and on society. In the Muslim world, in the wake of the dissolution of the extended family under the pressures of modernity, divorce and domestic violence within the nuclear family are on a sharp rise. Although the social tensions characterized by broken homes, juvenile delinquency, single motherhood, and homosexuality have not yet penetrated Islamic societies as pervasively as they have in the West, the recent necessity for revised family codes in many Muslim countries to prevent injustices toward women and children is a sign that something has gone terribly wrong.

THE DIVINE PRINCIPLE OF DUALITY

The divine archetype of marriage is present in all of creation. As with all divine revelations, Islam places marriage beyond the human realm because it is created and willed by God. The divine concept of archetypal pairs is explicit in the Qur'an. It is parallel to the doctrine of *Yin* and *Yang* in the Chinese tradition, *Purusha* and *Prakriti* in Hinduism, and the Holy Spirit and the Virgin Mary in Christianity. Reference to the divine concept of duality can also be found in the Hebrew Bible: "All things are double, one against another, and He hath made nothing defective. He hath established the good things of every one. And who shall be filled with beholding His glory?" (*Ecclesiasticus*, 62:25–26).

In Islam, the Creator is one. However, His creation begins with multiplicity and multiplicity necessarily originates with two, a duality. Like the Bible, the Qur'an frequently refers to the existence of pairs (*zawjayn*) in creation: "And of everything [God] created a pair" (Qur'an 51:49). Although the Qur'an continually reiterates the miracle of the pairs as a basis for creation, the essential message of Islam, considered as the final revelation in this cycle of humanity, reaffirms the Oneness of God. The Qur'an, believed by Muslims to be the direct word of God, is itself a miraculous reflection of Divine Unity (*tawhid*). The sacred text of the Qur'an is woven into a miraculous tapestry that threads together the Divine message but continually draws us back to the central doctrine of unity.

One of the most important threads of this Divine text refers repeatedly to the totality of the universe as it appears to us from the human vantage point. From the human perspective, the universe consists of the Earth and the Heavens. The phrase "the Heavens and the Earth" (*al-samawat wa al-ard*) occurs over 200 times in the Qur'an. This cosmic pair was the first "pair" in creation, and the Qur'an alludes to the Divine archetype of duality through reference to this primordial pair. The Heavens and the Earth refer to the whole of the universe and beyond. The phrase that often follows this in the Qur'an is *wa ma baynahuma,* which means "and that which is between them"—in other words, all of the rest of creation. The Qur'an's description of God's creation of the Heavens and the Earth recalls the creative act that brings duality into existence from unity and establishes the "pairs" as the fundamental components of existence. Moreover, the Qur'an also teaches us that the Heavens and the Earth existed together in an undifferentiated state before creation: "Do those who disbelieve know that the Heavens and the Earth were of one piece; then We parted them, and We made every living thing of water? Will they not then believe?" (Qur'an 21:30).

The first great pair of Heaven and Earth is miraculously repeated at every level of creation: in animals and plants, the sun and the moon, gold and silver, and lightness and darkness. It is even affirmed in the conceptual categories that we use: in affirmation and negation, motion and rest, cause and effect, and origin and return. The story of the Prophet Noah, which is recounted in the Qur'an much as it is in the Bible, is not only an account of the great flood that covered the earth but also a symbol of Divine duality: "Embark therein, of each kind two, male and female" (Qur'an 11:40).

As a corollary of the spiritual principle of duality, the Islamic concepts of the "Pen" and the "Tablet" also act as symbols of the twin poles of manifestation and creation or Divine Intellect and All-Possibility. Although the Qur'an mentions both Pen and Tablet in several verses, the Hadith literature provides more information about how these verses are to be understood. According to Hadith accounts, the Pen "wrote" the destinies of all humankind onto the Tablet at the dawn of creation. The word for "Pen" in Arabic (*qalam*) is masculine in gender. The word for "Tablet," (*lawh*), however, may be either masculine or feminine. In a famous verse, the Qur'an states that as the uncreated Word of God, the Qur'an is on a "Guarded Tablet" (*fi lawhin mahfuzin*) (Qur'an 85:22). In this cosmic, archetypal sense, the Tablet is a masculine concept. However, *lawha,* the actual tablet that children write on in Qur'anic schools, is a feminine word. Thus, if the concepts of Pen and Tablet are understood to represent manifestation and creation, they can also be seen to symbolize both the divine concept of pairs and the pair of male and female. As symbols, the concepts of Pen and Tablet also correlate with the concepts of Intellect and Soul, which are similarly masculine and feminine. Intellect (*'aql*) in Arabic is masculine, whereas Soul (*nafs*) is feminine. Both examples, Pen and Tablet and Intellect and Soul, illustrate how, in the religious language of Islam, divine duality pervades space, time, and language alike.

Divine duality exists on the human level as well. The Qur'an explains that God created human beings from one soul, a reflection of how the duality of male and female proceeds from the unity and oneness of God. The separation of the macrocosm into Heaven and Earth and the creation of the Pen and the Tablet have their equivalence in the creation of two souls from a single soul. These two souls, derived from the primordial single soul, became the first human pair, Adam and Eve: "Fear your Lord, Who created you from a single soul; from her/it, He created her/its mate, and sent forth from the two of them many men and women" (Qur'an 4:1).[1] Femininity and masculinity thus pervade the created universe and correspond to the primordial duality at the origin of creation. The "pairs" (*zawjayn*) at every level of creation are part of the divine plan. Divine duality also exists within every human being; that is, at the level of the microcosm, which metaphysically mirrors the macrocosm.

Thus, by examining the metaphysical and spiritual significance of marriage, it becomes easier to understand why Islam and the other great religious traditions consider marriage a divine institution, a "gift" from God. For the believer, whether Muslim or the follower of another faith, the commitment of marriage is first a pact with God and second a pact with one's spouse. Each marriage is thus part of the divine scheme of the universe. The divine aspect of marriage is also present at the physical level, as sexual union can be seen as a desire for wholeness, a symbol of union with God, and a foretaste of the bliss of Paradise. In a way, the joy felt in sexual union constitutes a sensual "glimpse" of Paradise. It is because of this divine aspect of sexuality that

Islam, like other religions, strictly regulates male and female relationships. It is also the reason why a full understanding of sexuality cannot be gained outside of the framework of tradition and sacred laws.

ISLAMIC MARRIAGE AS A SANCTIFIED CONTRACT

Unlike Christianity, which treats marriage as a sacrament, marriage in Islam is a contract, a legal commitment written up as such, sanctioned by God and acknowledged by society. It is a contractual agreement between two parties: the husband and the wife. Under this contract, each party agrees to fulfill certain duties in return for certain rights and privileges. The written contract is signed by both of the spouses, and the marriage agreement is made public to the wider community through festivities, the customs of which vary across the Islamic world. These festivities confirm that the couple has come together through a sanctified agreement in conformity with Islamic law. The Islamic bonds of marriage not only sanctify human sexuality and reproduction but also provide for companionship and mutual support. The stereotypical Western view of a Muslim marriage as a secluded harem of dark-eyed beauties that is ruled by a dominating and sexually insatiable male needs to be reassessed in the light of the God-given legislation based on the metaphysical principles sketched above. The socioeconomic situation of the Arabian Peninsula at the time of the Islamic revelation also needs to be taken into consideration.

Before God, all women and men in Islam are *nas* (singular *insan*), human beings. All human beings, whether they are males or females, are at once both slave (*'abd*) and vice-regent (*khalifa*) of God on Earth. Women and men are spiritual equals in Islam and are addressed as such in the Qur'an. Therefore, one of the underlying premises of marriage in Islam is the primacy of the individual human being before God. Within the context of a marriage, a man and a woman serve each other and their children as well as serve God, thereby extending their responsibilities as slaves of God and His vice-regent. As Lamya Farouki has pointed out, "Instead of holding the personal goals of the individual supreme, Islam instills in the adherent a sense of his or her place within the family and of a responsibility to that group."[2] For a Muslim, the ultimate goal of the individual is to please God. Besides the prescribed rites and virtues encouraged by the religion, the social obligations of both men and women are very explicit in the Qur'an, the Hadith, and the Sunna. One way of pleasing God is by carrying out marital and family duties. According to Muhammad Abdul-Rauf, "Moral restraint (imposed by marriage in Islam) is not an encroachment on human freedom, but a reasonable sacrifice for the sake of human dignity and in the interest of society and for the pleasure of God."[3]

At the social level, a major goal of marriage in Islam was to establish fairness and equilibrium in what was arguably a disordered society in the Arabian

Peninsula during the period before the Islamic revelation. This period is commonly known as the *Jahiliyya*, the "Time of Ignorance," in Arabic. Rules for marriage and norms of sexuality revealed by God through the Qur'an provided the needed protection for women, especially widows and orphans. However, it must not be surmised that the rules of Islamic marriage were only for pre-Islamic Arabia. Despite abuses of the system, the time-honored models of Muslim marriage and the family have existed successfully for centuries.

Islam brought a new social order to the Arabian Peninsula and ultimately to the entire sector of humanity for which it was destined. Islam, God's final revelation to humanity, elevated the status of woman as equal with man before God. The Qur'an granted women new rights and responsibilities in the social domain and repeatedly commanded men to treat all women, even divorcees, with kindness. Men were given new rights as well, but they were also given new responsibilities toward women. One of the final pronouncements of the Prophet Muhammed before his death was, "Take care of your women." Throughout his life, the Prophet was a model of kindness and justice toward the women who were entrusted to him. His general rule for the behavior of husbands is summed up in another famous hadith: "The best of you is he who treats his wife in the best way."

Because of the spiritual significance of marriage and the necessity for stable families and societies, volumes have been written by Muslim jurists on the rights and responsibilities of marriage. In the Muslim world, the laws, rights, and responsibilities of marriage and divorce have caused much debate in works of Islamic jurisprudence. The topic continues to be addressed by modern Muslims, who find themselves caught up in societies in transition, between traditional Islamic values and Western cultural patterns. However, the rise of the incidence of divorce in Muslim societies and the urgency to revise personal status codes in Muslim countries show that many Muslims have lost the understanding of the deeper significance of marriage in Islam and no longer have the same commitment to marriage as those who lived in previous generations. This neglect of the marriage contract is often paralleled by a similar neglect of the "contract" that human beings have with God.

MARRIAGE AS AN ABODE OF PEACE

When asked what had prompted him to enter Islam, one young American Muslim that I know said he was struck by the happiness of middle-aged Muslim couples he had met and the peace and tranquility that characterized their lives. On the level of human relations, the ideal Islamic marriage should provide a sense of inner and outer peace—peace within the home and peace within the individuals who inhabit the home. Our relationship with our Creator has a direct influence on our relationships with our spouses and our families. True happiness can only be found in God. When this is understood, relationships with spouses are understood from a higher and more all-encompassing perspective and are thereby liable to be smoother and more tranquil.

In Arabic, one of the words for "home" is *maskan*. Literally, a *maskan* is a "residence" or a "dwelling." This concept is related to the important Qur'anic term, *sakina,* which comes from the same Arabic root as *maskan*. The Arabic root *sakana* means "to dwell" or "to become quiet," thus giving *sakina* the sense of "an indwelling presence that provides stillness or peace." The Hebrew term *shekhinah* also carries a similar meaning. Thus, a *maskan,* a home, is meant to be an abode of peace and tranquility, a refuge from the tumult of the outside world. How can the home become an abode of peace? It can become such only if the relationships within the home are harmonious. The primary relationship in a household, upon which all other relationships are built, is the intricate relationship between husband and wife. This relationship can only be successful if both parties realize that marriage and the creation of a family are "signs" and gifts from God and if they respect this privilege by treating each other with respect and selfless service. As the Qur'an makes clear, recognition of the spiritual significance of marriage is crucial to the success of the relationship between husband and wife: "One of His signs is that He created for you, from among yourselves, spouses (*azwajan*) that you may find peace in them (*li-taskunu ilayha*). Then He ordained that you treat them with affection (*mawadda*) and mercy (*rahma*). Verily in this are signs for a people who reflect" (Qur'an 30:21).

If a home is meant to provide an abode of peace for those dwelling in it, such peace can only be created by a family, headed by a couple committed to the long-term stability of the marital relationship. Through this commitment, the couple take it upon themselves to surrender some of their desires and personal freedoms for the greater good of the family. A Muslim home permeated by the sacred presence of *sakina* is dwelt in by a couple, their family, and sometimes an extended family. The couple strive to place their responsibilities toward each other and their children ahead of their own interests for the benefit of all who live in the home.

Sakina is also produced by love and mercy, which should be continually refreshed in a relationship, particularly with one's spouse. The self-sacrifice of love is manifested through mercy toward one's spouse and one's children. The mutual sharing of love and mercy produces *sakina*—peace and tranquility—within the family. The ever-increasing strife and conflicts in today's world mirror the state of unhappy households. In both dysfunctional societies and dysfunctional families, individuals put their personal interests before those of others and thus cannot live harmoniously. Dysfunctional families also reflect the discord, unhappiness, and disequilibrium of individual souls. A soul's ultimate happiness and well-being are dependent upon its relationship with God. Worldly pleasures and success can provide temporary happiness, but if our relationship with our Creator is not in order, we will never find true contentment or peace nor will our relationships with others be easy.

RIGHTS AND RESPONSIBILITIES WITHIN ISLAMIC MARRIAGE

In Islamic jurisprudence, the laws pertaining to marriage are based on what promotes the greater good for the couple, the family, and the society as a whole. One of the things not normally understood in the West about Islamic marriage is that women have at least as many rights as men in a marriage. This is because it is understood that a woman's primary obligations to society are the all-consuming task of bringing up her children and creating an honorable lineage—young adults who are spiritually, physically, emotionally, and intellectually beneficial to themselves and to society.

Children require approximately 12 years of appropriate care, education, and supervision to assure their spiritual, moral, and educational development. The care and nurturing of a child is, in principle, a full-time occupation for the first 10–12 years of the child's life. In order to carry out these duties to the best of her ability, a mother needs the assurance of complete economic support and maintenance so that she can focus on this most important function. This is why man is required to bear the financial burden of maintaining the family in Islam. In addition, man also has a responsibility to protect both woman and children because of their being physically weaker than man is. In return, a woman protects and maintains the *maskan,* the household or abode of peace, in which her husband and children can find refuge from the pressures of the outside world. In a Muslim marriage, the husband is responsible for the outward aspects of existence—job, income, support, and protection— whereas the wife is responsible for the inward aspects of existence—the home and the good of those who dwell in it.

The primary source of Islamic regulations for the rights and responsibilities pertaining to marriage is the Qur'an, but their details are worked out through the Sunna and the opinions of legal scholars. However, the Qur'an is not vague in its prescriptions for a good and moral family life. It is quite specific about how men should treat women and vice versa, the rights of wives and divorcees, the rights of small babies and young children, and the treatment of orphans. In addition, the laws of inheritance are spelt out very clearly in the Qur'an, leaving little doubt about their application.

At the time of her marriage, a bride has the right to a dower (*mahr*), which in principle is a financial guarantee for her in case of divorce. Throughout the marriage, and even for specific periods after a divorce, a woman has the right to complete economic maintenance by her husband.

Islamic law insists that a woman should not be preoccupied by economic concerns so that she can devote all of her time and energy to nurturing, educating, and bringing up her children. Well brought up, God-fearing children who are able to take charge of their own lives and souls are the greatest legacies a human being can leave in this world. In order to carry out this important goal, Islamic law puts the responsibility of financial maintenance on the man so that the woman can devote herself to preparing her children to be responsible Muslims and constructive members of society. In fact, a man may find himself responsible for more females than just his wife, including his unwed sisters, his mother, or his aunts. Although most Muslim jurists agree that women have the right to work outside of the home or operate their own businesses, they are not required to contribute their income to the family coffers. In addition, some schools of Islamic law agree that a wife should be maintained under the economic conditions that she was used to in her own family.

Turning to the rights of men in marriage, the Prophet's cousin Ibn 'Abbas (d. 687 CE) reported that the primary right of a man in marriage is sexual access to his wife. Although this may seem "chauvinistic" to modern thinking, in an Islamic marriage a man has the right—within reason and normal expectations—to have a sexual relationship with his wife whenever he desires her, except during the times of a woman's menses, illness, fasting, or other inconvenient moments. Of course, a woman's privacy should not be abused. The purpose behind this right is to prevent adultery by ensuring sexual satisfaction. However, it must be pointed out that women also have a right in Muslim marriages to seek sexual satisfaction on a regular basis. Some schools of law state that impotence or lack of sexual performance on the part of the husband can become grounds for divorce.

Another right of men that is specified in Islamic jurisprudence is the right to maintain one's lineage, which means the right of the man to give to his offspring his family name. In Islam, an orphan keeps the original family name of her father and cannot take the name of the family who raises her, even if she would want to. Similarly, a Muslim wife keeps her father's name, thus preserving her own family lineage. Muslim women normally do not take their husband's family name. In most Muslim societies, a person's family name and lineage are important aspects of identity. To lose these is, in a sense, to lose oneself. The right to lineage is also a reason why fornication and adultery are forbidden in Islam. Not only do sexual relations outside of marriage break the bonds of trust between husband and wife, but also sexual relations before marriage, especially on the part of women, carry the danger of producing children who will suffer throughout their lives because they have no established lineage, and hence no clear family identity. In most local cultures of the Muslim world, such children are for all practical purposes unmarriage-able because it is feared that their lack of lineage will somehow "dilute" or morally "sully" the lineages of respectable families.

Another important right of husbands in Islamic law that may come as a surprise to the reader is the right of a father to have his children breastfed. The Qur'an even specifies the length of time for breastfeeding. A woman who is not able to suckle her own child may hire a wet nurse. Indeed, breastfeeding is considered so important that if a divorce occurs while a woman is breastfeeding a child, the husband must compensate his wife with payment during the breastfeeding period. Children who are breastfed by wet nurses develop very close relationships with them, almost as between biological mother and child. It is believed in Muslim cultures that a child absorbs some of the nature of the person who suckles him. "The Arabs hold that the breast is one of the channels of heredity and that a suckling drinks qualities into his nature from the nurse who suckles him."[4] This is why it is forbidden to marry close relatives of the wet nurse (*murdi'a*) in Islamic law. A man may not marry his "milk" mother, "milk" sister, or "milk" aunt under any circumstances. Similarly, Muslim girls are forbidden from marrying their "milk" brothers.

The schools of law differ as to whether housework is an essential part of a wife's duties. The requirement of doing household chores and the responsibility of looking after the children have become important causes of marital strife in many parts of the modern Muslim world where women have started to enter the workforce. Most traditional jurists agree that since a woman is responsible for her household, such responsibilities include household chores. However, many hadith accounts relate how the Prophet Muhammad regularly assisted in household work in his own home. The belief that women should be responsible for the endless chores generated by housekeeping is often abused by Muslim husbands who expect the wife to contribute to the family income as well as maintain the house and bring up the children.

Finally, mention must be made of the often disputed Qur'anic passage, "Men have authority over women in that God has favored some over others and in what they spend of their possessions for them" (Qur'an 4:34). Commentators on the Qur'an generally interpret this passage as meaning that men have a certain authority over women in so far as they maintain them economically. This is a plausible interpretation because of the wording of the passage itself. However, the Prophet's cousin Ibn 'Abbas, one of the great early commentators on the Qur'an, felt that the verse also referred to the willingness of men to give up some of their marital rights from time to time for the sake of their wives. By acting altruistically or "expending themselves" for their wives, they enjoy a sort of "precedence" as human beings. A similar idea is expressed in the following hadith account: "If a man's wife behaves in a disagreeable manner but he responds with kindness and patience, God will reward him as much as Job was rewarded for his forbearance."[5] This tradition and the opinion of Ibn 'Abbas express the concept of *husn al-'ishra*, "harmonious coexistence" or "mutual companionship," which is both a goal of

Islamic marriage and a right that both husband and wife can expect from each other. In an Islamic marriage, both spouses have a fundamental right to be treated with kindness, respect, and dignity at all times.

MARRIAGE AND MOTHERHOOD

> I am God (*Allah*) and I am the Merciful (*al-Rahman*). I created the womb (*rahm*) and I gave it a name derived from My own name. If someone cuts off the womb, I will cut him off, but if someone joins the womb, I will join him to Me.[6]

This divine tradition (*hadith qudsi*) expresses the sanctity and importance of the womb in Islam as a symbol of femininity and as a reflection of God's mercy in creation. This concept is also expressed in the first verse of *Surat al-Nisa'* (The Women) of the Qur'an: "Be mindful of God, by whom you claim rights of one another and be mindful of the wombs" (Qur'an 4:1). The connection in the Arabic language between the womb and the concept of mercy is clear in both form and meaning. The Arabic root *rahima*, "to be merciful," produces the noun *rahma*, "mercy," and the divine names, *al-Rahman*, the Merciful, and *al-Rahim*, the Compassionate, which open almost every *Sura* of the Qur'an. The same root produces the word *rahm*, "womb." This powerful linking of terms stresses the sacredness of the womb and provides a strong justification for the respect given to mothers in Islam. The divine attribute of mercy is reflected in the mercy bestowed by a mother on her children from pregnancy through birth, and even after her children are brought into the world. Divine mercy is also reflected in the care that a mother gives to the child that is born from her womb. The essence of motherhood in Islam is mercy, and mercy is the most important of God's attributes. As the Qur'an affirms, "Call on God (*Allah*) or call on the Merciful (*al-Rahman*)" (Qur'an 17:1).

For most women, carrying out the duties of motherhood comes easily, as nurturing is in the nature of femininity. The love and care that a mother extends toward her children is a reflection of the loving mercy of God toward all of His creatures. The importance of mercy as a sign of God is confirmed in the following hadith: "Verily, on the same day that God created the Heavens and the Earth, he created one hundred parts of mercy (*rahma*). Every part of mercy is analogous to the space between the Heavens and the Earth. Out of this mercy He sent one part to the world, and it is from this that a mother shows affection to her child."[7]

The quality of nurturing, so essential in bringing up and educating children, is a natural God-given gift to women. In man, nurturing is also possible, but it is less "natural" and usually has to be acquired. If the reward of compensation to mothers for their self-sacrifice in this world is not always evident, Islam guarantees it in the next world: "Paradise is at the feet of mothers" is a well-known hadith. It has already been mentioned that one of the primary responsibilities of men in Islam is to assure that females are protected and honored, precisely because of their role as the bearers and nurturers of new life.

FILIAL LOYALTY AND FAMILY BONDS

> Oh humankind! Be mindful of your duty to your Lord Who created you from a single soul; the He created its mate from it and from the twain He spread abroad a multitude of men and women. Be mindful of your duty toward Allah in whom you claim your rights of one another, and toward the wombs. Verily, God has always been a watcher over you.
>
> (Qur'an 4:1)

This verse, the opening of the chapter (*Sura*) of the Qur'an titled "The Women," reminds us of the responsibilities we have toward the wombs that bore us but also toward those born of the same womb, who are thus our closest kin. "Womb bonds" (*silat al-rahm*) such as these are created by marriage. The above Qur'anic verse reiterates the importance of generosity and loyalty toward those who are closest to us by virtue of kinship. This verse also implies that Eve was the bearer of the first womb: "And from the twain [Adam and Eve] He spread abroad a multitude of men and women." The marriage of a man and a woman has a great impact on other people, bringing together two sets of fathers and mothers, and then uncles, aunts, and other relatives. As we start moving outward, drawing greater circles of people into the marital bond, the total number may include up to a hundred people. Theoretically, we could continue drawing wider and wider circles of relationships, until we included everyone in the world, such that all of us become "universal brothers and sisters" descended from the common womb of *Sayyidatuna Hawa*, "Our Lady Eve" in Arabic.[8] This may be another reason why the Qur'an extols us not to sever the bonds of the womb.

Not only do we have a responsibility toward our nearest of kin, but we also have a responsibility to honor and sustain what was left behind. We owe gratitude to those who went before us, as we are sustained in their shadow. Marriage thus produces both family ties and filial loyalty. The Prophet Muhammad exemplified this perfectly by maintaining excellent relationships with everyone in his large extended family and circle of companions. Like marriage, the practice of filial loyalty, honoring those who came before us, has been an obligatory part of all the world's cultures except our modern culture, which prides itself on innovation and departing from the usages of the past. Filial loyalty, by contrast, prepares us for the future by encouraging us to honor the past.

Each traditional culture places a different emphasis on filial loyalty. The Islamic version of this concept focuses primarily on honoring the mother. For males, filial loyalty means that a father has the right for a child to take his name such that his name is perpetuated through continuing generations. Muslim children take their father's name but a wife retains her own father's name, thus honoring her own posterity. In their most extreme forms, rebellion against one's parents and the "Generation Gap" that have been so typical of our age are rebellions against filial loyalty. As such, if they are not prompted by actual cases of abuse but are simply expressions of disrespect, they constitute a rebellion not only against one's parents and traditions but also against God.

POLYGYNY AS A POSSIBLE RELATIONSHIP IN MARRIAGE

Some years ago, I was privileged to know and study under a well-known teacher of Qur'anic recitation, Sheikh Abdeslam Derkaoui of Salé in Morocco. The Derkaoui family has an honored spiritual lineage in Morocco because they founded a great spiritual brotherhood, the Darqawiyya Sufi order, in the eighteenth century. Sheikh Abdeslam moved from the mountains of northern Morocco to the Rabat-Salé area to teach the Qur'an in the public school system. Before moving, he had married a woman from his own clan. The couple never had children. When his wife had passed the age of menopause and it was clear that she would not be able to bear any children, the Sheikh took a second wife from his native mountain region. Before marrying his second wife, he obtained his first wife's permission. Within several years, at the age of 70, the Sheikh was the proud father of six offspring. The first wife retained a position of honor in the family until her death. The second wife, always in deference to the first, devoted herself to the upbringing of her children. In this way, the Derkaoui lineage, posterity, and traditions were preserved.

Let us now return to Ali, Wafa, and Aziza, the polygynous Egyptian family that we met at the beginning of this chapter. The marriage was successful because each partner in the triangular relationship was willing to sacrifice a lesser good for a greater benefit. Ali married a girl with a disability and vowed to sustain her economically and emotionally for the rest of their lives. Wafa agreed to Aziza's becoming part of the family, thus sacrificing some of her marital rights in return for the prospect of having children. Aziza sacrificed some of her marital rights by sharing her husband's attentions with Wafa, who had already been married to Ali for more than 15 years.

The objective of permitting polygyny in Islam is to regulate, albeit strictly, the desires that are natural to many men, with a view to preserving marital relationships within the framework of sacred law. This is in contrast to most Western societies, where sexual freedom has become commonplace and even adultery may be considered "normal." Islamic rulings seek to limit the irresponsible gratification of desires by sanctifying human sexuality and channeling desire to obtain spiritual and social benefits. In criticizing polygyny in

Islamic society, non-Muslims forget that, according to anthropologists, polygyny has existed in almost every society. The Qur'an clearly allows for polygyny, but it also points out, "You will not be able to treat all of [your] women equally, even though you may desire to do so" (Qur'an 4:129). Many women in the Muslim world are unaware that under most Sunni schools of law, a woman can stipulate monogamy in her marriage contract.

Most Islamic scholars today believe that the permission to practice polygyny in early Islam was a response to the needs of the time. During the early period of Islamic history, this ruling was a grace, since it allowed for widows and orphans to be cared for in an environment of constant warfare, which took the lives of many early Muslims and left many widows. Mention should also be made of the polygynous marriages of the Prophet Muhammad. One should not forget, however, that Muhammad's first wife, Khadija, was his only wife for the entire 24 years of their marriage. Later marriages of the Prophet coincided with the more social phase of his delivering the Islamic revelation. The Prophet's wives were called "Mothers of the Believers," and they have been likened to jewels in a crown. They considered themselves blessed and privileged to be members of the Prophet's household. Despite the inevitable difficulties that arose in the Prophet's household because of human nature, none of his wives ever wanted a divorce. In his Introduction to *Sura* 66 (*al-Tahrim*) of the Qur'an, Mohammad M. Pickthall summarizes the Islamic position on polygyny thusly:

> For Muslims, monogamy is the ideal, polygamy the concession to human nature. Having set a great example of monogamic [*sic.*] marriage, the Prophet was to set a great example of polygamic [*sic.*] marriage by following which, men of that temperament could live righteous lives. He encountered all the difficulties inherent in the situation and when he made mistakes, the Qur'an helped him to retrieve them. Al-Islam did not institute polygamy. It restricted an existing institution by limiting the number of a man's legal wives, by giving to every woman a legal personality and legal rights which had to be respected, and making every man legally responsible for his conduct toward every woman.[9]

MARRIAGE AS SPIRITUAL FULFILLMENT

Whereas some religions, such as Christianity and Buddhism, encourage celibacy as an important virtue and support for spiritual fulfillment, Islam strongly recommends marriage. "Marriage is half of religion," is a well-known hadith and is illustrative of the emphasis that Islam places on marriage. What does "half of religion" mean in this context? Marriage not only qualifies men and women to fulfill their social functions in life but also requires self-sacrifice, self-effacement, and humility. Because of this combination of virtues, Islam has been called "a society of married monks." What this metaphor means is that all people, both men and women, should aspire to a higher level of spiritual awareness within the context of marriage. Women in particular are offered many opportunities for practicing self-effacement because their active lives revolve around their children for many years. When her children are young, a mother gives freely of herself and her time in the interest of her offspring, a commitment that usually continues for the rest of her life. This type of self-sacrifice and the compromises that are necessary between partners in a successful marriage chip away at the solidity of the ego, which is pleasing to God. Spiritual masters of all of the great religions teach that the ego is a major obstacle to reaching God. Even if a person is less interested in reaching God than having a successful marriage, the latter still requires the sacrifice of self.

Many Muslim women find spiritual, social, and emotional fulfillment in marriage. Islamic tradition situates much of such fulfillment in the wife's service to her husband, a notion that is often misunderstood by Westerners who are committed to viewing Islam as antiwoman. However, when the Prophet Muhammad said, "Paradise is the reward of the wife who pleases her husband until death," he did not mean that a wife is the chattel of her husband. Instead, he sought to stress the spiritual maturity that comes from giving selflessly to others, a message that can also be found in Western sources, such as Leo Tolstoy's *War and Peace*. In a similar vein, the Prophet said, "The gates of Paradise will be wide open to welcome the woman who observes her prayers, fasts the month of Ramadan, preserves her honor, and obeys her husband."

Shortly before my marriage, I sought spiritual counsel and was told that marriage was a "school for the soul." After being enrolled in this "school" for over 25 years, I have often found that I have only begun to learn the lessons of this "school" because the notion of the "self" that shrouds the heart is very hard. To crack this hard shell of egoism, marriage encourages self-effacement and lays the soul open to the spouse who knows us intimately. The great mystical teachers of Islam have said that for the spiritual man, the beauty of a woman reminds him of the beauty of Paradise, which he carries within himself. For a woman, the goodness and virtue of a man is a support and confirmation of her own inner goodness.

However, we also find in the Qur'an: "Oh you who believe! Verily, among your spouses and your children there are enemies for you, therefore beware of them; but if you efface, overlook, and forgive [their faults], then Allah is Forgiving and Merciful. Your wealth and your children are a temptation for you, whereas with Allah is an immense reward" (Qur'an 64:14–15). How are we supposed to understand such verses? One way to understand them is to see marriage as a "double-edged sword," in the sense that attachments to children and spouses, as well as to material possessions, can cloud one's spiritual vision and prevent a person from moving toward God. The "Holy War" in a marriage is the struggle to find a balance between offering love and mercy to one's spouse and children and at the same time attending to those elements of one's own soul that turn one away from the remembrance of God. If a person is able to achieve this balance, she has indeed accomplished "half of the religion" through her marriage.

As Muslim societies race toward modernity, they often spiral into rampant materialism and purely material values. One flagrant repercussion of these material values is the neglect of personal commitments and responsibilities to family, friends, and other members of society. Because it is a reflection of the Divine duality, marriage is one of the most important commitments we can make in our lives. The union of a man and a woman symbolizes the unity of God and the potential union of the soul with the Divine Spirit. Seen positively, this sacred union has the potential to symbolically "re-create" the whole or complete human being through the marital union. Seen negatively, the dissolution of the marriage bond may "un-create"—through an artificial act of separation—the person, who is otherwise meant to be whole. By honoring through marriage their commitment to God and each other, Muslims fulfill their double earthly role of God's slave and God's vice-regent. As the Prophet Muhammad said, "The best of you are those who are best to their women."

NOTES

1. From the point of view of Arabic grammar, it is ambiguous as to which gender was created first, the male or the female. Since the word for soul (*nafs*) is feminine, this verse of the Qur'an could equally refer to the soul of a male or the soul of a female. Thus, the possessive pronoun "her" in the phrase that follows ("and created from her/it its mate") refers to the soul and does not necessarily imply that the original nature of both men and women is female. In terms of historical creation, however, the Qur'an reaffirms the general outlines of the Biblical creation story of Adam, in which man is created before woman.

2. Lamya Farouki, *Women, Muslim Society and Islam* (Plainfield, Indiana: American Trust Publications, 1994), 17.

3. Muhammad Abdul-Rauf, *The Islamic View of Women and the Family* (New York: Robert Speller and Sons, 1977), 49.

4. Martin Lings, *Muhammad: His Life Based on the Earliest Sources* (London, U.K.: George Allen and Unwin and Islamic Texts Society, 1983), 24.

5. Hamza Yusuf Hanson, "The Rights and Responsibilities of Marriage," course recorded on CD, delivered at Zaytuna Institute (Hayward, California: Alhambra Productions, 2002) with reference to Al-Ghazali, op. cit. II, 30.

6. *Sunan Ibn Maja* (Cairo: Dar al-Kutub al-'Arabiyya, 1952), Vol. 1, 594.

7. *Sahih Muslim* (Beirut: Dar al-Kutub al-'Ilmiyya, 2001), 1056 (hadith no. 2,753).

8. Hamza Yusuf Hanson, "The Rights and Responsibilities of Marriage."

9. *The Glorious Qur'an*, Text and Explanatory Translation by Mohammad M. Pickthall (London, U.K.: The Islamic Festival Publications, 1976), 750.

5

RESPECT FOR THE MOTHER IN ISLAM

Aliah Schleifer

The relationship of the Muslim with his parents should be of the highest order of human relationships. This includes spiritual, financial, and emotional responsibilities, and is ongoing, even beyond the point of death. Ordinances are defined in the Qur'an relating to this point and are further specified by Hadith, Islamic jurisprudence (*fiqh*), and commentary. The reward for satisfactory compliance with the Qur'anic ordinances is Paradise. Mu'awiyya ibn Jahma narrated that Jahma went to the Prophet Muhammad and said, "Oh Messenger of Allah, I want to fight and I have come to ask your advice." The Prophet asked, "Do you have a mother?" "Yes," Jahma said. The Prophet then said, "Then stay with her because Paradise is under her foot."[1] Abu Umama narrated: "They are your Paradise and your Hell-fire"—that is, the parents.[2]

Thus, the clarification of these ordinances becomes essential to a Muslim, who wishes to know exactly how he can attain this reward, and exactly what will block him from it. In general, most statements of responsibility to parents include both father and mother, but the mother, in Islam, is granted more in this respect. Abu Hurayra narrated that a man came to the Messenger of Allah and asked, "Oh Messenger of Allah, who is more entitled to be treated with the best companionship by me?" The Prophet said, "Your mother." Then the man said, "Then who?" The Prophet said, "Your mother," "Then who?" The Prophet said, "Then your father."[3]

Nawawi says that the Arabic term *al-sahaba* used in this hadith means "companionship." It is intended to urge one toward kindness to relatives, the most deserving of whom is the mother and then the father. Giving the opinion of the *ulama* (the Muslim scholars), he says that the reason for giving the mother preference is due to her exhausting efforts for the sake of her child; her compassion; her service; the great difficulty of pregnancy, delivery, nursing, and rearing of the child; her service and care for the child when it is sick; and so on. In the view of the ulama, the mother is the strongest member of the family in kindness and devotion.[4]

Two verses in the Qur'an provide general injunctions to the believers to practice good treatment of parents. The first says: "Worship Allah alone and be kind to parents" (Qur'an 2:83). In their commentaries on this verse, Tabari, Ibn Kathir, and Qurtubi are in agreement about the meaning of the accusative noun, *ihsanan*, which is usually translated as "be good to," but Ibn Kathir devotes more discussion to good speech toward parents, while both Qurtubi and Ibn Kathir stress parents' rights.

Tabari states that grammatically, the expression *wa bi'l-walidayni ihsanan* ("and be kind to parents") is connected to the preceding expression, *la ta'buduna illa Allah* ("worship Allah alone"), and thus their meanings are connected.[5] Speaking of the two connected expressions, Ibn Kathir says that these are the highest and greatest of rights, that is, the rights of Allah, Most Blessed and Most High, that He be worshipped alone, with nothing associated with Him; then, after that, is the right of His creatures, and He firmly commissions them and their children with the right of parents. Thus, Allah draws a parallel between His right and the right of parents.[6] Qurtubi says that Allah, the Great and Lofty, makes a parallel in this verse, between the right of parents and the Unity of Allah because the first formation (genesis) proceeds from Allah, and the second formation—upbringing— proceeds from the parents. Thus, Allah compares thankfulness to parents with thankfulness to Him, this being expressed explicitly in Qur'an 31:14, "Give thanks to Me and to your parents."[7]

By way of explanation of the meaning of *ihsanan*, Tabari says it is to show kindness to parents, courteous speech, the lowering of the wing of submission as a mercy to them, tenderness, compassion, prayer for good to come to them, and other similar deeds. Qurtubi reiterates this definition, adding that the believers should keep up relationships with the people their parents love.[8] To explain the meaning of *ihsanan*, Ibn Kathir refers to Hasan al-Basri's definition of another form of the word, *husnan*, which is also found in Qur'anic verse 2:83. Basri defines *husnan* with reference to speech, as such speech "that commands kindness, terminates objectionable remarks, and is gentle, and restrains one and pardons."[9] To further clarify his definition, Ibn Kathir quotes the following hadith: Abu Dharr narrated that the Prophet said, "Do not show the slightest contempt for the concept of kindness. If you do not find any good to do, greet your brother with a bright face."[10] Ibn Kathir concludes that Allah commands His creatures to speak good speech to the people after He has commanded them to do well to others in deed; thus, He unites between the extremities of goodness of deed and that of goodness of speech.

In their discussion of the second Qur'anic injunction of a general nature about parents—"Show kindness to parents, to kinsfolk and orphans, and to the needy" (Qur'an 4:36)—the three commentators express a restatement of their previous opinions on the subject. Qurtubi, however, includes an additional hadith, which succinctly expresses the importance of the child–parent relationship. According to Shu'ba and Hashim al-Wastiyan,

'Abdallah ibn 'Amr ibn al-'As narrated that the Messenger of Allah said: "The satisfaction of the Lord is in the satisfaction of the parents, and the displeasure of the Lord is in the displeasure of the parents."[11]

The following hadiths are a further illustration of the immense importance, in Islam, that is given to kindness and service to parents in general, and to the mother in particular. Ibn 'Abbas narrated that the Prophet said: "Safeguard the love for your parents. Do not cut it off or your light will be extinguished by Allah."[12] 'Abdallah ibn Mas'ud narrated: "I asked the Messenger of Allah which deed was the preferred one?" He said, "Prayer at its proper time." Then I asked, "Which is next?" He said, "Kindness to parents." Then I asked, "Which is next?" He said, "Fighting for the sake of Allah."[13]

'Abdallah ibn 'Amr ibn al-'As narrated that the Messenger of Allah excused a man from *jihad*. He asked, "Are your parents alive?" "Yes," the man replied. He said, "Then struggling in their service is your *jihad*."[14] Anas ibn Malik narrated that a man came to the Messenger of Allah and said, "I longed to go on *jihad*, but I was not able to do so." The Prophet asked, "Is either one of your parents alive?" "My mother," the man said. The Prophet said, "Allah has instructed us in devotion to her, so if you do thus, you are as one who has made the *Hajj* pilgrimage, the *'Umra* pilgrimage, and has participated in *jihad*."[15]

Ibn 'Umar narrated that a man came to the Messenger of Allah and said, "I have committed a great sin. Is there anything I can do to repent?" The Prophet asked, "Do you have a mother?" "No," the man said. He asked, "Do you have a maternal aunt?" "Yes," the man said. He said, "Then, be kind and devoted to her."[16] Talaq ibn 'Ali narrated that the Prophet said: "If I became aware of my parents, or one of them, and I had begun the evening prayer and had recited *Surat al-Fatiha;* and my mother called me— I would have answered her."[17] Ibn 'Abbas narrated that the Prophet said: "Do not leave your mother unless she gives you permission or death takes her because that is the greatest deed for your reward."[18] Ibn 'Abbas narrated that the Prophet said: "Whoever kisses his mother between the eyes has protection from the Fire."[19]

With respect to financial responsibility to needy parents, the Qur'an addresses this point clearly: "That which you spend for good is for parents, near kindred and orphans, and the poor and the wayfarer" (Qur'an 2:215). Thus, among the categories of needy persons for whom financial support is due, parents come first. The consensus of the three commentators is that this verse implies the appropriateness of voluntary charity to needy parents, above and beyond the annually required compulsory charity (*Zakat*).

Tabari states that the reference is to voluntary charity. Ibn Kathir concurs with Tabari's opinion but also presents Muqatil ibn Hayyan's opinion that this interpretation was subsequently abrogated by (the commandment to pay) *Zakat*. Qurtubi says it was not abrogated and that there are two different issues, one being voluntary charity and the other compulsory charity.

Tabari's explication reemphasizes the fact that the Qur'anic injunction refers to both parents, the mother as well as the father. Thus, he says the meaning of the verse is that your companions, Oh Muhammad, ask you what they should spend out of their wealth on voluntary charity, and on whom they should spend it. So say to them: What you spend of your wealth as voluntary charity, use it for your fathers and your mothers and your relatives, and the orphans among you and the needy and the wayfarers. Therefore, whatever you do of good, do it for them. Verily, Allah is aware of it, and He records for you, until you die, your reward for it on the Day of Resurrection. Also, He rewards you for what you give out of kindness. Thus, the *khayr*, the good, that the Most Lofty, May He Be Praised, stated in this verse of His, is your wealth, the spending of which the Companions asked the Messenger of Allah about, and Allah answered them in this verse.[20] Qurtubi specifies the Companion for whom this verse was revealed as 'Amr ibn al-Jamuh, who was at that time an old man. He said, "Oh Messenger of Allah, my wealth is great, so what should I give in charity, and on whom should I spend it?" Consequently, according to Qurtubi, this verse was revealed.[21]

Ibn Kathir records, in reference to Ibn Hayyan's comment above, that as-Suddi said there is speculation about this; in other words, it is not a generally accepted opinion.[22] Qurtubi clarifies his position on the question posed by Ibn Hayyan's opinion, stating that Ibn Jurayj and others said that *Zakat* is different from the spending mentioned in this verse; therefore, there is no abrogation of it. He goes on to say that it is clearly the spending of voluntary charity, and it is obligatory on the man of means that he spends on his needy parents what is suitable for their status and compatible with his financial status, for food and clothing, and so on.[23]

This primacy of concern for parents' needs is expressly illustrated by the following excerpt from a longer hadith:

'Abdullah ibn 'Umar reported that Allah's Messenger told the following story: Three persons set out on a journey. They were overtaken by rain and they had to find protection in a mountain cave, when at its mouth there fell a rock of that mountain, and this blocked them altogether. One of them said to the others, "Examine your good deeds that you performed for the sake of Allah and then supplicate Allah the Exalted, that He might rescue you from this trouble." One of them said, "Oh Allah, I had my parents who were old and my wife and small children also. I tended the flocks and when I came back to them in the evening, I did the milking and served that milk to my parents, before serving my children. One day, when I was obliged to go out to a distant place in search of fodder and could not come back before evening, I found my parents asleep. I milked the animals as usual, and brought milk to them and stood at their heads avoiding disturbing them from sleep, and I did not deem it advisable to serve milk to my children before serving them. I remained there in that state and my parents too until morning. Oh Allah, if You are aware that I did this in order to seek Your pleasure, then give us an opening that we may see the sky." And Allah gave them an opening.[24]

Sura 6, verse 151 of the Qur'an reemphasizes the parallel between submission to Allah, the One, and submission to His command of good treatment to parents: "that you ascribe nothing as a partner to [Allah] and that you act with goodness toward parents" (Qur'an 6:151). However, the commentary on this verse further reveals that this obligation is due regardless of similarity or difference of religion; that is, the Muslim is bound to offer respect and service to parents, whether they be Muslims, Christians, Jews, or even polytheists.

Qurtubi says that grammatically, the word al-ihsan ("goodness") in the above Qur'anic verse is a noun masdar in the accusative case, which is made accusative by a missing verb; thus, the implied meaning is to do the highest degree of good to your parents. He further defines al-ihsan to parents as respecting them, protecting them, caring for them, obedience to their commands, and not treating them as slaves but rather giving them the position of authority.[25] Ibn Kathir points out that the comparison between submission to Allah and reverence to parents is mentioned many times in the Qur'an and adds that if the parents are nonbelievers, showing kindness and respect to them is sufficient, thus implying that the Muslim is bound to his obligations to his parents, with the exception of parental commands that are contra-Islam.[26]

The following two accounts illustrate the insistence in Islam on reverence and kindness to one's mother, regardless of religious difference. Shaqiq ibn Wa'il said: "My mother died a Christian, so I went to 'Umar ibn al-Khattab (the second Caliph after the Prophet Muhammad, r. 634–644 CE) and told him this." He said, "Mount an animal and ride in front of her bier at the front of the funeral procession."[27] Asma' the daughter of Abu Bakr reported: "My mother, who was a polytheist, came to me when the Prophet entered into a treaty with the Quraysh tribe of Mecca." I inquired from the Messenger of Allah, saying, "Oh Messenger of Allah, my mother has come to me and she is afraid. Should I show her kindness?" He said, "Yes, treat her kindly."[28]

When parents reach the period of old age, this is the time which offers the Muslim the greatest opportunity to fulfill his obligations to them, and thus hope to gain Allah's pleasure. Muslims are counseled to keep in mind the fact that their elderly parents were devoted to them when they were in need of care as a child, while at the same time to remember that they are parents, not children, with all the rights and privileges due to them as such.

The Qur'an speaks directly to the question of the treatment of parents in old age: "Your Lord has decreed that you worship none save Him, and that you show kindness to parents. If one or both of them attain old age with you, say not 'Uff!' to them nor repulse them, but speak to them graciously. And lower unto them the wing of submission through mercy, and say: 'My Lord, have mercy on them both as they did care for me when I was little'" (Qur'an 17:23–24). The Qur'an also stresses the obligation to parents and its nature in the following verse: "[John the Baptist] was dutiful toward his parents; he was neither arrogant nor rebellious" (Qur'an 19:14).

In their discussion of Sura 17:23–24, Tabari and Ibn Kathir apply their previous comments on the child–parent relationship with some specification for the period of old age. Qurtubi, however, uses these verses as an opportunity to give his full exegesis on the subject. Tabari emphasizes that because of the words *wa qada rabbuka* ("your Lord has decreed"), this is a command from Allah to show kindness to parents, to do good to them, and to respect them. He says the meaning of the verses is not to grumble or utter a complaint about something that you see in one of them or both—a kind of muttering that people are hurt by, but rather, to be patient with them in anticipation of spiritual reward, as they were patient with you when you were young.[29] He then refers to Mujahid's statement that the reference in these verses is to the case where your parents are senile, in the condition of feces and urine, as you were as a baby, and you say "Uff!" to them.[30] As a further comment on the meaning of "Uff!" Tabari includes 'Ata'illah ibn Abi Rabah's statement, on the authority of Muhammad ibn Isma'il al-Ahmasi: "Don't brush your parents aside;" that is, do not treat them as if they were insignificant. Having stated what not to do, the verse then describes what to do by stating, *wa qul lahuma qawlan kariman* ("but speak to them graciously"), which is explained by Ibn Jurayj on the authority of al-Qasim: "The best that you can find of speech."[31]

Qurtubi says that reverence and goodness to parents is that you do not insult or blaspheme them because this is, without argument, one of the major sins. To qualify his statement and to illustrate the depth of its meaning, Qurtubi refers to the following hadith. 'Abdullah ibn 'Amr narrated that the Messenger of Allah said: "Verily, abuse of one's parents is one of the major sins." They said, "Oh Messenger of Allah, does a man abuse his parents?" "Yes," he said. "The man insults the father of another man, so the other man insults the first one's father, and he insults the other one's mother and vice-versa."[32] Also, in another hadith, the blasphemer of parents is placed on a par with the idol worshipper and the unwarranted innovator: 'Ali said, "Allah curses whoever curses his parents. Allah curses whoever sacrifices to other than Allah! Allah curses whoever accommodates an innovator. Allah curses whoever changes the boundary lines of the land."[33]

In his commentary on this account, Nawawi confirms that the cursing of the father and the mother is one of the major sins in Islam. To explain the rest of the account, he says that the connotation of *manar al-ard* (literally, "lighthouses of the land") is the limits or the boundary of the land. As for sacrificing to other than Allah, its connotation is one who sacrifices in the name of other than Allah the Most High, like he who sacrifices to the idols or to the cross, or to Moses, Jesus, or the Ka'ba, and so on.[34]

Qurtubi says that the condition of old age is specified in Qur'an 17:23 because this is the state in which parents need kindness owing to the change in their condition to weakness and old age. With regard to their condition, more kindness and compassion is required because in this state they become more troublesome. In addition, since the burden is the man's duty and is something he has to live with daily, irritation develops and vexation increases; then his anger toward his parents appears, and he flies into a rage at them and becomes arrogant with the boldness of his position and the lack of religion. Qurtubi says the despicable is what he exhibits by indicating his irritation by repeated "heavy breaths." Instead, he is commanded by Allah to receive his parents with speech characterized by respect, the doing of which is his security against shameful acts. Qurtubi includes Abu Raja' al-'Ataridi's statement that "Uff" is speech that is maligning, mean, and concealed. In reference to Mujahid's above-mentioned statement included by Tabari, Qurtubi says that the verse is more general than that and that it refers to the saying of "Uff" to everything that vexes or is a burden.[35]

It is related from a hadith of 'Ali ibn Abi Talib, according to which the Messenger of Allah said: "If Allah knew any type of rudeness worse than 'Uff,' He would have mentioned it. So do of the righteous acts what you want to do and you will not enter the Fire, but do of the disrespectful acts what you want to do and you will not enter Paradise."[36]

As a commentary on this hadith, the ulama said: "Accordingly, one's saying 'Uff' to one's parents becomes the worst thing because the rejection of them is an ungrateful rejection and repudiation of one's upbringing, and a rejection of the counsel given in the Qur'an." To prove his point that "Uff" is not an expression to be taken lightly, Qurtubi gives the example of the Prophet Abraham's use of it to show his rejection of idols and idol worshippers, in which Abraham said to his people, "Uff to you and all that you worship instead of Allah!" (Qur'an 21:67). In addition, Qurtubi states that the meaning of *al-nahr* ("repulsion") in Qur'anic verse 17:23 is rebuke and harshness.[37]

To explain the meaning of *wa qul lahuma qawlan kariman* ("but speak to them graciously"), Qurtubi refers to 'Ata's statement in which he says it is polite gentleness; for example, saying, "Oh my father and my mother," without calling them directly by either their first names or their last names.[38] In reference to this part of the verse, Abu al-Baddah al-Tujibi said, "I said to Sa'id ibn al-Musayyib that I understood everything in the Qur'an about reverence to parents except [Allah's] statement, 'but speak to them graciously.' Ibn al-Musayyib said, 'This refers to the sinner slave's speaking rude and harsh words to the master.'" Qurtubi goes on to say that the lending of affection and mercy to parents and submission to them is the submission of the governed to the leader, and that of the slave to the master, as Sa'id ibn al-Musayyib indicated. Thus, the intention of the ruling of this verse is that the person should put himself in a state of maximum submission with respect to his parents, in his speech and his silence and his looks, and should not give them sharp looks, as this is the look of the angered.[39]

In Tabari's explication of Qur'anic verse 17:24, he quotes a statement on the authority of al-Qasim, on the authority of Hisham ibn 'Urwa from his father, that 'Umar ibn al-Khattab said, "Do not refuse to do anything [your parents] want."[40] Qurtubi clarifies this point by stating that rudeness to parents is the contradiction of their desires that are legally permissible, just as respecting them is the acceptance of their desires that are legally permissible. Thus, if both or one of them commands, obedience to them is a must if that command is not a sin and if that which is commanded is permissible (*mubah*), likewise if it is recommended (*mandub*). Further, some people hold the view that the parents' command that is permissible for them becomes a recommended duty of the child and that their command which is recommended is increased to be even more highly recommended.[41]

Qurtubi mentions Abu Hurayra's hadith that kindness and compassion to the mother should be three times that to the father and relates it to his discussion of obedience. He mentions similar points as those made by Nawawi and adds that if you come to this conclusion, then the meaning is judged to be an obligation on the individual.[42] Then, he presents various opinions about this point and his own conclusion. First is a contrary opinion. It is reported about Malik (ibn Anas, founder of the Maliki school of jurisprudence, d. 795 CE) that a man said to him, "My father is in the country of the blacks (*al-sudan*) and he wrote to me that I should come to him, but my mother prevents me from doing so." Then Malik said to him, "Obey your father and disobey your mother." Thus, Malik's statement indicates that reverence to both parents is equal as far as he is concerned. Then al-Layth (ibn Sa'id, an early jurist) was asked about this question, and he commanded obedience to the mother, claiming that she gets two-thirds of the devotion of the child. Qurtubi concludes, however, that Abu Hurayra's hadith indicates that the mother gets three-fourths of the devotion, and that is proof for those who dispute the matter. Muhasibi affirms in his book *Kitab al-Ri'aya* (Observance of the Rights Due to God, Ed.; translation added for this volume) that there is no disagreement among the ulama that the mother gets three-fourths of the devotion and the father one-fourth, according to Abu Hurayra's hadith. But Allah knows best.[43]

In his discussion of the phrase *min al-rahma* ("of mercy") in Qur'anic verse 17:24, Qurtubi says that *min* means "the kind of," in other words, that the "lowering of the wing" be a kind of merciful submission of the spirit, not that it be in actions only. Thus, the Most High ordered His slaves to be merciful to their parents and to pray for them. Thus, you should be compassionate to them as they were to you, and befriend them as they did you, remembering that when you were an incapable, needy child, they preferred you to themselves, and they stayed awake nights, and went hungry while they satisfied your appetite, and were in need of clothes while they clothed you. So reward them when they reach old age in the condition that you were in as a child, in that you treat them as they did you, and give kindness to them priority.[44]

Ibn 'Abbas reported that the Prophet said: "He who ends the day with his parents satisfied with him and begins the day thus, to him two doors to Paradise are opened; and if it is one parent, then one door. But he who ends and begins the day and is the object of odiousness to his parents, for him, two doors to the Fire are opened; and if it is one parent, then one door." Then a man said, "Oh Messenger of Allah, what if his parents have mistreated him?" He said, "Even if they have mistreated him, even if they have mistreated him, even if they have mistreated him."[45]

In the commentary on Qur'an 19:14, the emphasis is on the importance of obedience to the parents, by way of the example of the Prophet Yahya (John the Baptist), who is praised for his consistent submissiveness and humility before Allah and his parents, doing what he was commanded to do and refraining from what he was forbidden.[46] The following hadiths are further illustrations of the requirement in Islam for such respect and submissiveness to one's mother and father, and an indication of what constitutes disobedience.

Al-Miqdam ibn Ma'dikarib narrated that the Prophet said: "Indeed, Allah has warned you about your responsibility to your fathers; indeed Allah has warned you about your responsibility to your mothers; indeed Allah has warned you about your responsibility to your mothers; indeed Allah has warned you about your responsibility toward your mothers; indeed Allah has warned you about your responsibility to your relatives; so look to your relatives."[47]

Abu Malik al-Qushayri narrated that the Prophet said: "If someone's parents, or even one of them, dies and then he enters the Fire, Allah will disassociate Himself from him and will destroy Him."[48] In other words, being kind to his parents would have saved him from the Fire. Abu Hurayra reported Allah's Messenger as saying, "Let his pride be in the dust; let his pride be in the dust; let his pride be in the dust." It was asked, "Oh Messenger of Allah, who is he?" He said, "He who finds his parents in old age, either one of them or both of them, and does not enter Paradise."[49] Nawawi comments on this tradition: "Let his pride be in the dust" for not revering his parents with his service to them or providing for them; thus, he lost his chance for Paradise.[50]

'Abdallah ibn 'Amr narrated that a man came to the Prophet pledging himself to go on the *hijra* (emigration) with the Prophet (from Mecca to Medina). He left his parents crying. The Prophet said, "Return to them and make them laugh as you have made them cry."[51] 'Ali said, "Whoever saddens his parents has disobeyed them."[52] 'Abdullah ibn 'Amr ibn al-'As narrated that the Prophet said: "The major sins are associating anything with Allah, rudeness to parents, killing anyone, and swearing a false oath purposefully."[53] In a longer hadith, Abu 'Isa al-Mughira narrated that the Prophet said: "Verily, Allah forbade you rudeness and disobedience toward mothers."[54]

Respect and kindness to the mother even extends beyond her death. This includes prayers for her forgiveness and the completion of various obligations to her. The Qur'an provides examples of such prayers on behalf of believing parents and a reminder to the Muslim to be grateful for having this opportunity: "Our Lord, forgive me and my parents and the believers on the Day of Reckoning" (Qur'an 14:41). "My Lord, arouse me to be thankful for Your favor, through which You have favored me and my parents" (Qur'an 27:19). "My Lord, forgive me and my parents, and the one who enters my house believing, and [all] believing men and believing women" (Qur'an 71:28).

The three commentators apparently find the meaning of these verses so obvious that they do not require additional explanation. However, in Qurtubi's previous discussion of "as they cared for me" in Qur'an 17:24, he mentions that the reference is to believing parents, as the Qur'an abrogated asking for forgiveness for the nonbelievers, even if they are the closest relatives: "It is not for the Prophet and those who believe to pray for the forgiveness of idolaters, even though they may be near of kin" (Qur'an 9:113). Thus, if the Muslim's parents are nonbelievers, he should treat them as Allah has commanded him to, with respect, kindness, and so on, except for the mercy to them after death as nonbelievers, because this alone was invalidated by the verse mentioned. An additional comment clarifies that prayers for mercy in this world for the nonbelieving parents that are still alive is not invalidated by this verse.[55] Abu Hurayra narrated that the Messenger of Allah said, "I asked my Lord's permission to ask forgiveness for my mother, but He did not allow me to do so. Then I asked for His permission to visit her grave, and He allowed me to do so."[56]

Nawawi's commentary on this hadith is that contained in it is permission for visiting the polytheist during liftetime and the grave after death. His argument is that if permission is given to visit the polytheist after death, then it must include during the lifetime, because this has more priority and is in accordance with Allah's command of the best of companionship to all people during one's lifetime. He goes on to say that contained in this hadith is the prohibition of asking forgiveness for nonbelievers after death.[57]

The following hadith indicates that a reward is forthcoming for the one who visits his parents' grave. Abu Hurayra narrated that the Prophet said: "Whoever visits one or more of his parents' graves once every week, Allah forgives him and he will be recorded among the righteous."[58] The next two hadiths indicate additional obligations due to parents after death and the reward for fulfilling them.

Abu Asad Malik ibn Rabi'a al-Sa'di said that when we were with the Messenger of Allah a man from Banu Salama came and asked: "Oh Messenger of Allah, is there any remaining chance to show devotion to my parents after they have died?" "Yes," he said, "prayer for them, asking forgiveness for them, fulfilling their contracts after them, keeping up the family relations that they used to maintain, and respecting their friends."[59] Ibn 'Abbas narrated: "Whoever performs the pilgrimage for his parents or terminates a debt for them, Allah sends him forth among the righteous on the Day of Ascension."

In summary, according to Islam, gratitude to parents is on the highest human level, such that it is compared with the ultimate gratitude, that due to Allah. Service to parents is second only to prayer and its fulfillment to elderly parents absolves one from participation in *jihad*. Good treatment of parents, in their lifetime and after death, is an established right due to them, not a gratuitous act, and involves all aspects of human behavior, great or small, to be expressed to the limits of human feasibility. Furthermore, utmost respect is due to them, regardless of religion, physical condition, or social status. The concern and respect for the mother, specifically, is a way of expiating sin and a clear way for the believer to become closer to Allah and to ward off the Fire.

NOTES

This chapter first appeared as a chapter in Aliah Schleifer, *Motherhood in Islam* (Louisville, Kentucky: Islamic Texts Society and Fons Vitae, 1996). It is reproduced here with minor modifications by permission of the publisher.

1. Muhammad Siddiq Khan, *Husn al-uswa bi-ma thabita min Allah wa Rasulihi fi al-niswa* (Beirut: Mu'assasa ar-Risala, 1976), 236.

2. 'Ala' al-Din ibn Husam al-Din al-Hindi, *Kanz al-'umal fi sunan al-aqwal* (Hyderabad, India: Da'irat al-Ma'arif al-'Uthmaniyya, 1364/1945), vol. 16, 463 (hadith number 45,453).

3. *Sahih al-Bukhari* (Chicago, Illinois: Kazi Publications, 1979), vol. 8, 2; Khan, *Husn al-uswa*, 235; see Ismail Abdul Razack and Abdul Jawad al-Banna, *Women and Family in the Sunnah of the Prophet* (Arabic text included), International Centre for Population Studies and Research, Al-Azhar University (Cairo: Dar al-Kutub, n.d.), 32, for another narration of this hadith.

4. Abu al-Hasan Muslim ibn al-Hajjaj, *Sahih Muslim bi-sharh al-Nawawi* (Cairo, 1924), vol. 16, 102.

5. Muhammad ibn Jarir al-Tabari, *Jami' al-Bayan 'an ta'wil ay al-Qur'an* (Cairo: Mustafa al-Babi al-Halabi, 3rd printing, 1388/1968), vol. 1, 390.

6. 'Imad ad-Din Abi'l-Fida' Isma'il Ibn Kathir, *Tafsir al-Qur'an al-'azim* (Cairo: Dar al-Qutub al-'Arabiyya, n.d.), vol. 1, 119.

7. Abu 'Abdullah Muhammad ibn Ahmad al-Qurtubi, *al-Jami' li-ahkam al-Qur'an* (Cairo: Dar al-Kitab al-'Arabi li-al-Taba' wa al-Nashr, 1387/1967), vol. 2, 13.

8. Tabari, *Jami' al-Bayan*, vol. 1, 390; Qurtubi, *al-Jami'*, vol. 2, 13.

9. Ibn Kathir, *Tafsir*, vol. 1, 120.

10. Ibid.

11. Qurtubi, *al-Jami'*, vol. 5, 183.

12. Hindi, *Kanz al-ʿulum,* vol. 16, 464 (hadith no. 45,460).
13. *Sahih Muslim,* vol. 2, 73.
14. Khan, *Husn al-uswa,* 236.
15. Ibid., 514.
16. Ibid., 237.
17. Hindi, *Kanz al-ʿulum,* vol. 16, 470 (hadith no. 45,500).
18. Ibid., 472 (hadith no. 45,504).
19. Ibid., 462 (hadith no. 45,442).
20. Tabari, *Jamiʿ al-Bayan,* vol. 2, 342.
21. Qurtubi, *al-Jamiʿ,* vol. 3, 36.
22. Ibn Kathir, *Tafsir,* vol. 1, 251.
23. Qurtubi, *al-Jamiʿ,* vol. 3, 37.
24. *Sahih Muslim,* vol. 17, 55–56.
25. Qurtubi, *al-Jamiʿ,* vol. 7, 132.
26. Ibn Kathir, *Tafsir,* vol. 2, 187–188.
27. Hindi, *Kanz al-ʿumal,* vol. 16, 577 (hadith no. 45,929).
28. *Sahih Muslim,* vol. 7, 89.
29. Tabari, *Jamiʿ al-Bayan,* vol. 15, 63.
30. Ibid., 64.
31. Ibid., 65.
32. Qurtubi, *al-Jamiʿ,* vol. 10, 238; see also, Abu Zakariyya Yahya ibn Sharaf al-Nawawi, *Riyad al-Salihin* (Beirut: Dar al-Fikr, n.d.), 108 (hadith no. 338).
33. Hindi, *Kanz al-ʿulum,* vol. 16, 480 (hadith no. 45,546).
34. *Sahih Muslim bi-sharh al-Nawawi,* vol. 13, 141.
35. Qurtubi, *al-Jamiʿ,* vol. 10, 241–242.
36. Ibid., 243.
37. Ibid.
38. Ibid.; see also Khan, *Husn al-uswa* 80, 114–115.
39. Qurtubi, *al-Jamiʿ,* vol. 10, 243–244.
40. Tabari, *Jamiʿ al-Bayan,* vol. 15, 65.
41. Qurtubi, *al-Jamiʿ,* vol. 10, 238.
42. Ibid., 239.
43. Ibid.
44. Ibid., 244.
45. Ibid., 245.
46. Tabari, *Jamiʿ al-Bayan,* vol. 12, 58.
47. Ibn Kathir, *Tafsir,* vol. 3, 35.
48. Ibid.
49. *Sahih Muslim,* vol. 16, 109.
50. Ibid., 108–109.
51. Hindi, *Kanz al-ʿulum,* vol. 16, 478 (hadith no. 45,537).
52. Nawawi, *Riyad al-Salihin,* vol. 7, 45 (hadith no. 337).
53. Ibid., 108 (hadith no. 340).
54. Qurtubi, *al-Jamiʿ,* vol. 10, 244–245.

55. *Sahih Muslim,* vol. 7, 45.

56. Ibid.

57. Hindi, *Kanz al-ʿulum,* vol. 16, 468 (hadith no. 45,487).

58. Abu Dawud Sulayman ibn al-Ashʿath al-Sijistani, *al-Sunan* (Cairo: Maktabat al-ʿArab, 1863), vol. 2, 216–217.

59. Hindi, *Kanz al-ʿulum,* vol. 16, 468 (hadith no. 45,485).

6

Pregnancy and Childbirth in Islam

Aliah Schleifer

From the Islamic point of view, marriage is the desired state of affairs. The Prophet Muhammad said: "If the slave (of Allah) marries, he has completed half of the religion; so let him fear Allah (through worship and service) with the remaining half."[1]

Childbirth is considered the natural outcome of marriage. The Muslim woman sees pregnancy, childbirth, nursing, and rearing as spiritual acts. It is her exclusive opportunity to obtain Allah's blessings and rewards, as the difficulty of pregnancy and childbirth is a way that Allah has allotted only to the female sex. On the one hand, she has been endowed with suitable characteristics for the task, and on the other, she is to be rewarded for her efforts by her children. Thus, even if she does no more than simply bring them into this world, they are bound, as Muslims, to respect and have concern for her. The following two Qur'anic verses clearly indicate the obligation on the Muslim of reverence to the mother because of her childbearing responsibilities:

> We have enjoined on the human being concerning his parents: His mother bears him in weakness upon weakness, and his weaning is in two years. So give thanks to Me and to your parents. Unto Me is the journey.
>
> (Qur'an 31:14)

> We have enjoined on the human being kindness toward his parents. His mother bears him with reluctance, and brings him forth with reluctance. The bearing of him and the weaning of him are thirty months, till, when he attains full strength and reaches forty years of age, he says: "My Lord, arouse me that I may give thanks for the favor that You have granted me and my parents, and that I may do right unto You. And be gracious to me in the matter of my progeny."
>
> (Qur'an 46:15)

The Arabic phrase, *wahnan 'ala wahnin,* found in Qur'an 31:14, which has been translated as "weakness upon weakness" has a fuller meaning, which the commentators have attempted to describe. Tabari says it means weakness upon weakness, and straining upon straining. Qatada says it is effort upon effort, and thus Ibn Kathir comments that the Most High mentions the mother's rearing of the child and tiring herself, and her hardship staying awake night and day, in order to remind the child of her previous kindness to him. Qurtubi says it refers to the period in which she carried him in pregnancy, and she increased each day in weakness upon weakness. Muhammad Siddiq Khan summarizes in his statement: "It is said that pregnancy is *wahn*, the labor pains are *wahn*, and the delivery is *wahn*, and the nursing is *wahn*."[2] Then, in reference to *ilayya al-masir* ("unto Me is the journey"), Ibn Kathir says that the meaning is that Allah will give an abundant reward for giving thanks to your parents.[3] Sufyan Ibn 'Uyaina adds that he who prays the five prayers has thereby given thanks to Allah, the Most High, and he who makes *du'a* (a prayer of supplication) for his parents after his prayers has thereby given thanks to them.[4]

The Hadith explains the importance of the mother's task and the great reward she receives:

> Anas ibn Malik narrated: Salama, the nurse of [the Prophet Muhammad's] son Ibrahim, said to the Prophet, "Oh Messenger of Allah, you brought tidings of all good things to men but not to women." [The Prophet] said, "Did your women friends put you up to asking me this question?" She said, "Yes, they did." He said, "Does it not please any one of you that if a woman is pregnant by her husband and he is satisfied with her that she receives the reward of one who fasts and prays for the sake of Allah? When the labor pains come, no one in Heaven or on Earth knows what is concealed in her womb to soothe her. When she delivers, not a mouthful of milk flows from her and not an instance of the child's suck, but that she receives, for every mouthful and for every suck, the reward of one good deed. And if she is kept awake by her child at night, she receives the reward of one who frees seventy slaves for the sake of Allah."[5]

Because of the strong bond of affection that accompanies the great effort of the mother, the loss of children is a heavy burden, and if she accepts it as Allah's will, her reward is Paradise:

> The women said to the Prophet Muhammad: "Oh Messenger of Allah, the men have taken all your time from us, so give us a day with you." So he promised them a day. He preached to them and commanded them and amongst what he told them was: "There is not one of you that sends forth (in death) three of your children, but that this will protect her from the Fire." One woman asked, "Oh Messenger of Allah, what about two?" He replied, "And two."[6]

In another hadith the Prophet said, "Not one of you will have three children to die and accept it (as the will of Allah), but that she will enter Paradise." Then he added "Or two."[7] In addition, if the mother dies in childbirth, she is equal to the martyr who dies fighting in the cause of Allah.

'Ubada ibn al-Samit narrated (in a longer hadith): "A woman who dies in childbirth together with the baby, becomes a martyr."[8]

In Qur'an 46:15 above, the accusative noun *karhan* has been translated as "with reluctance." To further clarify this point, Tabari refers to the statements of Mujahid, Hasan (al-Basri), and Qatada that *karhan* means hardship, labor, and trouble. He goes on, in his interpretation of the verse, to say that the age of 40 years is when Allah has given man maturity and competence; the folly of youth has passed and he knows his duties to Allah and what is right in terms of respect to his parents.[9] Thus, Tabari indicates that a human being does not reach the state of full awareness of his mother's great efforts exerted on his behalf, until he or she has fully experienced the stage of parenthood himself.

Both Tabari and Qurtubi mention that verse 46:15 was revealed for Abu Bakr al-Siddiq (d. 634 CE, the first successor to the Prophet Muhammad as leader of the Muslim community). According to (the Prophet's cousin and son-in-law) 'Ali (d. 661 CE), both of Abu Bakr's parents became Muslims. This did not happen in any of the families of the *Muhajirin,* except that of Abu Bakr; thus, Allah advised him about his parents, and this became obligatory on all Muslims afterward.[10]

The last part of Qur'anic verse 46:15 means, "Make my descendents pious; make them successful in doing good works so that You may be satisfied with them."[11] This provides a guideline for the mother in her responsibility of rearing her children. The Hadith clarifies her role of providing her children with religious knowledge, piety, good conduct, and morals. In addition, a mother must discipline her children and teach them obedience. At the same time, she should be a good companion to them—sharing, understanding, and generous. One very important factor in child rearing is the equal treatment of children.

Ibn 'Abbas narrated that the Prophet said: "Pronounce as the first words to your children, 'There is no God but Allah,' and recite to them at death, 'There is no God but Allah.'"[12] The Prophet's wife 'A'isha narrated that the Prophet said: "Allah will not call to account the person who brings up a small child such that he says, 'There is no God but Allah.'"[13]

Ibn 'Umar narrated that the Prophet said: "What does a parent leave as an inheritance for his child that is better than good morals?"[14] Anas ibn Malik narrated that the Prophet said: "Be generous to your children, and excel in teaching them the best of conduct."[15] Ibn 'Abbas narrated that the Prophet said: "There is no Muslim, whose two daughters reach the age (of maturity), and he is good to them as a companion, that do not cause him to enter Paradise."[16] Abu Hurayra narrated that the Prophet said: "Set your children's eyes on piety; whoever wants to can purge disobedience from his child."[17] Jabir ibn Samra narrated that the Prophet said: "If one of you disciplines his child it is better for you than if you give half a *sa'* (a measure of grain equivalent to a large basket) in charity to a poor person."[18]

Ibn Qayyim discusses the matter of children's obedience in the context of explaining the Qur'anic verse: "Oh you who believe! Save yourselves and your families from a fire" (Qur'an 66:6). He includes a statement of 'Ali: "Teach them and train them in good conduct." He also mentions a statement by al-Hasan al-Basri (d. 728 CE): "Command them with obedience to Allah and teach them what is good." Then, he mentions the following hadith, which he says describes three kinds of moral conduct. 'Amr ibn Shu'ayb narrated on the authority of his father, on the authority of his grandfather, who said: The Messenger of Allah said: "Order your children to pray at seven, beat them about it at ten, and in sleeping separate them."[19]

The final counsel is that of equal treatment of children: al-Nu'man ibn Bashir narrated that the Prophet said, "Fear Allah and treat your children equally."[20] In another narration the wife of Bashir said: "Make a gift of your slave to my son and have the Messenger of Allah bear witness for me." Bashir went to the Messenger of Allah and said, "The Daughter of So-and-So (that is, my wife) asked that I make a gift of my slave to her son and said, 'Have the Messenger of Allah bear witness for me.'" Then [the Prophet] said, "Does your wife's son have any brothers?" "Yes," Bashir said. "Have you given to each of them the like of that which you gave to him?" asked the Prophet. "No," he said. Then the Prophet said: "This is not fair. I do not bear witness except to what is just."[21]

Ibn Qayyim argues that unequal treatment of children is morally forbidden (*haram*), based on the Prophet's refusal to bear witness in the above hadith, and on the fact that he said three times, "Treat your children equally," thus making equal treatment a required duty (*wajib*).[22]

In summary, although in Islam there are many ways to open the doors of Paradise, the vehicles especially chosen for the woman are those of pregnancy, childbirth, nursing, and the conscientious rearing of her children. The commentaries clearly point out the great effort and struggle these involve. However, for every ounce of effort exerted in this direction—be it physical, emotional, or mental—the mother is elevated to a higher position of esteem in the eyes of her family and society and has thereby gained a place for herself amongst the successful in the Hereafter.

NOTES

This chapter first appeared as a chapter in Aliah Schleifer, *Motherhood in Islam* (Louisville, Kentucky: Islamic Texts Society and Fons Vitae, 1996). It is reproduced here with minor modifications by permission of the publisher. The editor thanks Yulia Uryadova Salamo of the University of Arkansas for transcribing this chapter from the original.

1. 'Ala' al-Din ibn Husam al-Din al-Hindi, *Kanz al-'umal fi sunan al-aqwal* (Hyderabad, India: Da'irat al-Ma'arif al-'Uthmaniyya, 1364/1945), vol. 16, 271 (hadith no. 44,403).

2. Muhammad ibn Jarir al-Tabari, *Jami' al-Bayan 'an ta'wil ay al-Qur'an* (Cairo: Mustafa al-Babi al-Halabi, 3rd printing, 1388/1968), vol. 21, 69; 'Imad al-Din Abi'l-Fida' Isma'il Ibn Kathir, *Tafsir al-Qur'an al-'azim* (Cairo: Dar al-Qutub al-'Arabiyya, n.d.), v. 3, 445; Abu 'Abdullah Muhammad ibn Ahmad al-Qurtubi, *al-Jami' li-ahkam al-Qur'an* (Cairo: Dar al-Kitab al-'Arabi li-al-Taba' wa al-Nashr, 1387/1967), vol. 14, 64; Muhammad Siddiq Khan, *Husn al-Uswa bi-ma thabita min Allah wa Rasulihi fi al-niswa* (Beirut: Mu'assasa al-Risala, 1976), 159.

3. Ibn Kathir, *Tafsir al-Qur'an al-'azim,* vol. 3, 445.

4. Qurtubi, *al-Jami',* vol. 14, 65.

5. Ismail Abdul Razack and Abdul Jawad al-Banna, *Women and Family in the Sunnah of the Prophet* (Arabic text included), International Centre for Population Studies and Research, Al-Azhar University (Cairo: Dar al-Kutub, n.d.), 15.

6. *Sahih Muslim* (Cairo: 1924) vol. 16, 181; see also, Khan, *Husn al-uswa,* 471 and 392.

7. *Sahih Muslim,* 1924, 181.

8. Khan, *Husn al-uswa,* 493; according to Nawawi, Malik ibn Anas in the *Muwatta* includes a hadith that the martyrs are seven, one of which is the mother who dies in childbirth, i.e., together with her child. See *Sahih Muslim bi-sharh al-Nawawi* (Cairo: 1924), vol. 13, 62–63.

9. Tabari, *Jami' al-Bayan,* vol. 16, 15–17.

10. The *Muhajirin* were the emigrants from Mecca who came with the Prophet Muhammad to Medina in 622 CE. (Ed.)

11. Qurtubi, *al-Jami',* vol. 16, 194; see also, Tabari, *Jami' al-Bayan,* vol. 16, 17.

12. Shams al-Din Muhammad ibn Qayyim al-Jawziyya, *Tuhfat al-mawdud bi-ahkam al-mawlud* (Cairo: Maktabat al-Qima, 1977), 176.

13. Hindi, *Kanz al-'umal,* vol. 16, 456 (hadith no. 45,408).

14. Ibid., 460 (hadith no. 45,435).

15. Ibid., 456 (hadith no. 45,410).

16. Ibid., 448 (hadith no. 45,370).

17. Ibid., 457 (hadith no. 45,419).

18. Ibid., 461 (hadith no. 45,438); see also, Ibn Qayyim, *Tuhfat al-mawdud,* 176.

19. Ibn Qayyim, *Tuhfat al-mawdud,* 176; see also, *Sunan Abi Dawud,* vol. 1, 51.

20. Hindi, *Kanz al-'umal,* vol. 16, 445 (hadith no. 45,353); *Sahih Muslim,* vol. 11, 67; see also, Ibn Qayyim, *Tuhfat al-mawdud,* 178. In the version given by Ibn Al-Qayyim, the command "Treat your children equally" is repeated three times.

21. *Sahih Muslim,* 69. In another narration, the Messenger of Allah said: "Then get someone else to bear witness for this." See also, Abu Zakariyya Yahya al-Nawawi, *Riyad al-Salihin* (Beirut: Dar al-Fikr, n.d.), 433.

22. See Ibn Qayyim, *Tuhfat al-mawdud,* 178–179. Nawawi adds that equal treatment includes equal treatment of both girls and boys. However, he considers a breach of equal treatment as *makruh* (disapproved but not forbidden). Concurring with Nawawi's opinion are the jurists Shafi'i, Malik, and Abu Hanifa. See Nawawi, *Sahih Muslim bi-sharh al-Nawawi,* vol. 11, 66–67.

7

THE BIRTH OF ALIYA MARYAM

Seemi Bushra Ghazi

Gracious are the gardens in which in winter
New fruits ripen for every Mary

—Mawlana Jalaluddin Rumi

My lineage goes back to Adam (upon him be peace). In this respect, I am no different from anyone. I read once in a family manuscript, flowing in rivulets of elegant *nastaliq* script, about the threads of reputed origin, Prophets, scholars, pilgrims, and holy men, who moved from Yemen to Yathrib (present-day Medina) before the coming of Islam, who hosted the Prophet at their table in Medina, and arrived in India soon after the first Arab merchants. There they dispersed, taught, and preached, and established religious schools or *madrasas*. When I think of these men in my father's family as I encountered them in visits to India, Pakistan, and Afghanistan, they bore no resemblance to the wild-eyed mullahs of CNN with their hateful small-time religion. My "uncles" seemed powerful and delicate, majestic and fluid, with features of perfect Chinese brushwork and the poise of the blue heron on our shoreline at low tide.

The shoreline where my family and I live is the coast of British Columbia, where a renegade tropical current moderates the frigid Pacific as it narrows into the Burrard Inlet entering the city of Vancouver. It is a long way from the steppes of my Central Asian forebears, the dry riverbeds of Yemen, the mustard fields of Haryana. It is far even from the London of my birth, and the Boston and Chicago of my childhood. Mostly it is far from the cities that had always seized my imagination—Damascus, Cairo, Istanbul. I arrived here nine years ago wondering how it came to be that this ancient soul had been flung out onto the furthest rim of the newest world.

It was a question but not a complaint. I'd been forbidden complaint by my Turkish spiritual master, Sherif Baba, who, at the least sign of lament in any of his dervish students, would kiss whatever garment he happened to be wearing and sing, " I like my shirt," a reminder of the Prophet Muhammad's teaching, *Alhamdulillah 'ala kulli hal,* "Praise belongs to Allah in every sit-uation and spiritual state." Far then from Mecca and the shrines of our holy ones, I resolved to sanctify the life in which I found myself, making pilgrimage through urban blackberry thickets to the wild beach at Kitsilano and probing the shifting mandala of the Mary blue Pacific. Black and azure, grey and gold—the North Shore Mountains became my Layla, both veiled and revealed by the courtship of sunlight and cloud. With many pasts surging together, I sought presence here in nature and tried to imagine a future worthy of our ancient aspirations.

Here I will recite the Sura of Maryam (Qur'an 19), the Qur'anic chapter devoted to Mary the Blessed Virgin. Somewhere in Cairo, a friend is in labor. Her mother e-mailed me last night, "Pray for a safe delivery." Earlier in her pregnancy, in the months of gestation, I had recited the Sura of Yusuf (Qur'an 12), praying that her daughter might grow beautifully in the womb, as the young Prophet Joseph grew in the well and in the crucible of his prison cell, refined in inner and outer qualities—exquisite and visionary, a king. But by now, my friend's baby has known both union and separation, the coming together of her parents' seed and the myriad delicate divisions that gave rise to her form. We prayed for her formation for four months, but now her gestation is complete. As her journey to this world begins, we read especially of Maryam, her noble birth to a priestly lineage, her long devotions in the sanctuary, and the strange and poignant Qur'anic tale of her labor and birth.

I have read this Sura countless times for aunts, cousins, sisters, and friends. Though we live continents apart, a woman feels the pangs of labor, neighbors knock, the phone rings, and e-mails appear out of ether. In Karachi, London, Chicago, and here too in Vancouver, women leave their occupations, draw about themselves the tabernacle of silken shawls, and sing the same sacred song, praying that divine compassion might envelope their sister as the date palm bowed over our Maryam, nourishing her endurance.

I have read the Sura of Maryam for my nieces and nephews with all their beautiful names. I have read it on a Pacific outcropping where eagles circled as Haniya (Joy) was born; I have read it flying across the continent toward little Isra (Night Journey) emerging one month too early. I have read it on a bunk bed flanked by my nephews, Idris and Ilyas, as we awaited the birth of their brother, Isa, the last of a trio of Japanese-Pakistani-Canadian lads named for the venerable apostles, Enoch, Elias, and Jesus. And just once, six years ago, I read it for myself.

I say "once," because I have recited the Sura of Yusuf for myself many, many times. Two years before my daughter's birth and three years afterward, I read it for a full trimester. Though the two sons I bore too early and then buried—one a finger's length of a boy, the other a delicate seahorse—did not linger long, in their brief sojourn they revealed to me Yusuf's perfect beauty. They chose themselves names in jest and then in earnest, Pir Ali and Ibrahim; scattered small miracles for their expectant mother like so many red money packets at the Chinese New Year Parade; and cared for me even as they slipped away, announcing their departure and promising me protection. I folded them in white cotton, recited the Sura of Ya Sin for their passage, and buried them beneath daisies near the Coast Salish site at Jericho Beach. They appeared to me as six-year-olds, as teenagers, as young men. Once in a dream they stole upon me out at Spanish Banks, two strong sons who lifted me up, up by the arms like a girl, and ran laughing the length of the surf, Pir Ali with shining curls, gravity in mirth, and Ibrahim's dark eyes, mirth in gravity. Though briefly embodied, they made themselves known, rending the veil between the seen and the unseen and offering me so much of themselves and the world to which they were turning that I now fall silent, lest I transgress the boundaries of spiritual courtesy.

My daughter Aliya was another matter. She grew within me a full nine months but would not reveal herself. Sherif Baba cautioned us against speaking of her unnecessarily, and she assured our adherence to his guidance by eluding us entirely. In ultrasounds she turned away from the camera, briefly presenting one almond eye and then a pearl-strung languor of spine. The technicians, who had been charged with photographing the four chambers of her heart, suggested us to roll down the hospital greens to elicit her compliance. After 10 minutes of entertaining interns assembled under an arbor for a smoking break, I sat by a late blooming magnolia in conversation with my unborn daughter. "It is true that the chambers of your heart are no place for strangers to be probing, and I admire your discretion and clarity of will, both of which, God knows, I am lacking. Still, if you would indulge these people, it would save us both returning next week, by which time I intend to be well past somersaulting on public lawns." Minutes later, she turned just long enough to assure us of her heart's bivalve perfection. By the time I asked to see her face, she had sequestered herself again.

The first four months of my pregnancy with Aliya were not marked by wonder. I was nauseous, exhausted, and hypersensitive, with an animal sense of smell. I could not be in the remote vicinity of chicken or cologne. Though others assured me nothing had changed, the odors of municipal sewage seemed to permeate my home by way of the kitchen drain. At one point, I could not tolerate even the fragrance of my own clean skin. Then one morning I awoke and the sickness was over. Not having walked more than three blocks in that time, I announced to my bemused husband Osman that his child wished to go to the mountains. At Cathedral Lakes Provincial Park, which seemed to be 10,000 miles above Earth's northernmost desert, Osman and his friends hiked the advanced trails. My baby and I set out at our own pace, aided by a reliable walking stick. Together we traversed an improbable vista of rock scape, glacier, and alpine meadow. We stood, one foot on ancient ice and the other in a field of ephemeral bloom. I thought of Moses climbing Mt. Sinai, and of all who ascend. The scent of anguish fell away.

Perhaps here arose the seed of intention that brought us the name Aliya, "Raised High," or "Exalted."

Returning home, I was again afflicted, this time by insomnia. My mother, *Ammi,* had always retired early and arisen before dawn. As a girl, I awoke to the sonority of her morning devotions. God's breath in *Ammi's* breath called me before the first light. While my younger siblings slept, we shared the communion of dawn prayer, tea and toast with guava jelly, conversation, reading, and reflection. Even today, I relish the hours between 5:00 and 8:00 AM. But something was not letting me sleep until the hour when I usually arose. Though preferable to my previous nausea, sleep deprivation soon began to trouble my equanimity.

In the midst of this condition, I attended a celebration of the birth of the thirteenth-century poet and mystic Mawlana Jalaluddin Rumi. There I asked Sherif Baba whether he could suggest a prayer or divine name to alleviate my condition. He laughed, "Don't ask for sleep! The holy ones love the night. Perhaps the one within you is awakened. Bear with her. No frustration. Lie in bed peacefully and reflect upon whichever divine names and verses come into your heart." Late that night I left Osman sleeping and wandered out to a towering bonfire around which young dervishes were immersed in *dhikr,* the ceremony of divine remembrance. A woman beat a frame drum laced with iron rings. Their two faces flickered, woman and drum, golden moon skins shimmering with song. I sat on a bench with the *dhikr* around me, *Ya Jamal, ya Jalal,* Oh Beauty, Oh Majesty. *Ya Qabid, ya Basit, ya Hayy, ya Haqq.* Oh, Contractor of Hearts, oh Expander of Souls, oh Life and Vitality, oh You who are Real. *La ilaha illallahu. La ilaha illallahu.* There is no God but the one God (He). There is nothing but the One. *Hu, Hu,Hu, Hu.* I joined them on *Hu,* the breath of creation, remembering Allah's divine name *al-Rahman,* the creative womblike Compassion that exhaled a primordial and eternal *Hu,* warming and animating the damp clay of the original human being. I took that *Hu* home to my cabin and fell into a deep and restful slumber. Insomnia returned the next night and did not leave until Aliya was born, but my feelings about it had been transformed. I surrendered to the night's serenity, to intimate discourse with my unborn darling, and to a subtle presence that I had not experienced before, the presence of Hazrat Maryam.

Hazrat Maryam, Islam's "Noble Mary," was born into a priestly clan in the lineage of Aaron, Moses' brother. Her mother Hannah had promised to dedicate the child in her womb to the service of the Temple. That the child was born a daughter did not deter her. Under the spiritual mentorship of her Uncle Zakariyya, the young Maryam flourished.

Her Lord accepted her in beauty
And cultivated her in beauty,
Entrusting her to Zakariyya.
Whenever Zakariyya came upon her
In the *mihrab* (sanctuary),

He found her blessed with sustenance.
He said, "Maryam, whence comes this to you?"
She said, "It is from Allah.
Surely, Allah grants sustenance without measure to whomever He wills."

(Qur'an 3:37)

I first noticed this verse 12 years ago. It was inscribed in Sherif Baba's fanciful hand on the door of his library. He nodded toward it and then toward me with a glance that said, "Pay attention." Over the years, it has shown me much about transmission between generations, between genders, between teachers and students, within families, and especially between God and human beings. Zakariyya offered Maryam a sanctuary and trusted her cultivation of her inner world. The physical sanctuary in this passage was Maryam's prayer niche located within the Jerusalem Temple, but the literal signification of the Arabic term *mihrab* is "a place of struggle or battle." Though we revere Maryam for her serenity, she engaged in a profound inward struggle without which her *mihrab,* as a site of inward battle, could not have become her *mihrab* as a site of sanctity and retreat. Through struggle Maryam became her own *mihrab*, "Maryam Full of Grace." One manifestation of this grace was the sustenance she received from Allah "without measure," a miraculous sustenance that Islamic traditions describe as the fruit of winter in summer and the fruit of summer in winter.

Zakariyya asks Maryam a question, "Whence comes this to you?" although as her elder and spiritual mentor he must have discerned the answer. He attended to her story and honored the fruit of her communion with the unseen, allowing it even to nourish his own spiritual trust. Despite Zakariyya's advancing years, he had been granted no son. Maryam's experiences moved him to return to the sanctuary and to pray to Allah for a child. There in the winter of old age, he received the promise of summer's fruit: he would be blessed with a holy son named Yahya (John). This son, John the Baptist, would later foretell the birth of Maryam's own son Isa (Jesus), a fruit of summer conceived and borne in the winter of Maryam's maidenhood. Once, I asked a group of women, "What if we were to regard these verses as a promise?" What if Mary's daughters and sons were promised that whenever we turned to the sanctuary, we would be blessed beyond season? Does it ever happen that we turn from the merely incidental to the most sacrosanct place within, without receiving some immeasurable gift?

Lying awake in my bedroom sanctuary, I began to meditate on silence and night. I knew that when Zakariyya had received word of the birth of Yahya, the Angel Gabriel granted him a sign: that he should not speak to any human being for three *layali*, three nights, except in signs (Qur'an 19:10). I also recalled hearing in childhood of young Maryam's nocturnal devotions, and how she too had received angelic guidance and "fasted" a time from speaking

(Qur'an 19:26). In quiet solitude, I began to imagine nights that I called *Layali Maryam,* nights that Maryam had devoted to prayer, meditation, and fasting. I entered each *Layla,* each single Night: *Layla* of Mystery, *Layla* of Union, Moon *Layla, Layla* of Seventy Unveilings, *Layla* of Shining Constellations, and strangest of all, the *Layla*/Night when the *Ruh,* the Divine spirit, breathed into Maryam the baby Isa (Jesus), a child conceived like the first human being, Adam, of sheer Divine desire. (As the Qur'an tells it, Allah commanded, *Kun fa yakun,*"Be! And it was.")

With my daughter now dancing within her own sanctuary, brushing her wings against my womb and sending me delicate butterfly epigrams, I touched the improbability of human development. That any child should be conceived and thrive, and then emerge living for even one breath, became no less remarkable to me than the virgin conception of Isa.

> She conceived him and withdrew to a distant place.
> The birth pangs drove her to the trunk of a date palm. She said,
> "I wish I had died and were forgotten!"
> A voice called to her from below, "Grieve not. Your lord has placed a stream below you.
> Sway the trunk of the tree toward you. Ripe dates will shower down.
> Eat and drink, and be comforted. If you meet anyone, say, I have consecrated a fast to the Compassionate and cannot speak today to any human being."
>
> (Qur'an, *Maryam* 19:22–26)

Aliya began to enter this world on December 17, 1999. That evening we had gathered in the Quaker Friends Meeting Hall to celebrate the *Urs,* "Wedding," or death anniversary of Mawlana Jalaluddin Rumi. I lay on a narrow wooden pew, as around us dervishes in ethereal white whirled the dance of the cosmos and the soul's rebirth. Right hand raised, they sought grace, with left hand lowered in offering. They spun on the axis of the left foot, centered in the heart and in divine unity, but with the right foot turned to embrace all directions, all creation. I had been asked to recite Qur'an and perhaps lead the chanting at the conclusion of the ceremony but doubted my ability to do anything at all. And yet when the music suddenly stopped, as the dervishes folded up their flowering forms, I sat up and recited the Sura of *Qadr* (Qur'an 97), the Chapter of Divine Power. This Sura invokes *Laylat al-Qadr,* the Night of Power, destiny, and value, on which the Qur'an was first revealed. It is a night "better than a thousand months," an angelic night pregnant with spirit, a night of "peace until the rising of dawn" (Qur'an 97:3–5). Afterward, we invoked God's 99 names and I sang Rumi's Persian poem, "Come, come my sweet heart, come into all that I do. You, you are my garden. Whisper my innermost secret. Come, come my dervish. Do not leave my side. You, you are my own tress, you are my very self." I arrived home near midnight and began to feel my daughter's descent.

When Hazrat Maryam came to this moment, the Temple could no longer shelter her. She had conceived a child with no father and risked the opprobrium of her people. Young, unprepared, and utterly alone, "she conceived him and withdrew to a distant place" (Qur'an 19:22). I thought of her solitude as my pains increased and beautiful companions joined me. I had let Osman sleep to gain strength for the next day, but he awoke early, sparkling with vitality and goodwill. *Ammi* arrived in the afternoon on the first flight from Chicago. She had been reading the Sura of Maryam on the plane and disembarked to blow its blessings thrice over my body as we lingered near the baggage claim in International Arrivals. Her eyes told me that she would not cease until I had safely delivered her grandchild. Later I was joined by three women whom I had thought of as wise Sherpa guides. They would lead me, share my burdens, and teach me how to breathe in the thin, high altitudes of labor.

The first was Jackie, our *doula* or birthing companion. She had met Osman and me twice during the pregnancy and had helped us reflect on how we should experience this event. Mostly, I knew that I wished to be present and conscious to experience each moment of the journey and greet our child, clear-eyed and fully aware. Who would she be at the moment when she arrived? What would I become? I wanted to share a first glance unmediated by any sedative. I called Jackie on the afternoon of December 18th to say that I was still at ease, despite riding the waves of suffering and relief. An hour later, Osman phoned again, urging Jackie to come quickly. As soon as she arrived, Jackie filled the bathtub and crouched beside me all night. When the hot water ran out, Osman boiled some more, running back and forth like a midwife's apprentice in some earlier century. I must have fallen asleep before sunrise, for when I awoke I found that someone had carried me from the bathtub to the bed. How long had I been unconscious? Five minutes? Five hours? Jackie lay sleeping on the floor.

My friend Lou arrived later that morning in a penumbra of red-gold curls. Once a nurse in rural Newfoundland, skilled in low-tech labor support, she was now an anthropologist, psychologist, and harpist. One day I said to her, " Lou if I get to that point in labor where I can't continue, I think I will be alright if I can just look into your eyes." Now her eyes held my gaze and her body held my form, moving together in the Tai Chi of "Love your baby down." I shuddered through each season of pain, too much now and too long, and Lou absorbed it, sloughed it off, and filled me with her melodic light. My child would not descend. Why? Was an elbow askew? Was her chin in her palm? We wound up the Hawaiian music box my brother had brought back from his honeymoon and swayed with the mechanical hula girl as I wept, "Come down, baby, please come down." In Jackie's notes she says that *Ammi* approached me around this time saying, *Beti, Allah se bhi maango*, "Darling, also ask Allah." "You ask Allah, Mum, please. Talk to Allah. Right now I need to talk to my baby."

By the time Dr. Rachael arrived, the labor had been going on for 36 hours. She knelt beside me, "How are we?" I remember saying, "This is hard now, Rachael, really very hard." Rachael was an advocate for midwives and home birth. She could not recall the last time she had needed a knife and a needle. Rather than telling women to push, she urged, "Love your baby down," and called her work "catching," not "delivering" babies. I knew the first moment I had met her that I wanted her to "catch" mine. Though Rachael was herself five months pregnant, she had dropped in on her Sunday off just to see how I was doing.

A woman must open for a child to be born, open in every possible way. Medically, it is said, she must open 10 centimeters. After 36 hours of labor, I anticipated success, but somehow the examination revealed otherwise. "You have not yet begun to dilate," said Rachael, "there are 10 centimeters to go." My heart fell—after all that time! (Women are expected to dilate one centimeter per hour.) "But you are fully effaced," Rachael added, "That's the hardest part. You've done remarkably well." Rather than noting my failure to progress, Rachael offered her dazzling approval and made me feel like a hero.

Rachael felt confident that in Jackie's care we could continue to labor at home, but upon phoning the hospital we learned that a room had just opened in a new ward called Cedar where mothers could labor, deliver, and recover all in one suite. I had seen the windowless delivery rooms in the old basement wards and felt certain that I would feel caged and claustrophobic there. Cedar had spacious windows, pullout beds, endless hot water, and room for all of my companions. Room 7 was available and I did not want to lose it. How long would it take to get there? With green lights all the way and one red light on Broadway—two and a half contractions.

At one point, while preparing our birth plan I had become self-conscious. Women give birth every day in challenging circumstances. Why was I walking, swimming, and meditating? Why did I need five companions? Was this not self-absorption? Then one morning before dawn prayer, I dreamt of myself within a vast tent, a circular tent of white skins. The skins were supported by four peripheral poles and one great central pole. Smoke ascended skyward through an opening in the roof. Waking, I knew with certainty: the four "poles" were Osman, Jackie, Rachael, and Lou. Without each one of them, the tent would collapse. The central pole was *Ammi*, her unceasing recitations opening up to Hazrat Maryam. At first, labor would be like ascending a mountain, later like plunging into a burning sea, but *Ammi* would blow into me the presence of Maryam. Without each one of them, my will would fall into absence. Without each one of them, my baby would not be released.

At first, I bore the surge and the retreat. I called upon the divine names *Al Qabid, Al Basit,* "Contractor, Expander, grip and release me, draw this being from my being, let this child be born!" As the storm rose, so too did my endurance. The women told me, "Other pain is a signal of warning and danger, but not this pain. This pain is safe; it is the pain of creation, and you are safe with us." Somehow, this made a crucial difference. I feared the sensation of pain, but I never feared that it would harm me. I loved its work and its effect. The women knew these contours of the ocean, islands of respite, and depths of the sky. I shivered, trembled, and cried out. They embraced me in the ceramic hospital tub, pouring warm water down my spine. They would not let the ark of my body shatter on any reef.

I have read that even elephants give birth like this—elephant *doulas* and midwives stroking their elephant sisters, murmuring secrets remembered from ancient elephant times. Here is an elephant secret: at the height of labor, in a time called "transition," a time of vomiting, terror, and delirium, if a woman is held and comforted she can fall into a restorative sleep in the single minute between contractions. I had been awake more than 40 hours. Now, I slid to the bottom of an ocean, slept with strange aquatic angels, waking and slumbering, conscious and gone. Lou and Jackie sailed my body back and forth in their arms. My baby swam down, down, finally engaged.

Aliya did not want to be born in water, and I wanted strength beneath my feet. I crouched on the linoleum floor. Glancing up, the hospital bed seemed as remote and unstable as scaffolding or aerial wire. The urge to bear down became the most powerful instinct I had ever known, seven worlds thundering down into the depths of my abdomen. Though my friends surrounded me, I arrived at the place where Hazrat Maryam had begun and retreated into a wilderness where no one could find me. The Maryam who had arrived at this place was not the Queen of Heaven. She was a woman like every other woman—spirit, yes, but also flesh and blood, milk and bone. "The birth pangs drove her to the trunk of the palm tree" (Qur'an 19:23). She cried out in a voice so intimate, so colloquial, "I wish I had died and been forgotten!" It was the desire to become oblivion itself, to fall away traceless and unremembered. I could neither proceed nor retreat. *Ammi* had read the Sura of Maryam and blown its blessings over us unceasingly for one night and two days. In her murmuring, I heard the fugue of all my scattered kin. Sherif Baba would be reading from the Sura of "He Frowned" (Qur'an 80), "And then [God] eased the path" (Qur'an 80:20), but I knew now that nothing could ease this path. My child would never be born, nor would I survive. "I am dying now," I said, "I am going to die." I began to disappear but was drawn back by someone whispering, "If you have seen the door of death, then you are ready to have this baby. No woman can give birth, Seemi, without witnessing that door." Then there was screaming, a body rent, and Rachael exclaiming, "What a sweet face!" and our small slippery daughter crying out in my arms.

A root grows in the hills outside of Medina. The Bedouin women harvest small bunches of it and bring it to the graveyards of the Muslim martyrs. *Ammi* remembers it from her Indian childhood. The Hajj pilgrims would return from Mecca on great wooden ships, disembarking to garlands of marigold, jasmine, and rose. In return, they offered their loved ones vials of healing *Zam Zam* water and bunches of the root known as *Panja-e Maryam*, "Mary's Fist." They said that this same root grew in the hills near Bethlehem and that Maryam grasped it when she was overcome by birth pangs. *Ammi's* aunts used to soak it in a bowl of water until it was soft and grasped it in their own labors, calling upon Hazrat Maryam to stand by them in their pain.

My sister Saba had bought two Fists of Mary at the graveyard of Badr near Medina when she was but 12 and I was 17. Since then, they had accompanied her to Chicago, New York, and North Carolina. She used one root for the birth of her children and the other she saved for me. She told me how she had watched the "fist" unfold in her first labor, gradually tinting the water a delicate amber color. I too witnessed those deepening hues, and held the root in my hand, folding Maryam's strength within mine, sending *salaams* to her spirit.

Two nights and days had passed striving to give birth to Aliya. Night had come once again before she was finally born. It was December 19, 1999, the eleventh night of Ramadan, two hours before yet another midnight. As the postpartum nurses settled our daughter to rest, I turned to the glass bowl at my bedside and glanced at the Fist of Maryam, still floating carnelian and serene. Once gnarled, desiccated, and closed, it had slowly unfolded and softened in the animating medium of water. The fist had become a pliant hand, and now after 48 hours, it revealed something that no one had intimated. The root of Maryam had traveled from its ancient home to my daughter's land and become a tentative garden. On this, our last *Layla* together, Maryam's palm opened, offering green leaf and blossom.

8

EVEN AT NIGHT THE SUN IS THERE: ILLNESS AS A BLESSING FROM GOD

•

Virginia Gray Henry-Blakemore

A few years ago I was living in an English village outside Cambridge while researching my doctorate and working with the Islamic Texts Society, an academic organization that publishes important works from the Islamic heritage after having them translated into English.

One evening, as I reached to switch off the bedside lamp, I noticed that my arm would not stretch out to do so. In fact, I found I was not able to pull the blankets up about me except by using my teeth; neither arm seemed to function. When I tried to take a deep breath, it seemed as though my lungs were incapable of expansion. At the approach of a cough or a sneeze, I held my arms closely around my chest for fear the sudden and painful expansion of my breast would rip me apart. When I arose the next morning, the only way to get out of bed was to hang my knees over the edge and slide off since my upper torso had become powerless. I could not even raise my arms to brush my hair. Turning on the bathroom faucet was an excruciating affair. By holding the bottom of the steering wheel in my fingertips, I was able to drive to the village clinic. The doctor concluded I had some type of virus for which there was no treatment other than time.

A day or so later, my husband and I were to fly to Boston for the annual congress of the Middle East Studies Association. I viewed my affliction as an inconvenience that would ultimately pass and decided to ignore my condition. I noticed, however, that on the day we were to leave England, I began to have trouble walking, and getting upstairs was extremely difficult. By the time we reached the hotel room in Boston, more and more of my system seemed to be shutting down. I could no longer write or hold a teacup, bite anything as formidable as an apple, dress myself, or even get out of a chair unless assisted. Everything ached. I could not move my head in the direction of the person I was speaking to; I looked straight ahead, perhaps seeing them from the corner of my eyes.

Friends gave all kinds of advice that I simply shrugged off. The worst part was lying in bed at night. It was impossible to roll onto either side, and my whole body felt on fire with pain. It was terrible to have to lie flat, unable to make any shift whatsoever all night long. I thought to myself, "If only I could scratch my cheek when it itched, if only my eyes were not dry but cool, if only I could swallow without it feeling like a ping-pong-sized ball of pain, if only I could reach for a glass of water when thirsty during the long night!"

As we traveled on for work in New York, I continued to make light of my infirmity and to ignore suggestions that I seek help. On the plane, however, when it was necessary to ask the flight attendant to tear open a paper sugar packet for my tea, I suddenly realized, "I can't even tear a piece of paper!" I requested that a wheelchair await me in New York and that I be transferred to a flight home to my parents in Louisville, Kentucky. Since my husband was obliged to stay in New York, a kind soldier returning to Fort Knox helped me during that leg of the trip. I felt like a wounded fox that wanted nothing more than to return to, and curl up alone in, the nest of its childhood. My father met me at the airport and the next day he took me for every test imaginable. Nothing was conclusively established—was this rheumatoid arthritis, or lupus? I was brought to my parents' house and at last put in my childhood bed with a supply of painkillers, which I was not inclined to take. Since I found I could tolerate great pain, I wanted to observe the situation and know where I stood. I started seeing my body as a separate object and my mind passively witnessed its ever-declining condition. When my legs finally "went," with my knees swollen like grapefruits and my feet incapable of bearing me up, I mused with detached interest, "Oh, there go the legs!" The body seemed to be mine, but it was not *me*.[1] Later that night *it* happened. As I lay gazing out of my bedroom door and noticed the carpet in the quiet hall, I thought, "Thank God I'm not in a hospital and the hall is not linoleum and that I am not subjected to the clatter of ice machines and the chatter of nurses. I know I'm in trouble and I do need help, but *that* would be too great a cost for my soul."

A few moments later, I became aware that I seemed to be solidifying, my body had stiffened and seemed to be very much like a log: I was totally paralyzed. Then, I seemed to separate from my body and lift a distance above it. I glanced back and saw my head on the pillow and thought, "This is remarkable. I've read about this kind of thing. *I* am thinking but my brain is down there in my head! I must be *dead*." I considered what to do. When death comes in Islam, the dying person repeats the *Shahada:* "There is no divinity except God and Muhammad is the Messenger of God."

As I thought of the phrase, *La ilaha illa Allah* (There is no divinity except God), I seemed to be pulled back toward my heart, as if by a thread of light. However, there I was—quite all right in many ways, but utterly rigid and still.

The light of the moon comforted me as it passed through the leafless November branches, making patterns on the blankets. I thought, "Even at night, the Sun is there. Even in darkness and death, light and life are present." The fall season seemed to parallel my state.

Then I began to think about my future. I have friends who are paralyzed and who have always been placed along the sidelines for various events. Had I now joined them? Was I now out of the normal life of others? I began to see myself like a hunchback or a dwarf. I had always been known for my inexhaustible energy and activities. I could always, somehow, get to my feet and do one more thing. This was now over. I would no longer be able to *do* anything. I thought of people in this world who have impressed me most —the Mother Theresas of our world. I realized that what was exemplary in these people was not what they *did*, but what they *were;* the state of *being* that determined their movement was what actually inspired others. So I set upon a plan of inward action: The best thing I could do for others would be to sanctify my soul, to let my state of being become radiant. Having concluded this, I felt things were in order.

In the morning I was found, fixed in place; I was given eggnog through a straw—chewing was over. My husband came from New York and I recall marveling when I observed him. He could, without considering the matter in depth, shift his position in a chair, scratch his forehead, or lean over to pick up a dropped pencil—all painlessly! Imagine—reflex action! Occasionally, if I really wanted to move my fingers, for example, I would think to myself, "All right, now, I-am-going-to-try-to-move-my-fingers," and I would concentrate my entire attention on the task. With incredible pain and focus, I could at most shift a few millimeters. It struck me profoundly that when someone is able to move in this world without pain—that is, in health—that person has a foretaste of Paradise on Earth without ever being aware of it. Everything after that is extra.

Ultimately, it was decided that I should be given a week's course of cortisone so I could return to my children and the English specialist who might be able to figure out what I had. The cortisone was miraculous and frightening. I could actually walk and pick up things, yet I knew that I could not do this under normal conditions.

On my return to Cambridge, in order to speed up the blood tests, the doctor asked that I be removed overnight from the cortisone. I then discovered what withdrawal symptoms are—a level of pain that seems to consume one alive with fire. But the pain was nothing compared to the frightening mental confusion I experienced: I could not grasp proper thinking, or even normal reality. What I needed was not only a doctor but also a kind of scholar/saint who could describe to me the hierarchy of meaning in everyday reality, so that I would not be so painfully lost. I suppose true doctors are a combination of all three. The Islamic physician/philosopher was called a *hakim* (a sage or possessor of wisdom, *hikma*). I grasped some rosaries and clung to them like lifelines thrown to a drowning man, and I made it to the light of dawn on the invocation of God's Name, my sanity intact.

The English specialist could not make a conclusive diagnosis. Our Vietnamese acupuncturist suggested that toxins had built up in my entire muscular and nervous system and prescribed massage during steam baths to release them. This sounded definitely worth doing. However, at the same time, I had come to that point that the very ill always come to, where, although they take advice with gratitude, inside of them something has dimmed and they no longer wish to make any effort. Pleasantly, I had reached a great calm within. Each day I was brought downstairs, where I directed the preparation of meals and worried the children, who saw I could no longer sew on a button or sign a check. I was resigned to never moving again. I had never experienced such peace. It was touching to see that people prayed for me and it was lovely that so many asked after my condition. I felt like an upright pole stuck in the middle of a moving stream.

In the spring, my husband had work to do in Arabia and suggested that as he would be traveling by private plane, I could just as easily sit in a dry climate as I could in cold, damp Cambridge. I agreed to go. On my arrival, a dear friend managed to get me to Mecca because she thought that prayers in the mosque there would help. But when I found myself before the Ka'ba, I felt it would be wrong to pray that my affliction would be lifted, as its good had come to outweigh its bad, in terms of my heart and soul.

A few days later, I was asked to give a talk in Jeddah, Saudi Arabia. I declined, explaining that I was unable to research and prepare a topic properly. Friends said they would be delighted to do this for me, if I could come up with a subject. I answered, "All right, why does this Job-like trial happen to a person, in the view of Islam?" The passages they wrote down and translated into English from both the Qur'an and the Hadith—the sayings and recorded deeds of the Prophet Muhammad—all seemed to say the same thing. In Islam, illness is understood to be a great blessing. This is because it is an opportunity, if borne with patience and freedom from complaint, to purity oneself of past sins and burn away wrong thoughts and deeds.

As I delivered my talk, it began to dawn upon me why Muslims always reply with *Al-Hamdulillah* ("All praise belongs to God," the same as *Alleluia*) whenever anyone inquires as to their health. I had always wondered why one could ask someone who suffered from an obviously terrible physical or emotional pain or loss, "How *are* you?" and all one could get out of such a person was, "All praise belongs to God." I wanted them to talk about their pain with me, to share their suffering, and wondered why they would not do so. Suddenly, I realized that they were praising God for their state of being!

The suffering they endured, no matter how great, was an opportunity to be purified, which is the very aim of human existence. In an instant, I saw my own illness in a new light. I no longer patiently tolerated it—I *loved* it, I *flowed with it*. I saw how blessed I was to have been given not something small, but something as total as paralysis.

As I began to love my illness, my fingers began to regain movement. Bit by bit the movement in my hands returned, until at last in late spring, I was restored. What had been the most painful and difficult time in my life turned out to be the best thing that had ever happened to me. I had gained a deepened perspective, a sense of proportion and freedom. God had blessed me with near total dependence on others, a symbol reminding me of my utter dependency on Him. Even when I had not been able to move one inch, I was able to be in touch with His Divine Presence. This generous lesson from Allah taught me to say "yes" and to love whatever He wills for me, now and always.

(The illness described above was later diagnosed as Guillaume-Barre Syndrome.)

O God, to Thee belongs praise for the
    Good health of my body, which lets
    Me move about, and to Thee belongs
    Praise for the ailments which Thou causes to arise in my flesh!
For I know not, my God, which of the
    Two states deserves more my thanking
    Thee and which of the two times is more worthy for my praise of Thee:
The time of health,
    Within which Thou makest me delight
    In the agreeable things of Thy
    Provision, through which Thou givest
    Me the joy to seek the means to Thy
    Good pleasure and bounty, and by
    Which Thou strengthenest me for the
    Acts of obedience which Thou hast given me to accomplish;
Or the time of illness,
    Through which Thou puttest me to
    The test and bestowest upon me favors:
    Lightening the offenses that weigh
    Down my back, purifying the
    Evil deeds into which I have plunged,
    Inciting me to reach for repentance,
    Reminding me of the erasure of misdeeds
    Through ancient favor; and, through
    All that the two writers write for me.[2]

From Imam Zayn al-'Abidin 'Ali ibn al-Husayn (d. 712 CE), Great-Grandson of the Prophet Muhammad, *al-Sahifa al-kamila al-sajjadiyya,* "The Perfect Page of the Prayer-Carpet" (Translated by William Chittick)

NOTES

This chapter first appeared in *Parabola*, Vol. 18:1, Spring 1993, 60–65. It is reproduced here with minor modifications by permission of the publisher. The editor thanks Yulia Uryadova Salamo of the University of Arkansas for transcribing this chapter from the original.

1. "Islamic physicians saw the body of man as but an extension of his soul and closely related to both the spirit and the soul.... They envisaged the subject of medicine, namely man, to be related both inwardly through the soul and the spirit, and 'outwardly' through the grades of the macrocosmic hierarchy to the principle of cosmic manifestation itself. Whatever may have been the historical origins of Islamic Medicine, its principles cannot be understood save in the light of Islamic metaphysical and cosmological sciences." Seyyid Hossein Nasr, *Islamic Science* (London, U.K.: World of Islam Festival Publishing Co. Ltd, 1976), 159.

2. According to Islamic belief, there is an angel on either shoulder who records one's good and bad deeds.

9

CARING FOR THE ILL IN ISLAM

•

Kristin Zahra Sands

God will say on the Day of Resurrection, "Oh child of Adam, I was sick but you did not visit me." [The child of Adam] says, "My Lord, how could I visit you when you are the Lord of all beings?" God says, "But didn't you know that my servant so-and-so was sick and yet you did not visit him? Did you not know that if you had visited him, you would have found me present with him? Oh son of Adam, I asked you for food but you did not feed me." [The child of Adam] says, "My Lord, how could I feed you when you are the Lord of all beings?" God says, "Didn't you know that my servant so-and-so asked you for food and you did not feed him? If you had given him food, you would have found that in my presence. Oh son of Adam, I was thirsty but you did not give me water." [The child of Adam] says, "My Lord, how could I give you water when you are the Lord of all beings?" He says, "My servant so-and-so asked you for water but you did not give it to him. If you had given him water, you would have found that in my presence."[1]

This dialogue between God and the human race, recorded in a divine saying or *hadith qudsi*,[2] can be read—and should be read—as an urgent reminder of our obligation to respond to the needs of others. However, the wording of the hadith hints at deeper issues and broader possibilities than conventional notions of duty. What happens at moments when we are called upon by others? Why do we often turn away from those in need of us? Sometimes, there is irritation at the interruption or fear of one's own dependencies. There is the fatigue that sets in when one is asked to give again and again. Alternatively, there is the self-satisfied pride that follows some small sacrifice, the patting of oneself on the back for what was not at all difficult to give. What does it mean to say that God is present with the ill, the hungry, and the thirsty, and that one could find that presence in responding to those in need?

My approach to this question draws upon two sources: the textual sources of Islam and personal experience. The primary textual sources I am relying on are the Qur'an and selections from the literature of Sufism, also referred to as mystical Islam.[3] The literature of classical Sufism is characterized not only by its references to contemporaneous exegetical, theological, and legal discussions but also by its use of anecdotes and poems that express an ethical and emotional sensibility that is particularly suited to the topic at hand. This is *not* a chapter surveying practices of caring for the ill in Muslim societies. Instead, it is very much situated in my particular experience within a privileged middle-class and secular environment in North America. I care, along with my husband, for a daughter with spina bifida, hydrocephalus, and epilepsy, conditions that have led to a broad range of chronic, pervasive, and difficult challenges as well as acute emergencies. Our experiences, although profoundly personal, have also necessarily involved repeated in-depth encounters with the services of outside professionals and private and public institutions. These encounters have led me to question the relationship between private beliefs and the organizational structures of a community, particularly the secular assumption that beliefs and institutions can be separated. The issues addressed here, then, are as much about private faith as they are about the relationship between that faith and action in the world.[4]

THE SHOCK

> We hurl truth against falsehood and it smashes out its brains; suddenly, falsehood is nothing.

> (Qur'an 21:18)[5]

The usual resting state of my consciousness consists of a carefully maintained bubble, within which a sense of entitlement to comfort and ease exists in tension with a gnawing fear of loss. One of these imagined "losses" materialized six months into my second pregnancy, when a sonogram uncovered the fact that the child I was carrying had a significant disability. The first idol to fall was the one that had assured me that I could predict and control events, if only I was willing to follow the rules—in this case, those of the healthy living required for a healthy pregnancy. Finding myself in the uncomfortable situation of needing help from strangers, I entered the foreign and complicated world of specialists in the medical profession, starting with a superior physician in a prestigious medical center. As I lay in his examining room experiencing my first internal sonogram, he stared at the image of my daughter's spine on the screen and exclaimed with excitement, "It's a very large defect!" Then he called in what seemed to be an entire class of medical students from the university to see it. No matter the indignities, I reassured myself—we were fortunate to be receiving the best medical care in the world. Sitting afterward in his office, the physician gave us a well-written, thorough report on his findings. Then he abruptly mentioned the stress that children with disabilities have on families and handed us a small piece of paper with the name of someone who would perform what would have been an illegal abortion at that late date in the pregnancy. This was the first lesson of many for me that the qualities that support the long and arduous development of excellent physicians are not necessarily the same those one longs for in a highly fragile state. This is not to say that there are no doctors who combine rigorously practiced medicine with sensitivity to their patients. However, many do not combine these qualities.

The second idol to fall was my sense of entitlement to be treated in a certain way. Whatever slights I had suffered up to this point paled in comparison to this new kind of vulnerability. Having been raised to be as independent as possible, I found the task of petitioning others acutely painful to me. I had very few tools at my disposal for coping with the indignities of asking others for help, a situation many face far more frequently than I do, with far fewer resources. Visible to me now in the waiting rooms of medical offices and in hospital wards, these are the (mostly) women who fight on a daily basis on behalf of their children and other family members, demonstrating extraordinary levels of courage, intelligence, patience, and persistence, all of which frequently goes unrecognized. However, from my position of privilege, the events of my daughter's birth were shattering.

> A madman in Baghdad throws a stone into a shop selling glasses and all the glasses shatter with a great crash. When people ask him why he caused such damage, he answers: "I so enjoyed the crash and the tinkling sound! Whether it causes damage or is of any use to others, that has nothing to do with me as a madman."

> (Farid al-Din 'Attar d. 1220 CE)[6]

CALLING FOR HELP

> Oh humanity! An example has been made, so listen to it carefully. Those whom you call upon beside God are not even able to create a single fly, even if they were to join together to do it. And if a fly steals something from them, they cannot get it back. How feeble are both the seeker and the sought!

> (Qur'an 22:73)

There are many false gods to call upon, some more obviously fake than others and more easily exposed. Belief in the omniscience and omnipotence of modern medicine is sustainable only by those who have had very limited interactions with the medical profession and its institutions. Many of the doctors I have worked with have expressed their awareness of the limits of their prescriptions, tests, and interventions, and my confidence in them is in direct proportion to their humility. However, what has been even harder to bear than the limits of knowledge in the medical profession and its institutions are the limits in its ability to provide comfort; one could say that I have searched for a personal and caring god here without success. One arrives in an emergency room with the expectation that all will be taken care of. Instead, obtaining necessary care in today's medical system is more often than not a sustained struggle that requires tactical skills. Although a bewildering array of people provide services in emergency rooms and hospitals, they are empowered to act only in carefully demarcated areas. In New York State, hospitals are required to post and give patients a copy of the "Patients' Bill of Rights." Among the rights given to patients is the right to "know the names, positions, and functions of any hospital staff involved in your care and refuse their treatment, examination or observation."[7] Everyone who cares for patients in hospitals must understand this right along with the other rights of patients. Once, I sat in an emergency room perched on the edge of a gurney for three hours before finally being told by a kind worker that there was no one available that evening who had the authority to examine a child beyond the initial triage.

To return to the "Patients' Bill of Rights," the language used here is significant: it is the language of legal ethics, not the ethics of medical care. What is odd about this is that one is certainly not looking to pick a fight in a hospital or an emergency room, yet a strategic, rational analysis of the system followed by assertive and sometimes aggressive action is frequently necessary to get needed care. It is extremely important for a patient to understand who has the power to do what in the hierarchical structure of hospitals. It is also important to understand that the primary task of the hospital is to care for the body, not the person or the soul that inhabits the person. The responsibility for attempting to relieve the fear, grief, boredom, and exhaustion that patients and caretakers experience comes under the rubric of auxiliary services: the social workers, chaplains, and recreational therapists who are entrusted with the power to soothe and help patients within limited parameters. So, although the hospital is invaluable in its rationing out of resources for keeping the body functioning as well as possible, it makes for a very poor god.

Second only to the fear for the well-being of one's child is the fear of how one will be able to pay for extraordinary medical costs. It has been suggested by some scholars that the concept of God's providence has been replaced in modern societies by a belief in the providence of the state and the economic structures that are tied to it.[8] The safety net for expensive medical costs in the United States is insurance, provided by and partially paid for by employers, privately purchased, or, as a last resort, provided by the state. Although the reimbursement guidelines for these organizations are relatively clear, anyone with extensive medical bills knows that getting all of the bills paid appropriately requires an endurance marathon of phone calls and e-mails if one does not want to end up with thousands or even tens of thousands of dollars in bills. If the primary organizing principle of hospitals is hierarchical, the organizing principle of health maintenance and other kinds of insurance organizations is bureaucratic, a structure that seems to lend itself to labyrinths of inflexible, complex, and sometimes absurd procedures for obtaining the resources that are the right of the members.

A key characteristic of these organizations is that there is no way to develop a personal relationship with any individual. In hierarchical organizations like hospitals, it is relatively easy, once one understands and respects what each person can and cannot do, to make personal connections. However, in most health maintenance organizations and insurance companies, a series of barriers separate the member and those who have the power to reimburse claims. Most use automatic phone systems that are presumably designed to increase efficiency but that unnecessarily delay members whose problems can only be addressed by speaking with a live customer service representative. When a live representative is finally reached, he or she is instructed to identify himself or herself by their first names only, and it is more than likely that one will never speak to the same representative twice. When an initial, single error compounds itself into a series of errors that require multiple phone calls, each phone call will be answered by a new representative who will piece together what happened by means of their computer records, feeling no personal responsibility for the preceding errors and therefore no corresponding sense of urgency concerning the problem. While this system perhaps succeeds in its function of equitably distributing limited resources to members with the requisite stamina, this success comes at the cost of an outrage. The more you and your dependents have suffered through medical procedures, hospital stays, and doctors' visits, and the more your time and resources have been stretched to the breaking point, the more you will be subjected to frustrating struggles with anonymous company representatives and systems. The point here is not to complain, as I am acutely aware of how fortunate I am to have good insurance and access to good medical care, but to point out the deficiencies of the providential god of the insurance society.

BARGAINING WITH GOD

Call upon [God] in fear and longing.

(Qur'an 7:56)

Of course, hospitals and insurance companies make for rather silly idols. Another trick of the religious imagination is more personal: the attempt to bargain with God. Uncharacteristically for me, I adopted this approach wholeheartedly in the period in which my daughter was having repeated *grand mal* seizures. No medicine seemed to work and the violent seizures increased, making it difficult to leave her alone for even a moment. It was difficult to do anything but sit and wait for the next seizure, whether that would be in a few minutes or a few weeks. Little by little, I found myself unraveling. God did not appear to help me like the Superman I watched on TV and in movies as a child or in the news coverage of real-life Superman stories. When a child who has fallen down a well is saved, I am the first to start weeping. However, I am also the first to raise the moral question of the other children who are not saved but die horribly instead. Are there not enough Supermen to go around? But, regardless of my misgivings as to the integrity of the process, I began, in my distress, to do what I had assiduously avoided up to this point in my life: I began to pray to God, the merchant. What would it take to buy the end of my daughter's seizures? I was willing to put everything I had on the table.

There is a degree of legitimacy to this approach; sometimes God sounds like a merchant in the Qur'an. The ultimate bargain, after all, is the afterlife. You work hard and try to behave yourself for a few decades and obtain happiness for eternity, which is a pretty good deal. But there is a problem. Justice of this sort, and the arguments of theodicy that assure you that everything will be fine in the end, work best when you are sitting on the fence at a distance, not sitting waiting for the next seizure.[9] The problem is in the moment, not later. Within the moment, there is no good reason for suffering, especially the suffering of those without blame. A passage from Fyodor Dostoevsky's novel *The Brothers Karamazov* is often quoted in discussions of theodicy.[10] This passage questions the notion that harmony in the afterlife can justify horrific suffering, especially the suffering inflicted on others by human beings. When the character Ivan Karamazov visits his brother Alyosha, who is training to be a priest in a monastery, Ivan uses a number of horrible examples of tortured children and animals to argue that innocent suffering could never be part of a larger scheme of justice, or at least not one that he would want to be a part of.

> I don't want harmony, for love of mankind I don't want it. I want to remain with unrequited suffering. I'd rather remain with my unrequited suffering and my unquenched indignation, *even if I am wrong*. Besides, they have put too high a price on harmony; we can't afford to pay so much for admission. And therefore, I hasten to return my ticket. And it is my duty, if only as an honest man, to return it as far ahead of time as possible. Which is what I'm doing. It's not that I don't accept God, Alyosha. I just most respectfully return him the ticket.[11]

I have always sided with Ivan. In the moment or string of moments of horror and terror, do we have to tolerate the intolerable? Is *this* what has to be put on the bargaining table? A point comes where the language of prayer moves from the mercantile to the *crie du coeur* (cry of the heart), from the rational bargaining of resources, goods, rights, and entitlements to cries into the unseen. What kind of prayer is appropriate when you are alone with your child in a hospital room in the middle of the night and an excruciatingly painful and invasive medical procedure must be done, especially when you are not totally convinced that it is necessary? I do not have an answer to this other than to relate something I heard from a 13-year-old girl. Some years ago, I was with a group of young Muslim girls who were talking about whether it is acceptable to pray to get good grades at school. Several of them were shocked at the very idea of asking God for something so petty, thinking prayer should be saved for more serious matters and for the benefit of others. This girl, however, vehemently denied this line of thinking; she kept repeating, "There are no boundaries! There are no boundaries!" The desire to obtain good grades or a soul mate, and the pleading to stop the suffering of oneself or another is, in the end, all the same. Prayer, at the point where the bargaining stops and honesty begins, is a dive off a cliff into the unknown.

> In the beginning, when I was a novice in love,
> My neighbor could not sleep at night from my whimpers.
>   But now, as my pain has increased, my whimpering has decreased.
> When fire takes over something completely, smoke dwindles.

(Ahmad Ghazzali d.1126 CE)[12]

THE TRIAL

The human being was created weak.

(Qur'an 4:28)

The human being was made of haste.

(Qur'an 21:37)

The human being was created with anxiety.

(Qur'an 70:19)

Say: Even if you were to possess the hidden treasures of the mercy of my Lord, you would cling to them, afraid of expending them. The human being is ever niggardly.

(Qur'an 17:100)

The love of worldly desires has been made attractive to human beings: the desire for women, sons, piles of gold and silver, fine horses, livestock, and fertile land.

(Qur'an 3:14)

Souls are prone to selfish greed.

(Qur'an 4:128)

You love possessions with an ardent love.

(Qur'an 89:20)

The human being wearies not of praying for good; but if something bad touches him, he is despairing and hopeless.

(Qur'an 41:49)

Alongside the terrifying moments of acute medical crises, there is the grind of chronic conditions, and it is in this daily grind that one has the time to experience the breadth and depth of one's faults and weaknesses. The quotes from the Qur'an above suggest that the very substance of the human being is comprised of weakness, impatience, agitation, selfishness, self-pity, greed, and the narcissistic need for material things and other people. The angels themselves were aghast when power was entrusted to this strange and frightening creature with its all-consuming desires and lack of self-control:

When your Lord said to the angels, "I am putting a deputy on the earth," they said, "Why put on it one who will cause corruption on it and shed blood while we glorify You with praise and proclaim your holiness?"
He said, "I know what you do not know."

(Qur'an 2:30)

Although the angels could not understand what God understood, they were prescient in their assessment. They knew that the weaknesses with which Adam and Eve were created would lead to the actions that caused their fall from the Garden and their subsequent actions on earth. The seal on the fate of human beings was "Go down, each of you an enemy to the other" (Qur'an 2:36, 7:24). This is a curse suggesting that, down here on earth, enmity flows more naturally between human beings than does altruism, mutual aid, or care for one another. The ferocity with which humans deal with one another is met in equal part with the burdens experienced by the vulnerability of the body on earth, with its burdens of illness, hunger, thirst, and need for shelter. To be human is to experience corporeal and emotional vulnerabilities: bodily pain and discomfort, fatigue, anguish, grief, and fear. As the Qur'an says, "We created mankind in trouble" (Qur'an 90:4).[13]

Among those who do not consider themselves practitioners of a religion, there is a common perception of religion as a kind of security blanket for believers, offering some degree of defense for its holder against fear and despair. Although this may be true for some believers, there are also many examples of religious figures who express the pain of life without trying to minimize it, even as they turn toward God. The classic literary expression for this spiritual attitude is the lament or complaint. In the Qur'an, Mary is described as having to face the pain of giving birth to Jesus alone, her sense of isolation intensified by a community that is quick to condemn her. As she is overwhelmed by the agonies of childbirth, she cries out, "Would that I had died before this and been a thing forgotten!" (Qur'an 19:23). The Prophet Jacob has to bear not only the lies and deception of his sons but also his grief for the son that has been taken away from him:

> And he turned away from them, saying, "Oh my sorrow for Joseph!" His eyes were full with of grief but he suppressed his anger. They said, "By God, will you never stop remembering Joseph until you are overcome by disease and then death?" He said, "I complain of my sorrow and grief to God alone, and I know from God what you do not know."

> (Qur'an 12:84–86)

The Sufi master 'Abdullah Ansari (d.1039 CE) cries out in his rhymed *Munajat* (whispered conversations with God):

> Oh God, this is not living but torture.
> This is not life, but a structure reared on water.
> Without Your grace, we are undone.[14]

Another Sufi, Abu al-Qasim Muhammad al-Junayd (d. 910 CE), has a much dryer style. This is especially useful for dispelling the mental trick that seeks escape from the realities of pain and suffering by imagining that the particular events of one's own life are unusual, thereby granting one the illusion that one is somehow special in one's pain. Instead, life's indignities and cruelties are only too normal for countless numbers of people. Junayd said, "I don't perceive what I endure from the world as something loathsome. For I accept it as a basic fact that the here and now is a house of grief and sorrow, of torment and affliction, and that the world is utterly bad. Thus, it is normal if it confronts me with everything I find repulsive. If it confronts me with what I like, that is something above the normal. But the original, normal situation is the first case."[15]

The famous Sufi and poet Jalal al-Din al-Rumi (d. 1273 CE) was amazed that we remain attached to a world that causes so much pain:

> Look not at time's events, which come from the spheres and make life so
>   disagreeable.
> Look not at this dearth of daily bread and means of livelihood! Look not
>   at this fear and trembling.

Look instead at this: In spite of all the world's bitterness, you are passionately
and shamelessly attached to it.[16]

The trial or affliction of being human, then, is the experiencing of our
vulnerability both from without and from within, from those who would
hurt us, from the afflictions of the body and poverty, and from the endless
refilling of our desires and fears.

According to the Qur'an, humanity brings additional pain and suffering
upon itself in three primary ways.[17] I have already mentioned the absurd
intensity and diligence with which one can look for help in all the wrong places. This is the cognitive error that the Qur'an refers to as idolatry (*shirk*).[18]
Another cause of pain for human beings is the disconnection between stated
belief and actions, a phenomenon that the Qur'an refers to as hypocrisy
(*nifaq*). The problem most often referred to, however, is called *kufr*, a word
that is usually translated as "unbelief" or "infidelity." "Unbelief" is a prob-
lematic translation because the English word "belief" suggests a cognitive
function that is implied only secondarily in the Arabic. "Infidelity" is better,
but it still fails to capture the full sense of the Arabic word, which connotes
the refusal to acknowledge the favor or benefit that has been conferred upon
one; its antonym is thankfulness (*shukr*).[19] The Qur'an says, "Verily, We have
displayed for humanity all of our signs in this Qur'an, but most people refuse
to acknowledge them, except by rejecting them (*illa kufuran*)" (Qur'an
17:89, 25:50). The primary meaning of *kufr*, then, is relational. In English
one can say, "I believe in you," which implies wholehearted support for
another person. The word *kufr* refers to the rejection of this kind of belief.
To be an "unbeliever" (*kafir*) is to think badly of God.

The Qur'an uses two words to describe alternative attitudes that will ultimately lessen pain and lead to happiness. The first attitude is "submission"
(*islam*), which strikes at the very heart of human restlessness and agitation.
The Persian poet Rabi'a bint Ka'b (fl. tenth century CE) writes, "I acted like
a wild horse not knowing: to struggle only draws the noose tighter."[20] To
be "one who submits" (*muslim*) thus means to stop running and hand
oneself over to God. To struggle in the midst of physical pain or emotional
suffering only increases one's pain. The only way out is to do what is counter-
intuitive: to relax and submit to the pain. To be "one who submits" is thus to
recognize one's smallness and the fact that self-aggrandizement adds to the
pain. According to the Persian Sufi Hakim Sana'i (d. 1131 CE),

Humility[21] suits you but violence does not.
A naked man frantic in a beehive is out of place.[22]

The second attitude is faith (*iman*), which entails thinking well of God
(*husn al-zann*).[23] As with the term "infidelity" (*kufr*), the meaning of *iman*
is less cognitive than relational. In the following verses, Sana'i compares our
careless cruelty (*jafa'*) to God's loyalty and fidelity (*wafa'*):

You have been unkind
Yet He keeps his faith in you.
He is more loyal to you
Than you are to yourself.[24]

To think badly of God is to lose faith in one's potential as a human being, to lose faith in discovering what was meant when God said to the angels, "I know what you do not know" (Qur'an 2:30). Human beings are a mysterious mixture of the high and the low: "We created humanity in the best kind of symmetry and then We turned him into the lowest of the low" (Qur'an 95:4–5). "By the soul and that which shaped it and inspired it in its shamelessness and its consciousness of God (*taqwa*)" (Qur'an 91:7–8).

Sufi writers have not been above pointing out the apparent contradictions in God's plan, even as they admit that it is impolite to do so. In another one of his *Munajat,* Ansari writes:

Oh God, You poured the jewels of purity into Adam's lap
And sifted the powder of rebellion upon Satan's head.
You mingled these two opposites.

In courtesy to You I should say that we did wrong,
But in reality, You provoked the mischief![25]

To return to the matter of justice, the problem is clear. The deck is stacked against human beings in a grand way, and yet the beauty of being human lies precisely in the tension between man's extraordinary capacity to behave badly and the equally extraordinary possibility of acting well. To accept this situation wholeheartedly requires giving up the "logic" of human notions of justice and embracing the "illogic" of pure giving.

CHOOSING A NEW ECONOMY

Be contented with your lot;
But if you have any complaints,
Go and take them to the judge,
And obtain satisfaction from him.
That's how the fool's mind works![26]

(Sana'i)

I have mentioned how hospital and insurance systems run on the principle that there is a finite amount of resources; their job is to distribute these resources as equitably as possible to patients and members. However, given the fact that the resources are limited and organizations are not always efficient in what they do, the smart caregiver quickly realizes that one of her many jobs is to fight with persistence and resolve to make sure that the patient and the patient's family get the help they need. The principle of equitable distribution and the fight for justice is similar to the mercantile bargain with one's soul, albeit with the addition of a stronger guarantee of justice: if you are good and do what you should, you will be rewarded—if not here, then in the afterlife. The Qur'an states repeatedly that there will be no injustice in the end: "You will not be treated unjustly by even so much as the thin membrane in the groove of a date-stone" (Qur'an 4:77; see also 4:49 and 17:71). Although seeking and attaining justice is a praiseworthy goal that is both necessary and liberating, it is ultimately unsatisfying if it is not itself liberated by the qualities of forgiveness and generosity. Likewise, the pragmatic goal of securing essential needs for oneself and one's family becomes oppressive if it is not balanced with the acceptance of uncertainty. Otherwise, fear may manifest itself as a form of niggardliness:

> The mean live in fear
> for their daily bread.
>
> The generous never eat
> yesterday's reheated leftovers.[27]

                                                                          (Sana'i)

Sana'i's playful metaphor in these verses unexpectedly locates pleasure in giving without fear, a voluntary embrace of insecurity. The word "generosity" refers to something beyond responding to the needs of others. It refers not only to the act of giving but also to an attitude behind the act that renounces any claims to recompense or guarantees that one's needs will be met equally in the future.

The act of giving to another may start from a principle of equity—if one has more than someone else, it is only right to give up some of what one has—but giving past the boundaries of this logic is something else altogether. Abu al-Qasim al-Qushayri (d. 1074 CE) describes three different degrees of generosity, using a different word in Arabic for each: "According to the Sufis, *sakha'* is the first degree of generosity. *Jud* comes after it, and then *ithar*, preferring others to oneself. Whoever gives a part and keeps a part [of his wealth] possesses *sakha'*. Whoever freely distributes most of it but keeps something for himself possesses *jud*. The man who suffers need but prefers that someone else have enough possesses *ithar*."[28]

The first degree of generosity described by Qushayri is necessary for social cohesion. It is hard to imagine a society that could exist without some degree of redistribution of wealth and resources from those who have a great deal to those who have very little. It is also hard to see this as much more than enlightened self-interest; societies with gross inequalities are not secure societies. Individuals who are not giving in their relationships tend to have unstable relationships. To not respond at this level is to demonstrate ignorance of this fact, as well as a complete contempt for others, whether crudely justified or not. "And when it is said to them, 'Spend out of that which God has given you,' those who are ungrateful say to those who have faith, 'Should we feed someone who, if God had willed, He could have fed?'" (Qur'an 36:47).

However, giving out of enlightened self-interest is still the same as bartering. The Qur'an accepts this as such and offers reassurance: "Whatever you spend in the way of God will be paid back to you in full and you will not be wronged" (Qur'an 8:60). Although the Qur'an accepts the concept of bartering, the phrase "Spend out of that which God has given you" in Qur'anic verse 36:47 suggests that the premise of personal ownership, whether of resources, honor, or security, is a faulty one. It is very easy to take health and privileged social and economic circumstances for granted. However, if what you possess is as much the result of good fortune as it is of individual exertion, then the concepts of personal property and personal rights have to be understood in a larger context. Enlightened self-interest would recognize that self-sufficiency is not permanent; familial or communal aid is needed by everyone at some point in one's life. The essential logic is still one of bartering, but within a wider context of time and justice that recognizes that "what goes around comes around."

Beyond the level of generosity understood as enlightened self-interest, there is a kind of generosity beyond the principle of the "fair deal" and the basic logic of functional families and societies. Rather than a one-to-one exchange, the premise here is that there is more than enough to go around and that the very act of giving leads to the multiplication of resources and energy. Qushayri uses the word *jawad* to describe someone who keeps a little for himself but gives away most of what he has; such a person practices the type of generosity known as *jud*. This word comes from the same Arabic root as *jawd*, which is used to describe a plentiful rain. The Qur'an uses an agricultural metaphor to describe this kind of generosity that moves beyond the level of bartering: "The likeness of those who spend their wealth in the way of God is like a grain out of which grows seven ears and in every ear there are a hundred grains. God multiplies for whom He wills. God is vast [in providing], knowing" (Qur'an 2:261). "The likeness of those who spend their wealth seeking God's pleasure and for the strengthening of their souls is like a garden on high ground. Heavy rain falls and its produce is doubled and, when the heavy rain does not fall, there is still dew" (Qur'an 2:265).

All kinds of generosity require the letting go of fear. To accept the barter arrangement, a degree of faith in other people is necessary, as well as faith in the ultimate, if not always immediate, likelihood of fairness. Accepting the principle of abundant generosity is different in that it involves letting go of the need to stockpile one's resources, whether those resources are emotional or material. While the logic of bartering is necessary for smooth familial and communal functioning, the logic of giving up one's stockpiles is more difficult to accept. Certainly, it is not a "natural" impulse in human beings. As the Qur'an says, "Humankind is ever niggardly" (Qur'an 17:100). However, generosity is a trait that can be conditioned culturally or individually. The Arabic word *birr* (righteousness founded on generosity) comes from the same root as the word *barr*, a wide open space. This word is used in the Qur'an to describe the human quality of kindness and generosity that requires discipline: "You will never attain *birr* until you spend of what you love" (Qur'an 3:92). Giving up one's stockpiles is difficult but ultimately more rewarding than clinging to one's emotional resources and material possessions.

Qushayri's text mentions a third level of generosity, *ithar*, which means preferring another to oneself. He relates the story of a Sufi who was aware of a hidden niggardliness within himself, even though he was considered generous by others.

> 'Abdallah ibn Ja'far was told, "You lavish much when you are asked, but you won't ask the slightest thing from those to whom you have given!" "I give my money freely," he said, "but I'm stingy with my mind." 'Abdallah ibn Ja'far went out to his country estate. He stopped by somebody's palm garden where a young black slave was working. When the boy got his food, a dog came into the enclosure and approached him. The boy threw him a piece of bread and he ate it. Then he threw him a second, and a third, and the dog ate those too. 'Abdallah ibn Ja'far watched this. "Young man, how much of your food meets this fate every day?" he asked. "As you see." "Why do you prefer this dog to yourself?" "This is not dog country," the boy said. "He must have come a very long distance out of hunger, and I hate to turn him away." "And how do you fare the day?" "Today I will go hungry." "And am I scolded for too much generosity?" 'Abdallah ibn Ja'far exclaimed. "This fellow is much more generous than I am!" So he bought the youth, the garden, and the tools that were in it, then freed the boy and gave it all to him.[29]

While there is a clear logic to bartering and sharing one's resources with others, preferring others to oneself makes little sense. Qushayri related, "I heard Abu 'Abd al-Rahman al-Sulami say...that al-Daqqaq said, 'It is not generosity when the one who has gives to the one who has nothing, but it is generosity when the one who has nothing gives to the one who has.'"[30]

Although people can be trained to act as if they prefer others to themselves, as in the cultural conditioning of gender and classes, the conditioning runs only so deep. The kind of generosity described here, actually preferring others to oneself, is not disciplined self-denial but effortless, weightless self-lessness. Note the wording in the following quotation from the Qur'an, which describes those who helped the refugees fleeing Mecca for Medina in the early years of the Muslim community: "Those who made their abode in the city and in faith before [the refugees] love those who emigrated to them. They find no need in their hearts for what has been given them and prefer [the refugees] to themselves even if they are themselves in dire poverty" (Qur'an 59:9).

Those who are in dire poverty "find no need in their hearts for what has been given them!" Given the niggardliness of the human soul, it is difficult to imagine how one would not feel one's own need. However, the feeling of preferring others to oneself is a feeling that most people have experienced: it is the feeling of being in love and of preferring the beloved to oneself. In the state of love, one feels an effortless and pleasurable selflessness that is not the same as renunciation or the negation of desire. The vortex of self-interest has been calmed, and instead of feeling grim self-denial, one instead feels playful. The supposedly "insane" person who has been freed from the niggardliness of his soul feels more pleasure, not less, even as he accepts the reality of suffering, his own included. 'Attar writes: "A madman rides about on a hobby-horse with a smile on his face and cheerfully singing like a nightingale. Someone asks him: 'Why are you riding around so quickly?' He answers: 'I have a craving to ride all over the world before they chain my hands and feet, and not a hair on my body can raise itself any longer.'"[31]

Qushayri presents the different kinds of generosity as a progression, with each degree indicating a greater ability to put others before oneself. But in the daily struggle with our interactions with others, the reality seems to be that there are moments where one is capable of giving freely out of what one has and other moments where one can barely manage to act with basic decency. The moments when one prefers another to oneself are rare but defining. Caretakers are often given the advice to take care of themselves first, which is good advice. However, the difficulties of caring for the chronically ill are not fully addressed by this advice; something more is needed that acknowledges the burdens of seemingly unending demands and struggles and one's feelings of inadequacy in trying to respond to them with at least a modicum of grace. The Sufi writings quoted above offer an elegant aesthetic for behavior, which accepts human weaknesses while pointing toward unexpected possibilities.

To return to the issue of the systems and organizations that exist for providing care and distributing resources, it is hard to imagine a social structure that could function like 'Attar's madman. The levels of generosity that Qushayri mentions, however, suggest that the virtue of generosity can be realized in different ways at different times. It is possible to develop organizational structures that encourage and foster responsiveness toward others; caring for the well-being of others cannot be forced, but it can be nurtured at all levels of a hierarchy and in all the nooks and crannies of bureaucracies. While organizational change works best when it is initiated and supported by those with the most power within the organization, it is also possible for any individual at any point in the system, including the petitioner in need, to choose to act with generosity. Every person who has power over another (and, if we take these stories to heart, there is no such thing as a person without power) has the choice to exercise that power for self-interest, for justice, or in gratuitous acts of generosity.

THE PRESENCE OF GOD

We began with an imaginary dialogue between God and humanity at the end of time, in which God asks the children of Adam why they did not care for Him when He was ill, hungry, and thirsty. Although from a strict Islamic theological viewpoint, such questions are improper—because God in Islam can never be ill, hungry, or thirsty and is far beyond the need for care—this story makes an important point. It addresses the common human problem of looking for God in the wrong places by suggesting moral localities in which the presence of God can be found. God locates His presence precisely at the point where the corporeal and emotional vulnerability of the human condition meets the anxious, greedy, and selfish human characteristics that so horrified the angels at the time of humanity's creation. To turn away from the discomfort of the moments when one is asked to respond to the suffering of others is, in a sense, to turn away from the presence of God, thereby dimming one's potential as a human being. As Sana'i says,

> The person who does not turn his face towards the Real—
> Considers everything he has and knows as an idol.
>
> As for one who turns away from the presence of the Real,
> In reality,[32] I cannot say that this person is a human being.[33]

In the face of suffering and in being asked to respond to the needs of others, the person of weak faith might ask, "Where is God?" However, for a Muslim, that is the wrong question to ask. When all is said and done, as Sana'i says:

> You are you.
> From this comes kindness and enmity.
>
> You are you.
> From this comes both faith and ingratitude.[34]

NOTES

1.   Quoted in William A. Graham's *Divine Word and Prophetic Word in Early Islam: A Reconsideration of the Sources, with Special Reference to the Divine Saying or Hadith Qudsi* (The Hague: Mouton, 1977), 179–80. Graham notes the resemblance of this divine saying to Matthew 25:41–45 in the Bible. The translation here is Graham's, with slight modifications.

2.   A *hadith* (pl. *ahadith*) is a saying attributed to the Prophet Muhammad. A *hadith qudsi* is a saying attributed to Muhammad in which God Himself is said to have spoken.

3.   Two excellent introductions to the history and thought of Sufism are Carl W. Ernst's *The Shambhala Guide to Sufism* (Boston, Massachusetts: Shambhala, 1997) and Annemarie Schimmel's *Mystical Dimensions of Islam* (Chapel Hill, North Carolina: The University of North Carolina Press, 1975).

4.   This chapter relies heavily on conversations and experiences I have shared with others, of whom I would particularly like to acknowledge Tahira Sands, Leila Ispahany, Mohammad Mehdi Khorrami, and Samuel Conway.

5.   The translations of the Qur'an here are drawn from those of A.J. Arberry's *The Koran Interpreted* (New York: Macmillan, 1975); Muhammad Asad's *The Message of the Qur'an* (Gibraltar: Dar al-Andalus, 1984); and Abdalhaqq and Aisha Bewley's *The Noble Qur'an: A New Rendering of its Meaning in English* (Norwich: Bookwork, 1999).

6.   Farid al-Din 'Attar, *Musibatnama*, 8/4. Quoted in Helmut Ritter's *The Ocean of the Soul: Man, the World and God in the Stories of Farid al-Din 'Attar*, Translated from German by John O'Kane with Editorial Assistance of Bernd Radtke (Leiden: Brill, 2003), 255. I have made one slight change in O'Kane's translation, substituting "madman" for the word "fool." The Persian word is *divaneh*.

7.   Patients' Bill of Rights, New York State Hospital Code Section 405.7. This Bill of Rights is posted throughout hospitals in New York State.

8.   Joseph A. Amato, *Victims and Values: A History and a Theory of Suffering* (Westport, Connecticut: Greenwood Press, 1990), 89.

9.   The term "theodicy" was coined by the philosopher Gottfried Wilhelm Leibniz (d. 1716) to refer to "the attempt to demonstrate that divine justice remains uncompromised by the manifold evils of existence," Eric L. Ormsby, *Theodicy in Islamic Thought: The Dispute over Al-Ghazali's "Best of All Possible Worlds"* (Princeton, New Jersey: Princeton University Press, 1984), 3.

10.   See, for example, Brian Hebblethwaite's *Evil, Suffering and Religion* (London, U.K.: SPCK, 2000), 5–6.

11.   Fyodor Dostoevsky, *The Brothers Karamazov*, translated and annotated by Richard Pevear and Larissa Volokhonsky (New York: Farrar, Straus and Giroux, 1990), 287 (Part II, Book V, Chapter 4).

12.   Ahmad Ghazzali, *Sawanih: Inspirations from the World of Pure Spirits*, trans. Nasrollah Pourjavady (London, U.K.: KPI Limited, 1986), 44.

13.   The word translated here as "trouble" is *kabad*. Muhammad Asad notes that it comprises the concepts of "pain," "distress," "hardship," "toil," and "trial" (*The Message of the Qur'an*, 952 n.3). The word for liver, *kabid*, which comes from the same Arabic root, was considered the source of the passions and even enmity in pre-modern Arab culture. See E.W. Lane, *Arabic-English Lexicon* (Cambridge, U.K.: The Islamic Texts Society, 1984), 2:2584.

14.   *Munajat: The Intimate Prayers of Khwajah 'Abd Allah Ansari*, trans. Lawrence Morris and Rustam Sarfeh (New York: Khaneghah and Maktab of Maleknia Naseralishah, 1975), 39. The *Munajat* has also been translated into English in *Ibn 'Ata' illah: The Book of Wisdom and Khwaja Abdullah Ansari: Intimate*

Conversations, trans. Victor Danner and Wheeler M. Thackston (New York: Paulist Press, 1978).

15.   Quoted in Ritter, *The Ocean of the Soul,* from *Hilyat al-awliya' wa-tabaqat al-asfiya'* of Abu Nu'aym Ahmad b. 'Abd Allah al-Isbahani (d. 1038 CE), 10/270; and *Sharh al-Hikam* of Muhammad b. Ibrahim b. 'Abbad al-Nafzi al-Rundi (d. 1390 CE), commentary on the text *al-Hikam* of Abu'l-Fadl Ahmad b. Muhammad Ibn 'Ata' Allah al-Iskandari (d. 1309 CE), 1/32.

16.   Jalal al-Din al-Rumi, *Mathnawi,* 6:1733–1735, trans. William C. Chittick in *The Sufi Path of Love: The Spiritual Teachings of Rumi* (New York: State University of New York Press, 1983), 57.

17.   When the Qur'an criticizes entire communities, it is such beliefs, attitudes, and actions that are being criticized. The terms "one who submits" (*muslim*) and "one who is faithful" (*mu'min*) are used to describe the adherents of several faiths. Similarly, Sufi writings are replete with references to the idolatry, hypocrisy, and infidelity that Sufis locate within themselves.

18.   *Shirk* means to associate anything or anyone with the Absolute, which is God.

19.   Lane, *Arabic-English Lexicon,* 2:2620.

20.   Peter Lamborn Wilson and Nasrollah Pourjavady, trans., *The Drunken Universe: An Anthology of Persian Sufi Poetry* (Grand Rapids, Michigan: Phanes Press, 1987), 65.

21.   The Persian word translated as "humility," *zari,* also means "lamentation," or "cry for help."

22.   Hakim Sana'i, *The Walled Garden of Truth,* trans. David Pendlebury (New York: E.P.Dutton, 1976), 18. Pendlebury's work is an abridgement and revised translation of Major J. Stephenson's translation and edited Persian text of *The First Book of the Hadiqatu'l-Haqiqat* (New York: Samuel Weiser, 1970). This selection from Sana'i appears on pages 42 (English translation) and 27 (Persian text) of Stephenson's work.

23.   The concept of "thinking well" (*husn al-zann*) of people and of God is a common expression in Sufi writings. See Schimmel, *Mystical Dimensions of Islam,* 118, 128.

24.   Sana'i, *The Walled Garden of Truth,* trans. Pendlebury, 23; Stephenson, *Hadiqatu'l-Haqiqat,* English 59, Persian text 37. I have modified Pendlebury's translation here.

25.   Ansari,*Munajat,* trans. Morris and Sarfeh, 45. I have made slight modifications in the translation. For the impoliteness of pointing out God's part in the moral failings of human beings, see also *The Mathnawi of Jalalu'ddin Rumi,* Translated by Reynold A. Nicholson (London, U.K.: Luzac, 1972), 1:1488–1494.

26.   Sana'i, *The Walled Garden of Truth,* trans. Pendlebury, 17. See also Sana'i, *Hadiqatu'l-Haqiqat,* trans. Stephenson, 37 (English translation) and 24 (Persian text).

27.   Sana'i, *The Walled Garden of Truth,* trans. Pendlebury, 26. See also Sana'i, *Hadiqatu'l-Haqiqat,* trans. Stephenson, 63 (English translation) and 40 (Persian text).

28.   Abu al-Qasim al-Qushayri, *Sufi Book of Spiritual Ascent (Al-Risala al-Qushayriya),* trans. Rabia Teri Harris, ed., Laleh Bakhtiar (Chicago, Illinois: ABC

International Group, 1997), 231–232. There is another partial English translation of this work by Barbara R. von Schlegell, *Principles of Sufism*(Berkeley: Mizan Press, 1992).

29.   Al-Qushayri, *Sufi Book of Spiritual Ascent*, 235.

30.   Ibid., 240.

31.   Farid al-Din 'Attar, *Ilahinama*, 14/20. Quoted in Ritter's *The Ocean of the Soul*, 254–255.

32.   There is a play on words here, in repeating the word Sufis frequently use to refer to God, "the Real" (*al-Haqq*) with the emphasis of the phrase "in reality" (*bi-l-haqq*).

33.   Sana'i, *Hadiqatu'l-Haqiqat,* trans. Stephenson, 29 (English translation) and 18 (Persian text). I have modified Stephenson's translation here.

34.   Sana'i, *The Walled Garden of Truth,* trans. Pendlebury, 19; and *Hadiqatu'l-Haqiqat,* trans. Stephenson, 43 (English translation) and 28 (Persian text). The translation here is my own.

10

THE MIRACLE OF PAIN

Daniel Abdal-Hayy Moore

With blisters the size of Brazil
and headaches the size of Manhattan—
why is spiritual pursuit so associated with
    physical pain?

Abd al-Qadir Jilani used to
tie his hair to a nail on the wall to
snap his head back if he dozed off
    reading Qur'an.
Christian mystics endure endless permutations of
    difficulty, including spontaneously
        bleeding from the
wounds of Christ.
Sitting in Buddhist meditation on puffy black cushions
    crosslegged for hours to
focus the mind nearly
    drove me up the wall I was facing.

Birth is no picnic. Death often
    less so. Life in between: a
tough love event.

Yet it all brings us to God.

These blisters on feet around
    Ka'ba marble
around and around,
the headache that comes from
    odd short hours of

sleep in order to
wake up the heart before Allah in the
last watches of the night—
    the abode of lovers—

is the price to pay for *ma'rifa*[1]—
as all creatures of this earth must
crack open the shells on acorns or mussels to get
    the meat, the
earth splits apart revealing
    deep fissures of ruby, whole
generations drown and later generations
come—a

tear of joy forms in the eye of one
    who sees *The One Who*
        Sees!

NOTES

This poem first appeared in Daniel Abdal-Hayy Moore, *Mecca/Medina Time-Warp*. Reprinted here from a Zilzal Press chapbook, by permission from the author.
  1. *Ma'rifa* means "recognition of the Divine Reality."

11

DEATH AND BURIAL IN ISLAM

Rkia Elaroui Cornell

As a young married woman and the mother of a two-year-old daughter, I worked at one of the largest Islamic centers in the United States, the Islamic Center of Southern California in the city of Los Angeles. It was 1980, a time when the Muslim community of Los Angeles was going through significant changes because of their large population growth. This demographic boom warranted an increased need for various religious services to be rendered. This in turn created job opportunities for immigrant Muslims with expertise in Arabic language teaching and Qur'anic studies.

I had just moved to the United States with my husband, who was then a graduate student in Islamic Studies at the University of California, Los Angeles. At the Islamic Center I established an Islamic Sunday School program, taught Arabic and the Qur'an, acted as a religious and spiritual advisor for female community members, provided information on Islam for non-Muslims, and assisted new converts and those on the verge of converting to Islam to know more about the religion they were about to embrace. When I was not teaching, advising, developing educational programs, or coordinating some of the Center's social activities, I acted as an administrative assistant to the Center's director and its nine trustees. Preparing bodies for burial was not part of my job description. However, when circumstances forced me to take on this responsibility, it turned out to be one of the most challenging and important services that I rendered for the Center and the community.

Although 26 years have passed, I still remember the dreadful phone call that I received in my office at around ten o'clock on a Monday morning. The voice was that of a young Muslim man from Canada, informing me of the sudden death of his bride in a West Hollywood hotel room. They had been in Los Angeles to celebrate their honeymoon, and the woman's death had snatched the young man's wife away from him in the blink of an eye. The police ran their investigation, the autopsy results revealed no foul play, and since embalming is not allowed in Islam, the body had to be cleaned, shrouded, and buried as soon as possible.

In this case, an autopsy had to be performed because of the woman's young age and because the cause of death was unknown. In California, the law dictates that such a procedure must take place even if it is objectionable to the religious beliefs of the deceased person's family. The death certificate is then signed by the Medical Examiner, and the Board of Health approves the body for burial.

Earlier, an elderly woman had passed away, but the cause of her death was unknown too. Her family refused to allow the coroner to perform an autopsy. They appealed to the Islamic Center for help. They asked the Center to explain to the authorities the religious reasons behind their stand. The Center's response to the coroner's office was that contemporary Islamic legal scholars were of two views on the matter of autopsies. Some do not object to an autopsy being performed, but others argue against it. Those who argue against autopsies feel that the relationship between the body and the soul continues after death. They believe that the dead person never loses her senses or feelings. According to this belief, the dead person is aware of what is going on around her and suffers because of this. The family's objection to subjecting the body of their deceased mother to the pain of an autopsy followed this opinion. They were also of the view that the body should not be used for organ donation or for any medical or scientific experimentation. This was because the body has to be intact on the Day of Judgment. In this particular case, the authorities honored the family's request. Because of the woman's advanced age, they did not insist on the rigid application of the law and waived the autopsy.

The poor young Canadian husband was not so lucky. He had no choice but to abide by the law because of his deceased wife's young age and because he did not want to be incriminated for her death. Having dealt with this harsh reality, he found solace in trying to fulfill the remaining religious obligations allowed to him before putting his wife's body to rest. He needed a Muslim woman to perform the cleansing of the body (*ghusl*) and a Muslim Imam to perform the funerary prayers (*salat al-janaza*). I informed the Center director of his call. He immediately called his wife and told her that a Muslim woman had died and that the young husband needed our help in preparing the body for burial.

The trip from the director's house to the funeral home was a long one. It took us nearly two hours to get there because of the lunch-hour traffic. During the trip, there was a minimal exchange of words among us. The sudden death of this young woman had immersed us in deep reflection on our own mortality. The fact that I was heading toward an experience that is usually considered taboo for young women in Muslim countries demanded an explanation.

In Islam, preparing bodies for burial is a religious duty that is not incumbent upon everyone but is only incumbent upon a sufficient number of people in the community (*fard kifaya*). Those who perform this service exempt the rest of the community from this responsibility. However, if no one performs the service, the blame would fall on the entire community. On this occasion, the director's wife and I were the only women available to perform this task. I could not allow myself to fail the community. However, I had doubts about my commitment because of the stigma that my Moroccan culture attached to young women who perform such a task. As a child, I was taught that if a young woman prepares a body for burial, the food she cooks will lose its taste and flavor. I shuddered at the idea but chose to disregard it as a cultural myth. After all, we were not in Morocco, where plenty of older widows are available to free young women from the burden of preparing bodies for burial. I saw the issue as one of the challenges that Muslim women living in non-Muslim countries have to face. In such circumstances, when a myth competes with a religious rule, the myth should lose and the needs of religion should prevail.

As I rode in the car to the mortuary, I could hear my mother reminding me not to fall into temptation, and not to forget the two angels watching over me at all times—one sitting on my right shoulder recording my good deeds, and the other on my left shoulder recording my bad deeds. These "Honored Scribes" (Qur'an 82:11) record every thought, every decision, and every act of a person in a big book or register and deliver their report on the Day of Judgment. In my religious Moroccan family, accountability to God is what life is all about. Thus, I was duty bound to render a service to the husband of the dead woman and nothing else mattered.

DEALING WITH DEATH

Important and serious thoughts about death came to my mind. Tragic deaths that happened during my childhood began to unfold in my memory. First, I remembered the politically motivated assassination of one of my parents' neighbors. This happened in the early 1950s. The assassination was carried out by some Berber traitors, who were known to work for the French at a time when Morocco was struggling to gain its independence. Although the assassination happened in the year that I was born, the house where it took place was attached to ours, and the fact that the murdered person was considered a martyr (*shahid*, literally, "witness") made the case very memorable.[1] I knew the family of the murdered person and the honor that the community bestowed on them. The second death that I remembered was that of my only brother, who died at the age of 18, along with two of his friends and schoolmates. After taking a swim in a nearby river, they caught a fever and died within 24 hours. Their death was a shock to everyone, and its memory filled me with sadness and grief. My parents could never recover from the loss of the only son they had, but they found consolation in the belief that my brother, along with all who died in their youth, would be one of the Grooms of Paradise (*'ara'is al-janna*). The third death that I remembered was the accidental drowning of my one-year-old nephew, who had fallen into a well. He is still remembered by everybody in the family as one of the Birds of Paradise (*tuyur al-janna*). His parents, my eldest sister and her husband, were told that he would join the other children who had died very young and would bring water to relieve the thirst of the people who stood in line, waiting to be judged for their deeds, on Judgment Day.

I also remembered three other deaths, two of which involved murder and one that was a rare case of suicide. The case of suicide involved one of the students who went to my high school and was a year ahead of me. She was intelligent, beautiful, and very competitive. However, the pressures and anxieties associated with the nationwide exams that took place at the end of every academic year in Morocco led her to take her life. Her case was especially tragic because of the stigma Muslims attach to suicide, which is forbidden in Islam. The Qur'an forbids suicide unequivocally: "Do not kill yourselves, for Allah is merciful toward you. Whoever does this, whether out of enmity or oppression, We shall cast him into a Fire, which is an easy matter for God" (Qur'an 4:29–30). The Qur'an also warns believers, "Do not destroy yourselves by your own hand, but instead do acts of goodness, for Allah loves those who do good" (Qur'an 2:195). In Islam, taking life is the responsibility of God, the giver of life. The Qur'an is very clear that it is not the right of the human being to "play God" by arbitrarily deciding when one's own life or that of another should end. "Do not take life, which God has made sacred, except as a matter of justice" (Qur'an 6:151).

By killing herself, the girl confirmed that she despaired of God's mercy, which rendered her an outcast from the Islamic faith. Members of the community showed little sympathy toward her or for the reasons that led her to commit a crime against herself. They also did not offer much consolation to her family because her suicide was considered an offense against God. However, they did their duty and buried her, according to tradition. In most Muslim countries, the bodies of people who commit suicide are not buried facing the *Qibla*—the direction of Mecca—like other dead people. However, in the Middle Atlas Mountains of Morocco where I was raised, it was believed that God should decide this issue. Before burying the student, the gravedigger went to the last grave in the cemetery, took the pickaxe he would use to dig her grave, and threw it behind himself as high as it would go. Wherever the pickaxe fell would be the place where he would dig the grave. The direction of the axe head would determine the direction the girl's head would face in the grave. If the fallen axe head faced the direction of the *Qibla*, this would mean that God might forgive her and that she might yet have access to salvation. However, as a suicide, she would still be denied the funerary prayers that are made at the time of burial.

The two cases of murder that I remembered were as follows. The first case happened on the wedding night of a young Arab couple. On that night, the bride turned out not to be a virgin. The groom saw her lack of virginity as an affront to his honor and felt that it robbed him of something that was his right to possess on that special night. Enraged at what he felt to be an insult to his pride and dignity, he brutally murdered his young bride, mutilated her body, left a note describing the reason for the murder pinned to her chest, and disappeared before dawn. He has not been caught or seen to this day.

The second murder was that of a Berber woman in her late fifties. Twice divorced and with no children of her own, she sought companionship by marrying a third husband, an Arab man in his early sixties. Since he had lost his first wife, and his children were grown up and happily married, she found him to be a perfect match. However, she did not know about his jealousy and bad temper. One night, after attending a wedding, they returned home and got into an argument over a man who the husband thought was trying to seduce his wife. The argument ended when the husband struck his wife with his cane, which killed her. The husband confessed to the crime and was sent to prison for more than 13 years. He died only a few months after the King of Morocco commuted his sentence.

According to traditional beliefs in Morocco, all victims of murder go to Heaven. According to accounts of the Prophet Muhammad that are recorded in books of Hadith and in other works of tradition such as the *Muwatta* of Imam Malik ibn Anas (d. 795 CE), a place is reserved in Paradise for those who have been murdered, for mothers who die in childbirth, for those who die as children, for those who die as unmarried youths, and for those who die on the Hajj pilgrimage to Mecca. Suicide, as we have seen, is a crime punishable by Hellfire. As for murderers, besides serving the sentence imposed on them by the courts, they must also repent for taking a life that only God has the right to take. This is done by fasting for two consecutive months, by feeding 60 poor people, or by saving the life of another to atone for their crime. Only thus can they hope to attain God's forgiveness.

These memories took me back to how the news of a death would change my father's countenance. I recalled the things he said when he heard that someone had died. I could almost hear him in the background, reciting the verses of the Qur'an that every Muslim recites upon hearing of a death. "Surely we belong to Allah, and to Him we shall return" (Qur'an 2:185); "Every soul shall taste death" (Qur'an 3:185; 21:35; 29:57); "Everything perishes but [God's] face" (Qur'an 28:88; 86:88); "Whoever is on Earth shall perish, but [God's] face alone shall remain forever" (Qur'an 55:26–27). My father took these verses to heart as unwavering truths and made sure that they would hold true for me as well.

I remembered how the news of a death would plunge my father into a state of deep reflection. I vividly recalled how my father's state of mind would prompt me to listen to everything he had to say about death, the rituals it occasioned and all the paradoxes and enigmas associated with it. It was during these intense moments that I learned the most about the subject of death.

In general terms, I learned that death was a part of life and that everything my mind could conceive and even the things I could not conceive would eventually perish. My father would say that even the Earth and the Heavens would eventually go through a sort of cosmic death, like every other created thing. Even the Angel of Death would face death himself.

THE EXPERIENCE OF DEATH IN
ISLAMIC TRADITION

The "delirium of death" (*sakarat al-mawt*)—the moment in which the reality of death comes to one's consciousness (Qur'an 50:19)—was a matter of major concern for my father. He described it as a time of perplexity and bewilderment for the dying person—so much so, in fact, that one might even forget the *Shahada,* the Muslim Testimony of Faith.[2] At this point in the process of death, the soul reaches the collar bone (Qur'an 75:26) and then it rises up into the throat (Qur'an 56:83). The entire body feels as if it has been drowned in a floodlike state (*ghamarat al-mawt*), and the angels stretch out their hands, asking that the soul be given to them (Qur'an 6:93). At this point, the soul is about to escape from the body and the end is rapidly drawing near.

If I were to be with a person when such an event happened, my father's advice to me was to observe the following rules. Never leave the dying person alone, so that he will be safeguarded against Satan's temptation. Make sure that the dying person's head is facing the direction of the *Qibla*. Assume a state of calm and serenity; make sure to keep children away from him and do not allow any loud lamentations by women to disturb him. Remind the dying person to utter the Testimony of Faith (*al-Shahada*): "I bear witness that there is no god but God, and I bear witness that Muhammad is the Messenger of God." Once this is done, no further request to make the *Shahada* should be made. Apply drops of water to the dying person's mouth to quench the intense thirst that comes upon him at such moments. Doing so will help bring relief. At all times, trust that God's mercy and goodness will prevail over His wrath, and make sure to convey this to the dying person so that he will have positive thoughts about God. Thinking positive thoughts about God is the "price of Heaven" (*thaman al-janna*) and repentance is the "key to Heaven" (*miftah al-janna*).[3] The sweat on the forehead of the dying person is a good sign because it indicates that his suffering will soon be over and that the end is near. If these rules are implemented, my father would say, the transition from the physical world to the Angelic Realm would be smoother and less painful.

My father would then describe the threshold between life and death where the physical world vanishes, and the Angelic Realm (*'alam al-malakut*) is unveiled. This threshold is marked by the descent of angels from Heaven, dressed in white, with faces gleaming like shining suns. They come down from Heaven with a white silk shroud (*kufn*) and sweet, fragrant musk to wrap and anoint the soul of the believer after it submits itself in peace.[4] My father would say that every year on the fourteenth day of the Islamic month of Sha'ban, leaves from the Lote Tree of Heaven, inscribed with the names of those destined to die, fall to Earth. These leaves are collected by Azra'il, the Angel of Death, whose task is to collect the souls and bring them back to their Lord. "Say: The Angel of Death, who is responsible for you, will gather you up and return you to your Lord" (Qur'an 32:11).

At the time of death, the Angel of Death comes to the dying person and conveys God's greetings of peace (Qur'an 33:44). Then he sits by the person's head, addresses the soul, and asks it to surrender itself in peace. According to traditional Islamic belief, the soul of the believer (*mu'min*) will slip away quickly and easily, like water jetting from a waterskin. However, the soul of the unbeliever (*kafir*), who rejects God's truth and resists the reality of death, will shriek in protest before it finally yields itself.[5]

The "pulling out of the soul" (*naz' al-ruh*) from the body, which is undertaken by the Angel of Death, marks the relinquishing of physical life and is the most agonizing of the pains that death inflicts. It is at this stage, my father said, that the soul (*ruh*), the essence of the human being that was created before its association with the body,[6] feels the pain caused by the Angel of Death pulling it away from its earthly abode. According to Islamic tradition, the soul's true home is in the Angelic Realm, although it becomes habituated to life on Earth through association with the body. The association of body and soul starts in the womb, continues after birth, and does not end until death. However, the fact that this is a semirelationship and not a relationship of identity is revealed in sleep, when the soul's connection with the body is loosened,[7] and in death, when the soul actually leaves the body and ascends to the Angelic Realm.

THE SOUL AND ITS ASCENT

Once the process of physical death has taken place, the Soul at Peace (*al-nafs al-mutma'inna*)—the righteous soul called by God to return "well pleased and pleasing unto Him" (Qur'an 89:27–28)—embarks on its ascension through the seven Heavens escorted by angels.[8] These angels, the number of which my father would put between two and four, first take the soul past all of the bygone communities of humankind ("scattered about like swarms of locusts") before they reach the first Heaven.[9]

When the angels arrive at the first Heaven, they knock at its gate. When asked, "Who are you?" they reveal their identity and introduce the soul they are escorting. They testify that the soul is that of a believer whose creed (*'aqida*) is intact and free from associating partners with God (*shirk*). At the

gate of the second Heaven, the angels praise the person's observance of the
five daily prayers. At the third Heaven, the person's charitable deeds are
commended. At the fourth Heaven, the angels honor the person's practice
of fasting. At the fifth Heaven, they attest that the person's pilgrimage to
Mecca was done with the best of intentions. At the sixth Heaven, they
mention the care and respect that the person showed to her parents. Finally,
at the seventh Heaven, they testify that the person's repentance for her sins
was genuine.[10]

Having passed successfully through the gates of the seven Heavens, the
soul celebrates its arrival at the Uppermost Heaven (*'Iliyyin*), where it sees
its name inscribed on the register that is kept until Resurrection Day. This
highest Heaven is also known as the Lote Tree of the Furthest Boundary
(*Sidrat al-Muntaha'*).[11] Here, the soul attains its closest proximity to the
Divine Presence. My father would never speculate on whether the soul
actually witnesses God. However, he would say that the physical death
of the body is not real death. True death is in reaching a higher level of consciousness through the annihilation of selfhood. Once the soul is annihilated
from itself, it loses all sense of identity and subsists in God (*al-fana' wa
al-baqa' fi Allah*).

My father preferred not to talk about what happens to the soul of the
unbeliever or evil person. Instead of ascending through the seven Heavens
in peace, the soul of the evil person would receive a terrible reception from
the frightful and horrible angels of Hell. These angels would wrap the soul
in a shroud made of coarse hair, smear awful smelling substances onto it,
and then try to ascend with it through the seven Heavens, only to be denied
entry through their gates.[12] Eventually, the evil soul would slip out of their
hands and drop into Hellfire.[13]

At this point, the car in which we were riding suddenly swerved to avoid
hitting another car. This brought me out of my reverie and back to the reality
of where I was. I noticed that the traffic was still moving slowly and that
much time would have to pass before we arrived at the funeral home.

I then remembered that the soul would have to be brought back to Earth
once again to join with the body while it was being washed and prepared
for burial. The soul also had to be with the body for the Interrogation in
the Grave, after which it would remove itself to a medial station called the
Barzakh, the "interval," or "isthmus." In the Qur'an, the Barzakh is a
barrier set up by God to keep two bodies of water separate and distinct
(Qur'an 25:53). In Islamic eschatology, the term refers to the separation
between the world of the dead and the world of the living. Once they have
arrived at the Barzakh, the dead do not return to the world of the living.
While there, the soul awaits the coming of the Hour (*al-Sa'a*). At the coming
of the Hour, the soul unites again with the body to be resurrected and to
stand before God on Judgment Day. Denying the coming of the Hour
means denying God's justice and acknowledging the dominion of evil

(Qur'an 25:11). My father would say in Moroccan dialect, "Were it not for the Hour, the evil ones (literally, "the bastards") would succeed" (*Law kan ma kantsh al-Sa'a, lasilku ulad al-haram*).

My father said that the body without the soul is nothing more than flesh and bones. It will perish and later it will be consumed by worms. The soul, he would clarify, is what allows the dead to be conscious of what goes on around them (Qur'an 35:22). Those who care for the body after death must be aware that the dead person can hear and feel everything they say or do. Thus, they must take care to say or do nothing that would disturb the soul's tranquility.

THE WORLD AND THE HEREAFTER

Forest Lawn Cemetery and Hollywood Mortuary started to appear from afar. I could see from the window of the car that we would soon arrive at our destination. I thought if my parents were still alive, and if I were to share with them my shock upon hearing the news of the young woman's death and the experience I was about to undergo, what would their advice be? At that moment, I imagined my father reminding me of the following Qur'anic verses: "No soul can die except by Allah's leave and at a time appointed" (Qur'an 3:145); "No soul knows in what land it will die" (Qur'an 31:34); "Wherever you may be, death will overtake you" (Qur'an 4:78). He would also have mentioned the following Hadith as a comfort for those who were left behind: "A sudden death is a solace for the faithful but a sorrow for the unbeliever."[14]

My beloved mother was a woman of few words. Rather than giving long explanations, she would probably have used a pointed Moroccan aphorism: "Grave-diggers and burial providers can be found in every land" (*haffar u daffan fi kull al-bled*). Being known for her wisdom, she might have added, "Pursue your happiness wherever it might be. Spread through God's land and seek His bounty (Qur'an 62:10), and never worry about who will be there to care for your remains when your appointed time comes." This was an adventurous statement, especially since it came from a woman who seldom left her house! Thinking of my mother, I could see what had motivated me to seek my happiness in faraway lands and to end up settling in the United States.

I took the Qur'anic verses that my father referred to as a warning not to question the will of God for taking a young life prematurely and to content myself with serving as one of those "body washers and burial providers" that my mother alluded to in her astute dictum. I also came to realize how my conception of the Last Day (*al-Yawm al-Akhir*) as a fundamental article of the Islamic faith along with belief in God, His angels, His Books, and His Messengers (Qur'an 4:136) had moved me to a higher and deeper level of understanding than before.

My parents' warnings against being oblivious to the reality of the Hereafter and not allowing myself to be seduced by the deceptions of the material world (*al-ghurur*) now made more sense to me than before.[15] I could see this as a valuable lesson worth passing on to my young daughter as well. I appreciated my parents' advice to guard against the temptations of the material world (*al-dunya*) and to stay focused only on what would be of benefit in the Hereafter (*al-akhira*).[16] My parents inspired me to emulate those whose hearts live in constant remembrance of God, who do not hate or fear death but perceive it as an opportunity that the soul takes to escape from worldly existence into the divine realm.[17] My father likened the soul's escape from the world through the annihilation of selfhood to a metaphorical "death" before physical death. By teaching me that one could realize such an annihilation in prayer, in living the Word of God through the Qur'an, and in embodying the Prophet Muhammad's character through the Sunna, he brought me to a better understanding of what was meant by the concept of mystical death. Without this sensation, my father would say, life as we understood it would be devoid of meaning.

Being in proximity to Forest Lawn Cemetery made me think of the answers that the dead are supposed to give to the questions asked of them in the grave by Nakir and Munkir, the two Interrogating Angels. Softly, the phrases, "Allah is my Lord (*Allahu Rabbi*), the Qur'an is my Book (*al-Qur'anu Kitabi*), Muhammad is my Prophet (*Muhammadun Nabiyyi*), Islam is my Religion (*al-Islamu Dini*)," came out of my mouth. I felt a great sense of relief because remembering these words gave me the assurance that, were I to be the one that had died and were I to be the one to be interrogated in the grave, I would have passed my first test on the journey to the Hereafter. These four statements, which every Muslim must know by heart, are believed to be the key to deliverance from the torments of the grave. Failure to answer them correctly would result in frightful encounters with vipers, scorpions, and all sorts of chastisements and afflictions that are unbearable for any human soul.

TERRORS OF THE GRAVEYARD

The sight of the well-kept graves covering a huge area of Forest Lawn Cemetery brought back memories of many frightening cemetery stories that I heard when I was a child. Some of these stories instilled in me a great fear of visiting cemeteries, especially at night. Their moral teachings, while bringing those who have sinned to be accountable for their wrongdoings, rely on fear as a preventive measure and encourage the young to avoid such sins in their own lives.

The sinners who are the subjects of cemetery stories include those who break their fast during the month of Ramadan, who show no mercy toward their frail and elderly parents, who are unfair to orphans and never care for the poor or the needy, and who commit major sins such as theft or murder. All sinners receive punishments that are commensurate with their wrong-doings. Such punishments might include wild beasts appearing at their graves at nightfall to terrorize them. Some tombs might be set ablaze, and vipers and scorpions might cohabit with the bodies in their graves. Even the Earth itself might take revenge on them and would say to them, "You have had much fun on my surface, but today you will suffer inside of me. You used to delight in all kinds of delicacies on my surface, but today the worms will eat you inside of me."[18]

These punishments will continue until the Gathering of Bodies (*hashr al-ajsad*) on Judgment Day, which the Qur'an also refers to as the "Day of Separation" (*yawm al-fasl*).[19] The Balance (*mizan*), the scale that weighs the deeds of every individual, will be the measure through which justice is dispensed. "Allah it is who has revealed the Scripture with the Truth and the Balance. How can you know? It may mean that the hour is nigh" (Qur'an 42:17); "As for him whose scales are heavy [with good works], he will have a pleasant life [in the Hereafter]. But as for him whose scales are light, the Bereft and Hungry one [Satan] will be his mother. Ah, what will convey unto you what she is—Raging Fire" (Qur'an 101:6–11). The Bridge of Hell (*Sirat al-Jahim*), starting at the door of Hell and comparable in its thinness to the finest hair, will be crossed by every human soul that desires to get to Heaven. "Gather together those who did wrong, along with their wives and that which they used to worship instead of Allah. Lead them to the Bridge of Hell, and then stop them, for they must be interrogated" (Qur'an 37:22–24). Those without sin will cross the Bridge as lightly as a feather and will attain Heaven and all the benefits it entails. Failure to cross the Bridge will result in the soul falling down to *Jahannam* (similar to the Hebrew *Gehennah*), the top layer of Hell, and all the nightmares that go with it.[20]

When I was a child, the two cemetery stories that frightened me the most and made the greatest impression on me were "The She-Mule of the Graveyard" (*baghlat al-qubur*) and "'Ali Wants His Hand Back" ('*Ali bgha yaditu*). Both stories were narrated by candlelight or around the fireplace during the long cold nights of winter in the Middle Atlas Mountains. The storyteller, a woman from the Sahara desert who was known to perform wonders with her words, would receive gifts for her expertise, and her dedicated audience, both young and old, would honor her with respectful silence and complete attention.

Thursday night was the night dedicated to storytelling. My father's regular weekly travel freed the day for my mother to invite my aunts over to our house, along with their daughters and some of my mother's female neighbors, one of whom was the storyteller. The gathering would start after dinner and would not end until it was almost dawn, for my mother's objective was to get as many extra hands as she could to help with the wool carding, spinning, or weaving that she wanted to finish that evening. Listening to these stories provided our entertainment, and their length affected the degree of our productivity. Hot and sweet Moroccan tea, rich in caffeine, would be served to keep us all awake and alert. When my mother noticed that the heap of wool she had put out for carding and spinning was not going down fast enough, she would say, "Speak, but spin (*hadith u maghzil*)!" which was one of her favorite aphorisms.[21]

The story of the She-Mule of the Graveyard was about a widow who lost her husband, but who failed to keep herself chaste during the four-month and ten-day period (*'idda*) that every woman must observe after the death of a spouse. After her death, she was turned into a werewolf-like creature as a punishment for her sins. According to Moroccan tradition, during the period of grieving a widow must wear only white, she must never leave her house after dark, and she must not wear makeup nor dye her hair with henna. Above all, according to Islamic law, she must not have sexual relations with anyone. Islamic law is strict about making the *'idda* period mandatory to ensure that any child conceived by the husband before his death will be acknowledged as his heir. If the widowed woman is accused of having sex with a man during this period, the matter must be settled in the courts. The concern of the law is for the rights of the child, who in Islam takes the father's family name and has specific rights of inheritance. Failure to observe such a rule would result in the kinds of "Who's my daddy?" controversies that one sees on daytime TV talk shows in the United States. Since DNA testing is not available in most Muslim countries, other means, such as the *'idda* waiting period, have to be used to ensure that a child born after the death of a husband is actually his.

The story of the She-Mule of the Graveyard is meant to dissuade girls from ever thinking of cheating on their husbands, whether they are alive or dead. No girl would want to see her body transformed into this werewolf-like creature after sinning in such a way. The storyteller described the transformation of the She-Mule of the Graveyard as an excruciatingly painful process. As she emerged from beneath the dirt and stones that covered her grave, every limb and extremity of her body would be broken and bruised repeatedly. She would emerge from her grave on the fourteenth of every lunar month, when the moon is at its brightest. Each time this happened, she would undergo the same tortures and would emerge from the grave resembling a mule. She would be heavily shackled with chains from head to toe. The chains would cause great pain to her bruised body and their rattling sound would reveal her accursed nature to the living. Her beastly appearance, with eyes like balls of fire and long sharp teeth ready to inflict vampirelike bites on anyone who crossed her path, were meant as a warning for sexual transgressors. Those who lived pure lives were immune from any harm she might cause. The main victims of this creature were men who committed the sin of having sex with a widowed woman, thus transgressing the boundaries of a sacred period set by

Islamic law. Those who were bitten by the She-Mule of the Graveyard were robbed of their masculinity and rendered impotent, sometimes for the rest of their lives.

"'Ali Wants His Hand Back" was about a woman who had procured the hand of a dead man named 'Ali. She procured it for the magical powers she was told it would have over her husband's love for her. Having paid a large amount of money for the hand to the man who had washed 'Ali's body for burial, she put it inside her husband's pillow after making sure that 'Ali's burial had been completed without anyone being aware that the hand was missing. At this point in this story, when each of the listeners was thinking of what would come next, the storyteller brought 'Ali himself into the picture. She described how he emerged from the grave shrouded in white, on the night of the day he was buried, and made us walk with him to the woman's house to reclaim his hand.

He needed his hand in order to undergo the Interrogation in the Grave by the angels Nakir and Munkir. In Islam, the resurrection of the dead cannot take place unless the body is intact. We all felt sad for 'Ali and were curious about what the woman's husband would say or do when he found out what his wife had done. 'Ali knocked at the woman's door all night, repeatedly pleading for her to give his hand back. As she described 'Ali's actions, the storyteller would have us repeat this refrain: "'Ali wants his hand back. He wants it before the new day dawns." We would repeat this again and again, pleading along with 'Ali to restore his hand so that he could escape from the torments of the grave. Finally, just before dawn, the woman relented and confessed to her husband what she had done. 'Ali got back his hand, and the storyteller had us recite in celebration the answers that 'Ali would need in order to free himself from the grave: "Allah is my Lord, the Qur'an is my Book, Muhammad is my Prophet, and Islam is my Religion."

The issue of accountability is of paramount importance in Islam. All of creation is governed by a just God that sees to it that everything, including the universe itself, will answer to Him. In the story of 'Ali Wants His Hand Back, the particularity of such accountability lies within the human being as a microcosm, where one's limbs are brought forth to testify on the person's behalf as stated in the Qur'an: "On the Day when their tongues, their hands, and their feet will bear witness against their actions" (Qur'an 24:24). Thinking about the bodies and extremities in these stories brought me back to the body I was about to wash and prepare for burial.

WASHING AND PREPARING THE BODY FOR BURIAL

The director of the Islamic Center broke our silence by announcing that we should be ready to get out of the car and head to the mortuary, where the body was. He reminded his wife not to forget the bag containing the towels, the gloves, the sheets, the shampoo, the musk, and anything else that was necessary for washing and preparing the body for burial. He asked me to bring the tape recorder containing the tape with the appropriate Qur'anic verses that are customarily recited while the washing of the body takes place.[22] He also handed me a few sheets of paper containing instructions for performing the washing of the deceased according to Islamic principles.[23] The requirements for washing a body in Islam are as follows:

1. The person washing the body must be a Muslim.
2. The person performing the washing must be in a state of purity. He or she must have made their ablution before they start washing the body of the deceased.
3. A woman who has just given birth is exempt from washing bodies.
4. A woman who is having her menstrual period is not allowed to wash a body.
5. If the deceased is male, his washing must be performed by a male.
6. If the deceased is female, the washing of her body must be done by a female.
7. Husbands are allowed to wash the bodies of their wives.
8. Wives are allowed to wash the bodies of their husbands.

Preparing a body for burial is a process that requires preparation and the right materials. To prepare the body of the young bride for burial, the director's wife brought three towels to preserve her modesty: one towel was to cover the woman's breasts, another was to cover her private parts, and another was to cover the backside of the woman when she was turned over. A man would need only two towels to preserve his modesty. She also brought two other towels to dry the body after washing. In the United States, it is also customary to bring latex gloves to wear during the preparation of the body, a large sheet of plastic to put under the body, and a pair of scissors to cut the burial shroud. Other required items include soap to wash the body, shampoo to wash the dead person's hair, and musk to anoint the body. If musk is not available, an oil-based, nonalcoholic perfume is acceptable. The burial shroud (*kufn*) requires three sheets for a male and five sheets for a female. The sheets must be without a hem and made of white cotton. Nowadays, twin sheets are used for most people, but queen sheets may be used for a large person. The edges of hemmed sheets can be removed with scissors. Any sewing, seams, or embroidery on the sheets must be removed as well.

Before preparing the body for burial, it must be placed on high table, with the face up. In the United States, the best-equipped place for such a task is a funeral home. Muslims have been using such facilities for many years now, and their needs have been accommodated accordingly. The first step is to undress the body of the deceased while making sure that the private parts remain covered at all times. A large piece of plastic and paper towels are put under the hips to collect any rectal or urinary discharges. After undressing the body, the person who prepares the body for burial presses the stomach gently to get rid of any discharges. The soiled plastic and paper towels are discarded in a garbage bag along with the first pair of latex gloves, and the bag is sealed.

The preparer next washes her hands, puts on a new pair of gloves, and performs the ablution (*wudu'*) of the body. She starts by cleaning the teeth and the inside of the nose, and then performs the following ritual ablutions. These ablutions are similar to those done by a living person, with a few minor variations:

- Wash the hands up to the wrist three times (right hand first, then left).
- Put water over the mouth three times. A living person would rinse the inside of the mouth.
- Put water over the nostrils three times. A living person would wash the inside of the nostrils.
- Wash the face from the forehead to the chin and from ear to ear three times.
- Wash the forearms up to the elbow three times, right first, then left.
- Wipe with a wet hand over the whole of the head once only.
- Wash the feet up to the ankles three times, right, then left.

The Center director's wife then filled the mouth, ears, nose, and eyes of the deceased bride with cotton to prevent water from entering her body. She next washed the body with a washcloth and soap three times, first on the right side, then on the left. If the body is still not clean after the first washing, it may be washed as many times as needed. However, the number of washings must always be an odd number: one washing, three washings, five washings, and so on. To preserve the modesty of the dead person, one must not remove the towels covering the private parts but must wash under them. The last washings must be done without soap. For example, if washings one and two are done using soap, washings four and five must be done with plain water. Rinsing the body should be done by pouring the water gently over the body: the right side first, then the left side, then the right side again, then the left side. The last rinse must be done with scented or perfumed water.

The director's wife then shampooed and washed the hair of the young woman three times and rinsed it well. A woman's hair may be braided in three braids or placed to the sides or to the back. For men, the hair is simply combed neatly. Next, she removed the cotton that was used to cover the body openings and discarded it in the garbage bag, along with her second pair of gloves. Putting on a third pair of gloves, she dried the body with clean towels. Finally, she put musk on the woman's head, forehead, nose, hands, knees, eyelids, and armpits and placed perfumed cotton on her private parts. While, she was preparing the body, the tape deck was playing recitations of the Qur'an. Thinking about these procedures made me realize how unchanged they have remained throughout more than 14 centuries of

Islamic history. With the exception of a few modern additions such as latex gloves, plastic bags, and a tape deck, little of the ritual of washing and preparing the body for burial has changed over time. A major reason for this is that most of these rituals are preserved in the collections of Hadith.

For example, Umm 'Atiyya reported that when Zaynab, the daughter of the Prophet Muhammad died, the Prophet said: "Wash her an odd number of times, and put camphor or something similar on her body at the fifth washing." Upon completing this task, the women informed the Prophet that they had done as he had asked. Then he gave them his undergarment and said, "Put it next to her body." The women then braided Zaynab's hair in three plaits, two on the sides of her head and one on her forehead. Following the instructions of the Prophet, every task must start from the right side, and with those parts of the body upon which ablution is performed.[24] A common addition to this procedure is to add some water from the well of Zam Zam in the Sacred Mosque of Mecca to the water that is used to wash the body for burial, if such water is available.

The process of shrouding and covering the body has also changed little over time. The Prophet's wife 'A'isha reported that when the Messenger of God died, he was first shrouded in a material from Yemen. Then it was removed from him and he was shrouded in three sheets of white Yemeni cotton. The cloth was said to have been not from a garment or a turban.[25] In modern times, white cotton bed sheets are often used in place of bolts of white cotton cloth. Often, people making the pilgrimage to Mecca bring their burial shrouds from Mecca or buy them for friends and family members as gifts.

When we wrapped the body of the young woman who had died on her honeymoon, we used five sheets to make the burial shroud. First, we cut two sheets in half, which gave us four pieces of cotton cloth. We cut a hole in the center of one piece, large enough to go over the waist of the dead woman. This piece is to be slipped over the head and pulled down to the waist to act as a sort of pajama bottom. We cut a second hole in the center of another piece of cloth, large enough to fit over her head. This piece was to act as a sort of blouse, covering her chest. We next cut long, thin strips of the third piece to be used as ties. Any remaining cloth from this piece would be used as a scarf to cover the head. The fourth piece of cloth was kept as a snug-fitting wrap to go around the bosom.

The mortuary had provided us with a simple wooden casket in which to place the body. We put one of the tie strips in the bottom of the casket and then placed a whole sheet in the casket to be used as the outer sheet of the shroud. We then used another sheet for the first wrapping of the body. We closed the sheet around the body from head to toe, covering the face, and tied it off at the top of the head, the waist, and the feet. Then we took the half sheet with the larger hole, put it over her head and shoulders, and pulled it down to her waist, until the bottom of the cloth touched her ankles. Then we took the half sheet with the smaller hole and pulled over her head, fixing it like a blouse. We next took the third half sheet and wrapped it tightly around her bosom area. The final piece of cloth was folded into a triangle and placed on the woman's head like a scarf. This was folded under the chin. Finally, we lifted the body and placed it in the casket on the last sheet, face up. We closed the sheet completely around the body and tied it at the waist. Then we faced the body in the direction of Mecca and closed the casket.

When I entered Forest Lawn Mortuary for the first time, I was so shocked by the sight of the bodies laid out for embalming that I could feel my head spinning. When we arrived where the body of the young bride was, I could not bear to look at her. The Center director noticed how pale I was and immediately made me sniff some perfume. I felt like running out of the mortuary, but I could not do so. Because I had been called upon to take care of somebody that needed real help, I did not have the luxury to feel sorry for myself. I could not allow my ego to distract me from my sense of duty. After that first time at the mortuary, I was able to prepare other bodies for burial, including the bodies of children, without thinking of myself. Instead, I spent my preparation time silently asking God to grant the deceased mercy and peace.

THE FUNERAL PRAYER (*SALAT AL-JANAZA*)

Unlike the daily canonical prayers in Islam, funeral prayers do not require bending at the waist (*sujud*) or prostration (*ruku'*). The entire prayer is done while standing. Typically, the prayer is led by the Imam of the mosque where the deceased person used to worship most frequently, but the prayer can be led by any qualified person. In the case of the Canadian bride who died in Los Angeles, the director of the Islamic Center of Southern California led the funeral prayer. During the funeral prayer, the men stand in lines at the front, and women stand in lines at the back.

When the funeral prayer is performed, the body of the deceased is placed in front of the Imam. The Imam positions himself behind the middle of the casket if the deceased is a woman and by the left shoulder if the deceased is a man. The funeral prayer is begun like the regular *Salat* prayer, by raising the hands and saying, "God is greatest" (*Allahu akbar*). Then the Imam and those who pray behind him quietly recite *Surat al-Fatiha,* the opening Sura of the Qur'an:

All praise belongs to God, Lord of the Worlds,
The Beneficent, the Merciful,
Master of the Day of Judgment.
You alone do we worship,
And to You alone do we turn for aid.
Guide us to the Straight Way,

The way of those of whom You are satisfied,
Not of those who have angered You,
Nor of those who have gone astray.

(Qur'an 1:1–7)

The Imam and the congregation then say, "God is greatest" a second time but without raising the hands. After this, they make the *tashahud*, the recitation of the *Shahada* in the prayer: "I bear witness that there is no god but God, and I bear witness that Muhammad is the Messenger of God." They then say "God is greatest" a third time, without raising the hands. At this point in the prayer, all who are present make a silent supplication for the soul of the deceased. Then they say, "God is greatest" a fourth time and make a supplication for all Muslims. The prayer finishes with the congregation following the Imam in saying, "Peace be unto you" (*al-salamu ʿalaykum*), first to the right side and then to the left side.

After the funerary prayers were over, the husband of the deceased woman was sad but relieved to be able to return to Canada, where he would join with his family and that of his wife to observe the bereavement warranted by such a tragedy. On the way back to the Islamic Center, I remembered how neighbors and extended family members would take over the household of the family of the deceased. They would provide a fried Moroccan bread called *milwi* and hot tea for the large numbers of people, whether friends, acquaintances, or enemies, that would come from all over to present their condolences. During this time, enmities would be forgotten and the event would create an opportunity for people to make peace among each other. The family also used this time to take care of the legal matters associated with the loss of a loved one.

On the third day after the funeral, the family would observe two important rituals. Early in the morning they would visit the grave and give *milwi* soaked in butter, dates, and water to those who accompanied them to the cemetery and to anyone they met on the way. At the cemetery, they would recite some verses of the Qur'an or hire someone who had memorized the Qur'an to recite verses on behalf of the deceased. At night, they would prepare a huge and costly meal and invite the community to come and celebrate the memory of the deceased. Neighbors, extended family members, friends, and even strangers would help with the cooking and with the meal expenses. Such a communal event brings people together to care for each other in a very compassionate way. Humor, but without vulgarity, is often used at such events to bring solace to the family of the deceased.

On the fortieth day after the funeral, family members and friends pay another visit to the family of the deceased. As on the third day, a feast is held and Qur'an reciters are hired. When my father died, I was in the United States and could not be present on time to attend his funeral.

To commemorate his death, the Islamic Center held a funerary prayer for him and people shared their own experiences of coping with distance and loss far away from their communities back home. In place of my family in Morocco, I relied on my friends from Los Angeles and the Islamic Center, who cooked for my family and me and brought me comfort and sympathy.

Life in America has taught me much, but none of the lessons I have learned have been as significant as the lessons I learned when dealing with death in a faraway land. I was amazed to see how much tradition mattered to my fellow Muslims who had lost loved ones in their home countries. No matter how secular they might be in their daily lives, and regardless of their religious inclination or ethnicity within Islam—whether Iranian Shiite, American Sufi, or North African Sunni—when they faced the loss of a loved one, they all wanted the rituals to be performed according to the strict observance of the Qur'an, Sunna, and tradition. My experience of working in the Islamic Center of Southern California taught me that the majority of Muslims in the United States take religion most seriously at three crossroads in their lives: at marriage, childbirth, and death. At such times, even people who make a point of being "modern" and rational in their day-to-day occupations fall back on the support and solace of tradition. When I see modern Muslim ideologues attempting to reform Islam by dismissing traditional practices as "superstitious" or "ignorant," I wonder what they will rely on when death and tragedy overtake them. The "human margin" of religion can be both a curse and a blessing. Sometimes, tradition can create its own tragedies, such as when a modern Anglo-Pakistani executive marries off his daughter, who has never been to Pakistan, to an unknown man from his native village in Punjab. However, at other times, such as moments of death and loss, the lack of tradition creates an emptiness and sterility that leaves the heart desolate and bereft of solace. As this chapter has shown, I am grateful for the traditions I have learned from many people in my native town and region, both literate and illiterate. What continues to amaze me is how much these traditions not only resonate with but also follow the teachings of Islam as they have unfolded throughout history.

NOTES

1.   The Qur'an says about martyrs, "And say not of those who are slain in the way of Allah, 'They are dead.' Nay, they are living, although you do not perceive it" (2:154).

2.   In a hadith, the Prophet Muhammad says, "Oh God, please help me bear the delirium of death." See, for example, Abu Hamid Muhammad al-Ghazali (d. 505/ 1111), *Ihya' 'ulum al-din* (Beirut: Dar al-Ma'rifa, n.d.), vol. 4, 461–465.

3.   Anas ibn Malik reported that the Prophet Muhammad said: "One must not die unless he holds positive thoughts about God. Verily, trusting in Allah's goodness is the Price of Heaven." Shams al-Din ibn Abi 'Abdallah Muhammad al-Qurtubi

(d. 671/1272–3), *Al-Tadhkira fi ahwal al-mawta wa umur al-akhira*, ed., Muhammad 'Abd al-Salam Ibrahim (Beirut: Dar al-Kutub al-'Ilmiyya, 1421/2000), vol. 1, 27.

4.   "And there will come forth every soul; with each will be [an angel] to drive it, and [an angel] to bear witness for it" (Qur'an 50:21). See also, *The Message of the Qur'an*, transl. and annot. Muhammad Asad, 2nd ed. (Gibraltar: Dar al-Andalus, 1984), 798. Asad interprets the "driver" (*sa'iq*) and the "witness" (*shahid*) in this verse as not meaning angels, but psychological constructs: "And every human being will come forward with [his erstwhile] inner urges and [his] conscious mind" (n. 13 and n. 14).

5.   Shams al-Din Abu Bakr Ibn Qayyim al-Jawziyya (d. 701/1301–2), *al-Ruh*, ed., al-Dimashqi (Amman, Jordan: Maktabat Dandis, 2001), 69.

6.   This fourth stage in the creation of the human being is distinguished by God's spirit being breathed into humankind. "Then [God] fashioned [the human being] and breathed His Spirit into him" (Qur'an 32:9). "They ask you about the Spirit. Say: 'The Spirit comes from God's command'" (17:85).

7.   Sleep, in Moroccan culture, is said to be the "little brother" of death. I remember my mother referring to death and saying that death had "a foolish little brother" called sleep, who never gets to finish the job he starts.

8.   "You shall surely ascend from one heaven to another heaven" (Qur'an 84:19); also, "[God] who has created the seven heavens one above another" (Qur'an 67:3).

9.   Qurtubi, *al-Tadhkira*, vol. 1, 50.

10.   Ibid., 50–51.

11.   "Near the Lote-Tree beyond which none may pass" (Qur'an 53:14).

12.   "For those who reject Our signs and treat them with arrogance, no opening will there be of the gates of heaven, nor will they enter the Garden, until a camel can pass through the eye of the needle. Such is Our reward for those in sin" (Qur'an 7:40).

13.   "If anyone assigns partners to God, he is as if he had fallen from heaven and been snatched up by birds, or the wind had swooped and thrown him into a far-distant place" (Qur'an 22:31). A fierce blast of wind, the wrath of God, comes and snatches the soul away and throws it into a place far from anywhere one could imagine, into the Hell of those who defy God. See Asad, *The Message of the Qur'an*, 859 n. 2806.

14.   Qurtubi, *al-Tadhkira*, vol. 1, 26; this hadith comes from the collections of Abu Dawud and Tirmidhi.

15.   *Al-Ghurur* is a term that the Qur'an uses to describe the multilayered self-deception of the person who is involved with the particularities of the material world and who forgets about the realities of the Hereafter. See Fazlur Rahman, *Major Themes of the Qur'an* (Minneapolis, Minnesota and Chicago, Illinois: Bibliotheca Islamica, 1980), 107.

16.   The literal meaning of the Arabic word *dunya* is "that which is very near," in other words, an immediate objective, the "here and now" of life. *Al-Akhira*, on the other hand, means, "that which comes at the end," the long-range results of the human being's life on earth.

17.   The Qur'an refers to such people as "those for whom neither trade nor commerce can divert them form the remembrance [of Allah]" (24:37).

18.   This tradition goes back in time to medieval Islam. See Jane Idleman Smith and Yvonne Yazbeck Haddad, *The Islamic Understanding of Death and Resurrection* (Albany, New York: State University of New York Press, 1981), 39.

19.   Qur'an 37:20–21; on Judgment Day, our limbs and faculties will be the strongest witnesses against us if we use them for evil purposes instead of the good purposes for which they were given to us. "On the Day when their tongues, their hands, and their feet will bear witness against them and their actions" (24:24).

20.   Smith and Haddad, *Death and Resurrection*, 78–79.

21.   "Speak but spin!" is a Moroccan aphorism that connotes doing multiple tasks at once, and it is used in many contexts outside of the home. In the present case, my mother used it as a reminder to follow the story, but stay focused on the task. It is equivalent to the American saying, "Walk, and chew gum at the same time."

22.   The most common Qur'anic Suras that are recited when washing bodies for burial are Sura 13 (*al-Ra'd*, The Thunder) and Sura 36 (*YaSin*, the Arabic letters Y and S).

23.   In the United States and Europe, Islamic organizations have taken it upon themselves to provide handbooks for the preparation and burial of the Muslim dead. One such handbook is the *Islamic Funeral Handbook* (1991), produced by the Muslim community of Chicago, Illinois. Many people cooperated in the preparation of this handbook, including local Imams, attorneys, funeral directors, and representatives of the Chicago Board of Health.

24.   See, for example, *Sahih Muslim,* trans. Abdul Hamid Siddiqi (New Delhi, India: Kitab Bhavan, 1978), vol. 2, 446.

25.   Ibid., 447.

12

Reflections on Death and Loss

———————————————— • ————————————————

Feisal Abdul Rauf

Great and important insights can be gained by understanding how those of another faith handle the experience of death. This chapter consists of two spontaneous reflections that were sent to the friends of the late Muhammad Abdul Rauf, a great Egyptian scholar and Imam, by his son Feisal and daughter-in-law, Daisy, bringing many to tears by the intimacy and dignity of the account. In a second letter of thanks for the condolences that the family received, the terrible tsunami disaster of December 2004 had just occurred in Indonesia and the Indian Ocean, and the Muslim reaction to this calamity is also expressed.

—Virginia Gray Henry–Blakemore, Volume Editor

A BEAUTIFUL END TO A LIFE'S JOURNEY

Inna lillahi wa inna ilayhi raji'un.
(Verily we belong to God, and to Him is the return.)

As-Salamu 'Alaykum: (Peace and blessings be upon you:)

This is to announce the passing away of my very dear and much beloved father Muhammad Abdul Rauf, on Saturday December 11, 2004, at Suburban Hospital in Bethesda, Maryland, a suburb of Washington, D.C., at 7:25 PM—just 16 days shy of his 87th birthday.

The last time I spoke to him was around 10:00 AM Thursday morning, the day of his medical emergency. He had called to tell me how much he found my latest book a continuation of his work and how much a source of pride it was for him. Then he prayed for God's blessings upon me. He was very lighthearted and extremely cheerful.

My wife Daisy saw him for the last time five days before that when she visited Washington, D.C., to be part of a women's conference hosted by

Karamah, headed by Dr. Azizah al-Hibri. Daisy found my father cheerful, remarked on the emptiness of his house, and noted that my father had donated away his library. He was preparing to visit Malaysia and then go to Egypt with my mother. He was obviously shedding his worldly attachments.

My father had frequently mentioned over the past year that his life's work was done. All he desired was to prepare himself for meeting his Lord. His thoughts revolved around making a final trip to his birthplace in Egypt, in order to die there and be buried next to his father in our village of Abusir Gharbiyya. It is apparent that he wanted to die a beautiful death, surrounded by us personally reciting the Qur'an for his soul's comfort in departing, for God ultimately arranged events toward that end.

My father was rushed from his home in Bethesda to the hospital on Thursday night (December 9) around 11:00 PM after he complained of abdominal pain and became unresponsive to my mother's entreaties. The doctors discovered that he had an aneurism of the abdominal branch of the aorta, a tear in the thinning wall of the artery that provides blood to the abdominal region. They were surprised to find him still alive; for this condition is one that normally results in fatality by the time the individual reaches the hospital. Following surgery and in spite of three doses of clotting factor and 30 units of blood transfusions, he was still hemorrhaging. Obviously his meeting with God was destined, a reality for which he was fully reconciled and prepared.

During this period, my father was generally aware of our presence. Although his eyes were closed, and he could neither speak nor move, I discovered that he was able to communicate to us by squeezing our hands in his softly clenched fists. From about 10:00 AM onwards, my brother Ayman, our dear friend Waleed Ansary, and other family members recited from the Qur'an, with frequent recitations of Sura Yasin (Qur'an 36). This Sura of the Qur'an was recommended by the Prophet to be recited for a soul in the throes of death; he called it the "Heart of the Qur'an." We also recited Surat al-Fath (Qur'an 48, The Victory), Surat al-Waqi'a (Qur'an 56, The Event of Judgment Day), Surat al-Mulk (Qur'an 67, The Kingdom), and other short Suras and assorted Qur'anic verses.

My father communicated to us by squeezing our hands. I learned to understand his special communiqués, such as squeezing my hand to express his desire and delight that I continued reciting the Qur'an to him. Five years ago, my father asked me to commit the time to recite the entire Qur'an to him so that he could ensure that I pronounced it with as perfect a *tajwid* (accuracy of pronunciation) as possible. We recorded the sessions, which continued on and off for about a year. His last published book was a book on *tajwid,* published in Malaysia. He also squeezed Daisy's hand whenever she mentioned news of the manuscript of his autobiography. This was the last work that he had been writing.

I recited continually until 6:30 PM, with my hand in his clasped hand, feeling his regular squeezing of my hand. That my father in a way "choreographed" how he wanted to pass on, surrounded by his family and with me reciting the Qur'an, was evidenced by a number of things. When we agreed with the doctors around 11:00 PM Friday night about the futility of giving my father more blood transfusions, their expectation was that he would pass away within a few hours. He did not. When at 4:30 PM the next day they stopped giving him the pressers to maintain his blood pressure, they thought he would pass away in minutes to an hour. His heart kept beating regularly and powerfully, to almost everyone's surprise, especially for an 87-year-old.

Finally, they decided to remove his respirator. I continued my final recitation of Sura Yasin holding his right hand and intoning it the way I knew he loved to hear it. My mother, Daisy, my daughters Leila and Amira, Waleed, and a few others also opted to remain in the room, holding his other hand and feet, with my mother moistening his mouth with water. He was now breathing on his own. He breathed softly and intermittently during that hour, as his heartbeat gyrated and began slowing down on the monitor. As I recited the eight-verse section ending with the words, *salamun qawlan min rabbin rahim* ("A greeting of peace from a Merciful Lord") his heartbeat flattened. Daisy patted my hand to point this out to me, and so we chanted this verse 111 times.

This eight-verse section of Sura Yasin (Qur'an 36:51–58) is worth repeating: "And when the trumpet on the Day of Resurrection shall blow, people shall rush forth to their Lord, Saying, 'Oh Woe unto us! Who has raised us up from our repose?' This is what the All-Merciful had promised, and the Messengers are now verified. It shall take no more than a single blast for them all to be brought up before Us! On this Day, a soul shall not be wronged in any way, nor shall you be rewarded except for what you did. Surely, the people of Paradise on this Day will be busy rejoicing with their spouses, reclining on shaded couches, enjoying therein fruit and whatever they ask for. A greeting of peace from a Merciful Lord!"

When I began to recite the next verse, Dad's heartbeat began to kick in on the monitor, to the delight of my mother. This was another of his communicative signs that he was indeed registering our presence and recitation, but this was also his final goodbye to us. His heartbeat slowed down within a minute, and I recited the remainder of the Sura. He died peacefully and beautifully, embraced by family and friends, among prayers and expressions of love and respect.

May Allah bless Dad's beautiful soul, forgive him for his shortcomings, forgive us for our shortcomings against him, and continue to reward him for the imprints of his good deeds that he left in the character and personality of the many whom he touched and taught.

My father was known for a religiosity steeped in and defined by deep spirituality and ethics. It was not a piety that was self-serving, but one that delighted in improving and transforming others toward their best behavior while overlooking their shortcomings, for he knew that we humans are imperfect and flawed creatures. He was never vindictive, instead leaving those who wronged him to Divine justice, and considered his patience in the face of others' wrongdoings toward him a means of drawing down upon himself God's forgiveness for his own shortcomings. His years of service were marked by many delightful stories of how he sought to transform hatred into love and heal broken friendships and relationships. He behaved in this way toward all: from those who were at the highest level of government and academia, to his students and those behind him either chronologically or in the ladder of spiritual ethics.

These were the most important imprints of his life. As an Arab poet once said, *Hadhihi aatharuna tadullu 'alayna. Fa'nzuru ba'dana ila-l-athari,* "These are our life-imprints, traces that point to us. So after our departure look at our life-imprints."

May the Benevolent Creator keep the blessings of Dad's life-imprints flowing upon us and admit him into the Divine Presence at the highest level of Intimacy, in the company of the Prophets and Saints.

Imam Feisal Abdul Rauf, Daisy Khan Abdul Rauf, and the Sharkawi Family

UNDERSTANDING DISASTERS AND PERSONAL LOSS

January 12, 2005

As-Salamu 'Alaykum,

To Our Very Dear Friends and Fellow Travelers on Life's Journey:

Our hearts are overflowing with enormous gratitude for your most generous outpouring of wishes, prayers, and goodwill in response to the news of my father Dr. Muhammad Abdul Rauf's passing on December 11, 2004. We wish we could personally thank every one of you for your most heartfelt sentiments.

Dad's fortieth day—marking the official end of mourning to which many Muslims traditionally adhere—falls on January 20, 2004, the evening in Islamic counting of the festival of *Eid ul-Adha,* an especially blessed day that marks Muslims' fulfillment of their required pilgrimage.

Many—even those who had never met Dad—expressed gratitude that we shared the narrative of Dad's last moments, and wrote to tell us of this. But we cannot ignore the news that precisely two weeks to the very hour after Dad's passing, more than 160,000 souls are now confirmed to have perished in the South Asian tsunami. "How could the Merciful and Compassionate God that we all believe in allow such a calamity to happen?" is a question that many, even in the media, have raised. They want to know how believers in God, and especially the Muslims—since we were the hardest hit and suffered the most casualties—are taught to think about such events and come to grips with them.

The Prophet Muhammad taught that among those receiving Divine grace are all who die unexpectedly by drowning, in an earthquake, in a fire, a plague, or an epidemic, from a stomach disease, and including women who die in childbirth. All of these souls are considered to have witnessed the Truth, and thus they receive a heavenly rank. However, God anticipates our next question pertaining to the survivors of such calamities and hastens to remind us, "We shall certainly test you by some [combination] of fear, hunger, loss of worldly goods, of lives and of [labor's] fruits. But assure those who are patient in adversity, who when calamity befalls them assert, 'Verily we belong to God and verily we return to Him (*inna lillahi wa inna ilayhi raji'un*).' Upon these shall flow their Lord's prayers and mercy, for they are guided" (Qur'an 2:155–157). This verse explains why Muslims urge their co-religionists who are touched by calamity to express patience (*sabr*) and utter these words of belonging to God and returning to Him. By complying with this Divine promise, we hope to merit God's prayers, mercy, and guidance.

Like students taking college exams, we go through divine tests to achieve the rewards that accrue from doing well on them. Thus, the tests facing the survivors of disasters include: How will we respond? Will we be angry with God, or will we be grateful for the ultimate grace that God has promised for those who are taken into His mercy? How will we contend with our fear, hunger, loss of worldly goods, and the fruits of our life's work? Can we remain steadfast in the face of adversity? Will we act in accordance with the best of what it means to be human: doing good, being compassionate and supportive to those who need our help, or will we be derailed from traversing the Way?

Some have suggested that modern man needs a Divine reminder and view the tsunami as a form of Divine scripture writ large on instant global television. They believe that the tsunami was meant to imprint onto our consciousness an image of the apocalypse, a terrifying time, according to the Qur'an, when the earth will quake, and "the seas swell and graves are scattered, with every soul keenly aware of what [deeds] it released and restrained" (Qur'an 84:3–5). These verses evoke an image that is intended to make human hearts receive and respond to the Divine sorrow and lament that God sustains for humanity, a humanity that is inattentive to the simultaneity of the overflowing of Divine mercy. God desires to forgive humans who are unaware of their need to ward off the Divine justice that confronts human responsibility. The final reminder in *Surat al-Infitar* (The Cleaving Asunder) underscores what many felt that the tsunami served to remind us of: namely, Who it is that has always owned, and will forever own the ultimate control and final say over our lives: "So how will you fathom Judgment Day? Again, how will you fathom Judgment Day? It is a day when one soul has no control over another and the sole command that Day is God's" (Qur'an 84:17–19).

A man once came to the Prophet Muhammad, asking him when this "Hour" of the Apocalypse that presages the Last Day will occur. "How have you prepared yourself for it?" the Prophet asked. "By loving God and His Messenger," the man answered. To this, the Prophet earnestly replied, "You shall be with those whom you love [i.e. in his case in the company of God and His Messenger]." Our individual moment of death is our "Hour," our precursor to the Last Day, and we shall be in the company of those whom we have loved. May we all have loved our Creator and whomever of His Messengers whose practice we have adoringly followed!

The Messenger of Allah, may Allah bless him and grant him peace, said, "There are seven kinds of martyr other than those killed in the way of Allah. One who is killed by the plague is a martyr, one who drowns is a martyr, one who dies of pleurisy is a martyr, one who dies of a disease of the belly is a martyr, one who dies by fire is a martyr, one who dies under a falling building is a martyr, and the woman who dies in childbirth is a martyr." (Malik ibn Anas, *al-Muwatta* 16.36). Some people asked, "Who else are they, Oh Messenger of Allah?" He said, "He who is killed fighting for Allah's cause is a martyr, he who dies in the cause of Allah is a martyr, he who dies in an epidemic is a martyr, he who dies from a stomach disease is a martyr, and he who dies of drowning is (also) a martyr." This hadith is narrated by Muslim.

Sa'id ibn Zayd reported that the Prophet, peace be upon him, said, "He who is killed while guarding his property is a martyr, he who is killed while defending himself is a martyr, he who is killed defending his religion is a martyr, and he who dies protecting his family is (also) a martyr." This hadith is narrated by Ahmad ibn Hanbal and Tirmidhi. The latter considers it a sound hadith.

Feisal and Daisy

13

DIE BEFORE YOU DIE

Daniel Abdal-Hayy Moore

Die before You Die.

—Hadith of the Prophet

We're never far from the appetites of our body.
Our senses are ready to spring at the slightest touch.
We stand on a bloody field to survey the booty,
but once collected, it soon becomes too much.

We walk inside our flesh-case like a brush
wielded by a painter making rapid splashes,
filling empty scroll-sheets with the blush
of skin-tones come alive in lightning dashes.

Existence comes and goes in furtive flashes.
Nothing belongs to us. It's all on loan.
We are those fleshly bursts like fluttering lashes
that open and close on eyes, and then are gone.

If we could see our real deaths we might die.
To die while still alive wakes up the eye.

5 Ramadan

NOTE

This poem first appeared in Daniel Abdal-Hayy Moore, *The Ramadan Sonnets* (San Francisco and Bethesda, Maryland: City Lights/Jusoor Books, 1996). The work was reprinted from Jusoor/City Lights Books and republished in the Ecstatic Exchange Series. The poem is reproduced here by permission of the author.

14

SUFI FOUNDATIONS OF THE ETHICS OF SOCIAL LIFE IN ISLAM

Kenneth Lee Honerkamp

> Sufism is ethical conduct.
> Whoever surpasses you in ethical conduct
> Surpasses you in Sufism.

—Muhammad ibn 'Ali al-Kattani (d. 838 CE)

Ethics has been a central issue of scholarly discourse in the Muslim world for over fourteen centuries. However, it is not just centuries of scholarly discourse that make ethics an important issue for Islam today. We live in a time when the ethical values that have traditionally formed the foundation of Islamic societies have come under question. In the eyes of many, these values are in need of reevaluation. Globalization, political activism, and radical religious ideologies have forced upon many people a view of the world in which the only ethical options are a choice between secular humanism and a pragmatic ethics of survival. The rhetoric of the "Clash of Civilizations" has marked our communities today such that the spiritual roots that have traditionally defined the moral basis of society seem unrealistic and even childish. Many people now question whether any religious tradition can meet the needs of today's diverse and changing world. This dilemma is not unique to Islam. However, given the clear-cut framework from which Muslims have traditionally drawn their ethical inspiration—the Qur'an and the traditions of the Prophet Muhammad—that such a dilemma should be facing the Muslim community at all today is disquieting.

This chapter focuses on the central role Sufism has played in the development of Islamic ethics. Sufism is rarely mentioned as a source of ethics, and the mentors of the Sufi path have almost been forgotten as ethical exemplars. In the following pages, the ethical teachings of the Sufis and their role in the formation and transmission of the ethical norms that have defined Islamic social life will be highlighted, in hopes of reintegrating this essential source of knowledge into the ongoing discourse on Islamic values. In particular, this chapter delineates the manner in which Islamic spirituality interfaces with Sufi ethical discourse, using original source materials from early Sufi works. Finally, in hopes that the reader might gain firsthand knowledge of the teachings and methods that the Sufis bring to ethical discourse, this chapter focuses on the teachings of Abu 'Abd al-Rahman al-Sulami (d. 1021 CE), a well-known exemplar of ethical teachings on the Sufi path.

ETHICS AND THE SPIRIT

The earliest definitions of Sufism that have come down to us clearly align the teachings of Sufism with ethical conduct.[1] The word for ethical conduct in Arabic is *akhlaq*. Many Sufis of the formative period defined Sufism as *akhlaq*. Abu al-Husayn al-Nuri (d. 908 CE) said, "Sufism is neither formalized practices nor acquired sciences; rather, it is ethical conduct (*akhlaq*)."[2] In the words of Muhammad ibn 'Ali al-Kattani (d. 838 CE) quoted at the beginning of this chapter: "Sufism is ethical conduct (*akhlaq*). Whoever surpasses you in ethical conduct (*akhlaq*) surpasses you in Sufism."[3] In the following generation, Muhammad b. 'Ali al-Qassab defined Sufism in the following terms: "Sufism consists of noble conduct that is made manifest at a noble moment on the part of a noble person among a noble folk."[4] Abu al-Qasim al-Junayd (d. 910 CE), renowned as the Master of the Folk of the Sufi Path, portrayed Sufism as a process of purification that was like a journey: "Sufism is departure from base character and arrival at lofty character."[5] The focus on ethical conduct as the guiding principle behind Sufi practice has continued to resonate throughout the Muslim world. As recently as the eighteenth century, the Moroccan Sufi and scholar Ahmad Ibn 'Ajiba (d. 1809 CE)[6] defined Sufism as, "The science of learning the manner of journeying toward the presence of the King of Kings; or [one could say] inward purification from base tendencies and inward beautification with lofty character traits."[7]

Quotations like those cited above challenge the widely held opinion that Sufism is preoccupied only with metaphysics and mystical experience. On the contrary, the teachings of Sufism affirm that the experiential aspect of human existence is most meaningful when it is understood within a context of spiritual transformation that is based on a normative code of behavior (*adab*) and ethical conduct (*akhlaq*). Sufism teaches that spiritual transformation is inherent to humanity, although within the individual it is only a latent or virtual possibility. From an Islamic perspective, participation in this process of transformation is one of the functions of religious life. Through its core teachings of *akhlaq* and the living examples of Sufi shaykhs, Sufism has played an important role in transmitting the ethical values of Islamic society.

Ruh is the Arabic term for spirit or soul, the substantial or essential aspect of the human being. The Arabic term *ruhaniyyat* refers to the teachings of Islam that deal most directly with the spirit. From the Sufi perspective, spirit defines the human condition, on the one hand, and is the essential substance of the process of spiritual transformation, on the other hand. When speaking of spiritual transformation, the Sufis have often employed the metaphors of a "path" that is followed by a "journeyer" or a "seeker," in which the journeyer passes through various stages or domains of knowledge of God as he encounters increasingly subtle states of the spirit. For example, Ibn 'Ajiba wrote, "The *ruh,* as long as it is engrossed in ignorance, is called the 'ego-self' (*nafs*) and will never access the divine presence."[8] For Ibn 'Ajiba, the process of self-transformation is an awakening of the *ruh*—in other words, a reorientation of the individual's ego-self until it awakens to its true nature and perceives the phenomenal world, not as a discrete entity separate from God but as a continuum of divine presences, or centers of divine manifestation. Spirituality, within the context of Sufi teachings, is thus a function of the process of transformation or reorientation of the ego-self. For the Sufis, this implied that the degree to which one participates in this process of transformation is the degree to which one participates in Islamic spirituality.

In the following narrative, Abu Nu'aym al-Isfahani reproduces a dialogue between two famous early Sufis, Abu al-Hasan al-Farghani and Abu Bakr al-Shibli (d. 945 CE). This narrative graphically illustrates the Sufi view of spirituality as an ethical journey of self-transformation based on a self-knowledge that results from an intimate knowledge of God:

> I asked Shibli, "What is the sign of one who knows God intimately (*'arif*)?" He said, "His breast is open, his heart bears wounds and his body is discarded [in the dust]." I said, "This is the sign of one who knows God intimately; who then is one who knows of God intimately?" He said, "He is one who knows God and His intent [for creation]; he acts in accordance with that which God commands and turns from that which God has forbidden, and he calls God's servants to God." Then I said, "This is a Knower of God, so who is a Sufi?" He responded, "He is one who has worked to purify his heart and has been purified; he has taken to the path of the Purified One (*al-Mustafa*) [Muhammad] and has cast the world behind him, making passion taste [the bitterness of] denial." So I said, "This is a Sufi, what is Sufism?" He said, "Being in harmony [with others], detachment, and avoidance of excess." I said, "Better than this, what is Sufism?" "It is submitting to the purification of the hearts at the hands of the All-Knowing of the Unseen." I said to him, "And better than this, what is Sufism?" He said, "Exalting God's command and compassion towards God's creatures." Then I said to him, "And better than this, what is a Sufi?" He said, "One who is clear of impurity, free of defilement, occupied with reflection; one for whom gold and clay are equal."[9]

THE SAINT-EXEMPLAR AS A TEACHER OF ETHICS

The key to understanding this process can be found within the basic sources of the Islamic intellectual tradition, the Qur'an and the Sunna.

To understand, however, the manner in which these two sources of Islamic thought relate to Islamic ethics, it is necessary to gain an insight into the examples afforded to us by the spiritual teachers or mentors of the Sufi path. These men and women, based upon Qur'anic terminology, are known as "Friends of God" (*awliya' Allah*). The stories of their lives, their teachings, and sayings have been preserved in the seminal works of Sufism. In his life, the Prophet Muhammad holistically exemplified the Qur'an[10] in such a way that he represented the foremost example of Islam for his community: "Indeed, in the Messenger of God you have the foremost example for the one who hopes for God's blessings, the Final Day and remembers God much" (Qur'an 33:21). The Friends of God represent within their own communities the highest aspirations and ideals of the Qur'anic and Prophetic models. Their role, didactic in nature, has long served to define Islamic spirituality. Herein lies their importance to our comprehension of Islamic ethics. The Friends of God are the embodiment of Islamic ethical teachings. They represent the fruit of such teachings and are a living testimony to the relevance of ethical conduct in daily life. They are mentors and teachers, who, by their example, restore their communities to the path of ethical conduct when people lose touch with the Qur'anic and Prophetic models. This role has earned them the high esteem in which they have been held in the traditional Islamic world. Their very presence in the community is considered a protection and a source of hope in the face of adversity. Their absence from a community is considered a sign that the community is turning away from God and His decrees.

The foundation of Sufi education is in compliance with the Qur'an and the Sunna, the example of the Prophet Muhammad. These two sources have long been considered the foundations of all religious knowledge and the keys to the direct and intimate knowledge of divine reality. In the early Sufi text *Darajat al-Sadiqin* (Stations of the Righteous), Abu 'Abd al-Rahman al-Sulami affirms the ethical nature of the journey he portrays for the disciple. He assures him that there is no path without the Qur'an and the traditions of the Prophet: "There can be no successful completion of the journey through the spiritual stations without a propitious beginning. He who has not founded his aspirant's journey upon the Qur'an and the Sunna of the Prophet will attain nothing of the knowledge of God."[11]

Submission to the religious law in Islam implies striving for perfect sincerity in the state of servanthood before God. This happens on two levels. On one level, it means perfecting servanthood outwardly as ethical conduct; on the other level, it means perfecting sincerity inwardly, as a set of ethical attitudes. In practice, this is accomplished by striving to imitate the Messenger of God through the Sunna, while never forgetting that in all spiritual states, the seeker is dependent on God. In a work dealing with the early Sufis of his native city of Nishapur, Sulami writes: "Among their tenets is that the state of servanthood is founded upon two essential things: the perfect awareness of one's total dependence upon God, and perfect imitation of the Messenger of God. In these the soul finds neither respite nor rest."[12]

Adherence to the Qur'anic and Prophetic models was more than a code of conduct; it provided the journeyer on the Sufi path with a means of conforming to the normative state in which God had originally created humanity, the *fitrat Allah*. From a Sufi perspective, this state mirrors God's intentions in the world. Ethical conduct thus becomes a means of conforming to God's will. Traditionally, the exemplar of ethical conduct within Islamic society was the Friend of God, for as a reflection of God's goal for humanity he or she represented what was most central to the spiritual life of the community. Peter Brown, writing on the role of the saint-exemplar in late antiquity, finds this same centrality within the context of Christianity. He defines the saint-exemplar as a "carrier of Christ," a figure who distilled in concrete and accessible form "central values and expectations." Brown also characterizes the relationship that binds the holy man as exemplar to his disciples as one of "esteem and love."[13] These perceptions of the saint-exemplar ring as true for traditional Islamic society as they do for the Christianity of late antiquity and go far in creating a common ground for understanding the spiritual realities and relationships that have long characterized the faith communities of humanity.

Just as the Qur'an and the Sunna manifest themselves through the saint-exemplar, the Sufi path, characterized by the pedagogic relationship between the mentor and the disciple, is a model of ethical comportment. This model relates directly to the Qur'anic and Prophetic models but goes beyond the prescriptive rules that are often associated with the idea of ethical conduct. The inclusive term for correct comportment in Arabic is *adab*.[14] Perfect *adab* is characterized as an attitude of complete detachment from one's individual inclinations and desires and a total commitment to self-effacement. For the Sufis, *adab* was the second of the two most important principles of spiritual transformation. It afforded the Sufi, so to speak, a "second wing" on his journey toward knowledge of God. In the following quotation by Sulami from *Darajat al-Sadiqin*, the perspective of *adab* as ethical comportment is well expressed:

> The comportment (*adab*) that brought them to this [initial] station [on the path] and this degree consists of their imposing upon themselves various spiritual exercises. Before this, they began with true repentance, perfect detachment, turning from all other than God, from the world and its occupants, the abandonment of all they own, distancing themselves from their personal inclinations, departure upon long journeys, denial of outward passionate desires, constant watchfulness over their inner mysteries, deference towards the masters of the Path, service to brethren and friends, giving preference to others over themselves in worldly goods, person and spirit, perseverance in [their] efforts, and regarding all their actions or states that may arise from them inwardly or outwardly with contempt and disdain.[15]

This passage reveals that as an inner attitude, *adab* is a norm of ethical conduct, although it is not directly derived from the Qur'anic and the Prophetic models. It comprises an inner dimension of ethical conduct that combines individual experience with the normative standards of self-evaluation that are central to the process of spiritual education. Normative ethical standards are a salient feature of Islamic ethics and have been characterized by some scholars as the rationale behind the religious disciplines. According to the Swedish Orientalist Tor Andrae, "The ethics of Islam consists of the observance of religious discipline."[16] Such conduct reflects the highest aspirations and values of Islamic society. Muslims see spiritual transformation as a central goal of their religious life. This attitude is not limited to an educated, urban elite. The Sufi teachings of Islam have had as much influence among the farmers and artisans of the Muslim world as they have had among the scholars.

Cultivating ethics in both its social and spiritual dimensions has far-reaching consequences. Inwardly, it is a means of counteracting the ego-self and its inclination toward pride, vanity, and self-satisfaction. Outwardly, ethical conduct occupies the ego-self with the demands of each moment in time, leaving it little time to indulge in momentary caprices. In the following quotation, Hamdun al-Qassar of Nishapur (d. 884 CE) stresses the all-inclusive nature of ethical comportment (*adab*): "Sufism is made up entirely of ethical comportment (*adab*); for each moment there is a correct comportment, for each spiritual station there is a correct comportment. Whoever is steadfast in maintaining the correct comportment of each moment, will attain spiritual excellence, and whoever neglects correct comportment, is far from that which he imagines near, and is rejected from where he imagines he has found acceptance."[17]

Journeying or traveling on the Sufi path (*suluk*) was thus a commitment to religious discipline in accord with the Qur'an and Sunna and submission to ethical conduct, both outwardly and inwardly. The goal of Sufi teaching was to infuse the ethical and spiritual comportment of the aspirant with an in inner understanding of each moment as God decreed it in the world. Thus the famous Sufi maxim, "The Sufi is the son of the moment." One's outward comportment was reflective of one's interior state. There could be no knowledge of God without ethically correct comportment and one's comportment could not be fully correct without a corresponding knowledge of God.

The saint-exemplar, the mentor, or "Man of God," is a key to the actualization of ethical comportment, as ethical comportment is a key to the actualization of knowledge of God. Finding a saint-exemplar is thus a major goal of the journeyer. The saint-exemplar's role vastly exceeds that of a "good example" or a "patron saint." As examples of ethical comportment, the "men of God" reflect an essential unity with all other saint-exemplars. In their very being, they reflect the inner unity that underlies outward diversity.

As Brown points out for early Christianity, " To be a 'Man of God' was to revive on the banks of the Nile all other 'men of God' in all other ages."[18]

The saint-exemplar is the key to the teachings he transmits; he is a sign of divine mercy for the journeyers on the path. In the following statement, Sulami accents the role of mercy as he describes the saint-exemplar, comparing his role in relation to his disciples with the role of the scholars of the Law in relation to the generality of believers:

[God] may reveal [the saint-exemplar] to people as an example and a refuge to which spiritual aspirants might turn in their quest of Him. In this, [God] permits the outward aspect [of the servant] to turn toward humanity as a mercy from Him to them. For were the saint's knowledge, character, and spiritual disciplines lost to them [referring to the aspirants], they would stray in their endeavor and their quest and fall into illusion. By the lights of these exemplars, their path is illuminated and by their counsel, they are rightly guided on their path to their goal. [Those among the saints who are returned to live with people] are the mentors of the aspirants to divine reality. They are the masters of hearts and lofty spiritual degrees. They are reference points for the travelers on the path, in them they find a guiding light and refuge. In the same manner, the generality of believers find a refuge in questions of law with the jurists.[19]

The saint-exemplar is the door through which the disciple passes on her way to God. Both while living and after death, these mentors are considered a means of realizing the fruits of the path to the knowledge of God. Thus, the memory of the saint-exemplars has been preserved after their deaths in the works of hagiography written on their lives and in the tombs and sacred precincts that so distinctly mark the landscape of Muslim lands. These tomb complexes continue to be visited today out of reverence for the saint-exemplars of the past and for the blessings that the faithful obtain in the spaces that are sanctified by their presence, where they taught, and where their teachings continue to be passed on from generation to generation. These sacred precincts are centers for spiritual transformation where Sufis meet to remember God, recite the Qur'an, and meditate. They often include hospices, schools, mosques, and soup kitchens for the poor and visitors. Such precincts draw men and women from all occupations. To the pilgrims, these precincts are locales of inner repose and peace, where, through the presence of the saint-exemplar, they experience God's proximity.

ZALAL AL-FUQARA': A TREATISE ON SUFI ETHICS

This section is an overview of a treatise on Sufi ethics by the tenth-century Sufi Abu 'Abd al-Rahman al-Sulami.[20] This text, a rich source of the teachings of the early saint-exemplars of Sufism, illustrates the centrality of the ethical teachings that Sufis derived from the Qur'an, the Sunna, and the tradition of *adab*. These values continue to resonate within Islamic society today. The full title of this work in translation is *The Stumbling of Those Who Aspire and the Ethical Comportment of the Folk Who Have Chosen Spiritual Poverty as Their Path*.[21] The shortened title of the work, *Zalal al-fuqara'*, means "The Stumbling of the Poor." *Faqir* (pl. *fuqara'*) is an Arabic term that for the Sufis referred to the practice of spiritual poverty (*faqr*). A *faqir* is a practitioner of spiritual poverty, and the term was often used as a synonym for "Sufi." For Sulami, all of the spiritual virtues admired by Sufis are contained in spiritual poverty. This is because spiritual poverty exemplifies the effacement of the ego-self that is central to the concept of *adab* as spiritual comportment: "This *faqr* or spiritual poverty is nothing other than a *vacare Deo*, an emptiness for God; it begins with the rejection of passions and its crown is the effacement of the 'I' before the Divinity. The nature of this virtue clearly shows the inverse analogy that links the human symbol with its divine archetype: what is emptiness on the side of the creature is plenitude on the side of the Creator." [22]

Zalal al-fuqara' is a work of formative Sufism by a spiritual mentor who emphasizes the ethical nature of spiritual conduct. The text's central theme is spiritual poverty (*faqr*), which from the Islamic perspective is an intrinsic attribute of all created beings and the active principle that underlies all ethical conduct. For Sulami, the prerequisite for the realization of *faqr* as a spiritual discipline was the realization of one's utter effacement before God. From the Sufi perspective, *faqr* is the spiritual attitude that resonates most distinctly with humanity's state of servanthood (*'ubudiyya*) before God. As stated in the Qur'an, the reason behind God's creation of humankind is servanthood: "I only created human beings and the *jinn* in order to serve me" (Qur'an 51:67). Servanthood and *faqr* relate to one another as do the two complimentary poles of *adab*, ethical conduct, on the one hand, and *akhlaq*, the inner awareness of morality and ethics, on the other hand. *Zalal al-fuqara'* is thus a practical guide to the Sufi way that relates human dispositions and inner attitudes to the outward aspects of ethical conduct.

In the Introduction to *Zalal al-fuqara'*, Sulami presents the fundamental precepts of spiritual poverty, which are derived from the Qur'anic concept of servanthood, humble submission to God's will. He reasons that utter need (*faqr*) is one of the traits of servanthood: a servant is capable of nothing on his own (Qur'an 16:75). In the state of servanthood, there is neither arrogance nor pride; therefore, anyone who claims a spiritual state or station for oneself is far from realizing true servanthood. In the remainder of the Introduction, Sulami discusses the norms of spiritual poverty and the accompanying ethical attitudes that are foundational to this mode of Sufi practice. These norms are founded upon an inward attitude of self-effacement and an outward commitment to serving others. The essence of spiritual poverty is to empty the innermost recesses of the soul of the world and all that is in it, while always being in a state of utter need for God. Sulami calls this state "praiseworthy *faqr*." From the practice's point of view, the disciple does

not abandon his daily profession, nor does he don a patched frock
(*muraqqaʿa*), nor does he flaunt his poverty. Such an outward show of
poverty reduces *faqr* to mere destitution, a state that is not fitting for those
who have found sufficiency in God. Rather, the true *faqir* passes unnoticed
among people: only those who are aware of his state know him (Qur'an
2:273). The true *faqir* makes his state of need known only to God. Humility
thus becomes an ethical precept that prevents the disciple from being
judgmental of others, for he regards all others as superior to himself. From
this perspective, anyone that finds satisfaction in one's own spiritual state or
pious act is only displaying gross ignorance.

Sulami then contrasts the true *faqir* to the pretender to poverty, the
deluded aspirant who forsakes the world and turns from it but condemns
those who follow worldly pursuits and regards other human beings with
scorn. Having thus elucidated the two poles of conduct in the practice of
poverty, Sulami then concludes his Introduction by affirming that true *faqr*
is to be attained only through inner detachment from the world and outer
commitment to the Shariʿa. Its incumbent attitudes are: reposing in God's
knowledge of one's state, sobriety, humility, relinquishing one's claims over
others, abandonment of one's natural inclinations, belittlement of oneself
while honoring others, nobility of character, detachment from worldly
sustenance, and reliance upon God, the One Who Suffices:

> One attains to the reality of *faqr* only after he enters therein by its principles and
> resides therein by its required comportment. Its precept of entry is to cast off all
> attachments [to outward things] from the innermost soul while putting formal
> religious knowledge into practice. The precepts of correct conduct [in *faqr*] are
> repose [in the knowledge that God knows our every state], sobriety, humility,
> preference of others over ourselves, relinquishing the self's claims, abandonment
> of natural inclinations, being disdainful of the self while honoring people, no
> bility of character, detachment from sustenance, and trust in the One Who
> Suffices, which is sincere reliance on His guarantee.[23]

In the body of *Zalal al-fuqara'*, Sulami discusses in detail the ethical
principles, attitudes, and corresponding modes of conduct that he dealt with
in general terms in the Introduction.[24] This treatise is a product of the
process of dialogue that went on between the textual sources of Islam and
the applied guidance of the saint-exemplars of Sufism. The nature of its discourse is interpretive, in that it contextualizes within a practical methodology
of inner and outer comportment the ethical ideals that are expressed in the
Qur'an and Hadith. Given the wealth of interpretive possibilities afforded
by these texts, it is not surprising to find in such works a preponderance of
Sufi sayings in comparison with the citations of the Qur'an and Hadith.
Sulami cites more than 60 narratives about the saint-exemplars of Sufism,
but only 10 Qur'anic verses and four Hadith texts. However, this apparent
imbalance does not reflect a lack of concern by Sulami for the centrality of
the Qur'an and the Sunna as sources of Islamic tradition.

The necessity of close compliance with the Qur'an and the Sunna is a theme that Sulami returns to repeatedly in his explication of the precepts of spiritual poverty. He writes, "The best [comportment] of a *faqir* is [his] ethical interaction with others, following the example of the Messenger of God in the Shari'a and actualizing intimate knowledge of God with regard to the Absolute Truth (*al-Haqq*)."[25] The following statement by Yahya ibn Mu'adh al-Razi (d. 864–865 CE), which is reproduced in Sulami's treatise, is representative of the way in which early Sufis based their ethical and devotional methods on practices outlined in the Prophetic Sunna. When asked at what point a *faqir* may claim to be truly on the path of Sufism, he replied:

> Not until he has prevailed over his ego-self in the following ways. He completely abandons the world, even while holding those who seek it in respect. At all times he is occupied with mandatory acts of devotion, devotional acts in the Sunna, or supererogatory acts. He is too preoccupied with his devotions to be concerned with whether he is accepted or rejected by others. He accumulates nothing. There is neither deceit in his heart nor malice toward any person and his devotions are not sullied by people's awareness of him. People's praise does not influence him and he would not slacken [in his devotions] were they to shun him.[26]

A salient aspect of *Zalal al-fuqara'* is the manner in which Sulami contextualizes the ethical ideals expressed in Islamic scripture within a framework of practical guidance that emphasizes the value of ethical practice. He cites Abu 'Uthman al-Hiri (d. 910 CE) as saying, "Ethical conduct is the mainstay of the poor in God (*faqir*) and the dignity of the wealthy in God (*ghani*)."[27] One of the results of ethical conduct is compassion and empathy for others who share the same trials and tribulations in life. According to the Sufi Abu 'Abdallah al-Jala' (d. 918 CE), "When a servant has realized the state of true *faqr*, he dons the raiment of contentment [in God], and in so doing increases his compassion for others, such that he conceals their faults, prays for them, and shows them mercy."[28]

For Sulami, the most essential inner attitude upon which ethical conduct is founded is disdain for the ego-self (*nafs*). Disdain for the ego-self and its abasement is a theme that has long been counted among the distinctive teachings of Sufism. This principle is well represented in *Zalal al-fuqara'*. Abu 'Uthman al-Hiri is reported as saying, "Everything that pleases the ego-self, be it obedience or disobedience, is passion (*shahwa*)."[29] Abu Ya'qub al-Nahrajuri (d. 941–942 CE) said: "Among the signs of the one whose state God has taken in hand is that he attests to the inadequacy of his sincerity, the heedlessness of his invocation, the imperfection of his truthfulness, the laxness of his discipline, and his lack of observance of what is required of spiritual poverty. Thus, all of his states are insufficient to him, both in his aspiration and in his [spiritual] journeying. He always feels his need for God until he is extinguished from all else but Him. For such a one, men's fortunes, as well as praise and blame have fallen away."[30]

The second distinctive trait of Sufi ethical practice for Sulami was the rejection of all pretensions to piety or advanced spiritual states. Disclaiming one's prerogative to special treatment is the foundation stone of service. Discussing this principle, Sulami writes: "It is obligatory for a sincere *faqir* to use the outward aspect of each of his moments to assist others, while not seeking assistance from them."[31] The disclaiming of all individual pretension is also an important step in the process of orienting oneself toward God. Abu 'Uthman al-Hiri said, "Fear of God will bring you to God, pride and self-satisfaction will sever you from God, and scorn for other people will afflict you with a disease for which there is no cure."[32] Among the fruits of avoiding spiritual pretentiousness was freedom from judging the states and acts of others. Addressing this issue, Hiri's disciple Mahfuz ibn Mahmud (d. 916 CE) said: "Whoever gives undue regard to the virtues of his own soul will be afflicted by the vices of people, but whoever looks to the faults of his soul will be freed from mentioning the vices of people."[33] Perhaps the most outstanding result of the Sufi disdain for pretentiousness was the flexibility it offered to traditional Islamic legal discourse. The following statement by Ruwaym (d. 915 CE), a revered Sufi of Baghdad, gives eloquent expression to this aspect of Sufi ethics: "Part of the wisdom of the *faqir* is in allowing a broad interpretation of the Law where his brothers are concerned, while enjoining strictness upon himself. This is because granting latitude to them is in accordance with religious teachings, while calling oneself to account assiduously is among the precepts of ethical accountability."[34]

If humility and self-effacement are inward consequences of disdain for the ego-self, an outward consequence would be a life of anonymity among the crowd, of hiding the true nature of one's inner states. For Sulami, this practice is another element in the process of spiritual transformation. He considered hiding one's inner states as a key to sincerity, which is a central principle of ethical conduct. In the following statement, he expresses the consequences of ostentation and through inverse reasoning demonstrates the necessity of anonymity in the realization of sincerity:

> Were a *faqir* to forsake an outward means of livelihood, he would surely be driven to importunity in seeking aid.[35] Were he to don the patched frock or show outward signs of spiritual poverty, he would likewise be showing importunity. Were he to make a show of his spiritual poverty before the wealthy, he would only show [his] esteem for the world and its place in his heart; for were there no esteem in his heart for the world, he would not flaunt his renunciation of it before others. Of such a one it has been said, "Verily, for one who esteems the world, God has no esteem."[36]

Among the consequences of hiding one's inner states is that an individual who attains true sincerity will have his awareness of a meritorious deed or state erased from his memory. He will thus be free of any compulsion to remember it. In the following quotation, Sulami narrates that his grandfather, the Sufi Isma'il ibn Nujayd (d. 976–977 CE), said: "The proof that one of your actions has not been accepted [by God] is that you come to take account of it. For that which is accepted is elevated and vanishes from sight. Not being aware of it is the sign of its having been accepted."[37] Even more indicative of the essential relationship between anonymity and the realization of true sincerity is the following statement by Ibn al-Jala', one of the most renowned mentors of the Sufi path in Iraq and Syria. When he was asked, "When is the *faqir* worthy of the name *faqir*?" He answered, "When there is no spiritual poverty left in him." Then he was asked, "How can this be?" To which he replied, "Were poverty his, it would not be 'his,' but were [poverty] not his, it would be 'his.'" [38]

Sulami concludes his discourse on spiritual poverty with a statement by Abu 'Ali al-Juzjani, one of the most illustrious Sufi teachers of Khurasan, the region that now comprises eastern Iran and Central Asia. Juzjani summarizes the distinguishing traits of the practitioners of spiritual poverty in a way that beautifully summarizes the balance between inner attitudes and outer behaviors that characterizes the Sufi approach to ethics:

> Obedience to God is their sweetness. Love of God is their companion. God is their need and He is their protector. Righteousness is their nature. With God is their commerce. Upon Him they depend. With Him is their intimacy, and in Him is their confidence. Hunger is their nourishment, nakedness their dress, renunciation their gain, ethical comportment their discerning trait, humility their disposition, and an open smiling face their adornment. Generosity is their profession, intimate fellowship is their companionship, the intellect is their leader, patience is their driving force, and abstinence is their provision. The Qur'an is their speech, gratitude is their ornament, the invocation of God is their yearning, contentment [with God] is their repose, and sufficiency is their treasure. Worship is their profession, Satan is their enemy, the world is their refuse heap, modesty is their garment, and fear is their natural temperament. The night is their meditation, the day is their reflection, wisdom is their sword, and the Truth is their guardian. Life is their path, death is their home, the grave is their citadel, and the Day of Judgment is their feast. [To stand] before God is their most ardent desire. In the shade of The Throne is their gathering-place. *Firdaws*[39] is their dwelling and the vision of God is the object of their yearning.[40]

The main body of *Zalal al-fuqara'* sustains the complementarity of interior attitudes and ethical conduct that Sulami outlined in his Introduction. The aspirant on the path to ethical excellence is self-effaced in his attitudes and conduct; he makes no claims to spiritual authority, nor does he seek personal satisfaction from his states or deeds of piety. In contrast, a pretentious man vies for worldly renown owing to his own inflated view of his piety. He thus falls from the path of seekers of sincerity and enters the path of the indigent and the destitute. This section of the text is rich in the teachings of Khurasan, Sulami's home region. Throughout this work Sulami opens a window onto a spiritual tradition that is as fresh today as it was in his own time, over 900 years ago.

The final sections of *Zalal al-fuqara'* comprise one of the most concise and eloquently written expositions of Sufi ethics that has been preserved in the rich heritage of Sufi literature. This section of the treatise is conspicuously lacking in citations of any kind. Here we encounter Sulami, the teacher and mentor, who has a unique ability to situate the subject of his discourse within a synthetic vision of the Sufi path. The passages of this section are derived from an earlier work by Sulami, *Suluk al-'arifin* (The Wayfaring of the Gnostics). In this work, Sulami depicts the various stages of the process of spiritual transformation from the point of view of the aspirant as he journeys toward his goal, the intimate knowledge of the Absolute (*al-Haqq*). As in *Zalal al-fuqara'*, spiritual poverty is essential to the process of finding God. In the final section of *Zalal al-fuqara'*, Sulami reiterates that the actualization of true spiritual poverty is extremely difficult to attain, for it is the spiritual state of the Prophet Muhammad himself. However, citing the Qur'an and the Hadith, he assures his reader that one who sincerely commits oneself to the process of spiritual transformation, and who sincerely orients oneself according to the compass of ethical conduct, will eventually attain the desired goal. "Anyone who patterns his life in the manner we have described and searches his soul for sincerity will be granted the blessing of truly realizing this way. The Most High has said: 'As for those who strive in Us, We surely guide them to Our Paths' (Qur'an 29:69). The Prophet—may the peace and blessings of God be upon him—said, "He who acts upon what he knows, God will endow him with what he does not know."

In his introduction to *Saints and Virtues,* John Stratton Hawley wrote, "Within each religion a powerful body of tradition emphasizes not codes but stories, not precepts but personalities, not lectures but lives."[41] In Islam, Sufism comprises such a body of tradition. The earliest traditions of Sufism define its method as a way of ethical conduct, *akhlaq*. The writings of Sufis in the formative period of the tradition clearly articulate that ethical conduct was practiced within the contexts of individual reorientation toward and a process of spiritual transformation. Transformation and change are inherent to the human state. The mentors and saint-exemplars of Sufism, as inter-preters of the Qur'an and the Sunna of the Prophet Muhammad, have since the earliest times provided their communities with guidance of how to achieve spiritual transformation. Ethical conduct, as exemplified in the figure of the saint-exemplar, has played a major role in defining the ideals and values of Islamic society from the earliest days of the community. A central tenet of Islamic spirituality is the process of individual transformation and reorienta-tion of the ego-self that accords with the foundational sources of the tradi-tion. The degree to which a person is a participant in this process depends on the degree to which he or she can participate in the ethical formation that was the mainstay of this process. Sufism, through its saint-exemplars, provided Islamic society with the axis around which the process of ethical development could be actualized on both the individual and the social level.

NOTES

1. For a good collection of early sayings defining Sufism, see T. Frank, "'Tasawwuf is...' On a Type of Mystical Aphorism," *Journal of the American Oriental Society* 104.1 (1984).

2. Abu 'Abd al-Rahman al-Sulami, *Tabaqat al-sufiyya*, ed. Nur al-Din Shurayba (Cairo: Maktabat al-Khanji, 1969), 167.

3. Abu al-Qasim al-Qushayri, *al-Risala al-Qushayriyya*, eds. Ma'ruf Zurayq and 'Ali 'Abd al-Majid Baltaji (Beirut: Dar al-Khayr, 1993), 271.

4. Abu Nasr al-Sarraj al-Tusi, *Al-Luma'*, ed. 'Abd al-Halim Mahmud and Taha 'Abd al-Baqi Surur (Cairo: Dâr al-Kutub al-Haditha, 1960), 45.

5. Abu Nu'aym al-Isfahani, *Hilyat al-awliya' wa tabaqat al-asfiya'* (Beirut: Dar al-Kutub al-'Ilmiyya, 1997), 55.

6. For more on the life of Ibn 'Ajiba see Ahmed Ibn 'Ajiba, *The Autobiography* (Fahrasa) *of a Moroccan Sufi: Ahmad Ibn 'Ajiba,* translated from the Arabic by Jean-Louis Michon, translated from the French by David Streight (Louisville, Kentucky: Fons Vitae, 1999).

7. Ahmad Ibn 'Ajiba, *Mi'raj al-tashawwuf ila haqa'iq al-tasawwuf,* in *Kitab sharh salat al-Qutb Ibn Mashish,* ed. 'Abd al-Salam al-'Imrani (Casablanca: Dar al-Rashad al-Haditha, 1999), 69.

8. Ibn 'Ajiba, *Sharh salat Ibn Mashish,* 29–30.

9. Abu Nu'aym al-Isfahani, *Hilyat al-awliya',* 55; this quotation is also cited by T. Frank, "*Tasawwuf* Is..." 76, translation by the present author.

10. When the Prophet's wife 'A'isha was asked about the ethical conduct of the Prophet, she responded: "The ethical conduct of the Messenger of God was the Qur'an." *Sahih Muslim* (746), "The Chapter of the Traveler's Prayer," sub-section: "Joining the Night Prayer."

11. Abu 'Abd al-Rahman al-Sulami, *Darajat al-sadiqin* in *Three Early Sufi Texts: Stations of the Righteous,* trans. Kenneth Honerkamp (Louisville, Kentucky: Fons Vitae, 2003), 127.

12. Abu 'Abd al-Rahman al-Sulami, *Risalat al-Malamatiyya,* ed. Abu al-'Ala 'Afifi (Cairo: Dar Ihya' al-Kutub al-'Arabiyya, 1945), 111.

13. Peter Brown, "The Saint as Exemplar in Late Antiquity," in *Saints and Virtues,* ed. John Stratton Hawley (Berkeley and Los Angeles, California: University of California Press, 1987), 9.

14. *Adab* is a term that has been used with a wide range of meanings, including correct beliefs, rules of conduct, and customs. For a survey of these meanings, see F. Garbrieli, "Adab," *EI 2,* vol. 1, 175–176. Treatises dealing with the *adab* of the Sufis have existed from the earliest eras of Islamic literature. For a detailed account of Sufi *adab* literature, see Etan Kohlberg's edition of Sulami's *Jawami' adab al-sufiyya,* (Jerusalem, 1976) 10–13. One of the best known Prophetic traditions on

the subject of *adab* was transmitted by Sulami in this work: "According to Shaqiq (al-Balkhi), according to 'Abdallah (ibn Mas'ud), the Messenger of God said: "God had instilled *adab* within me and has perfected it within me, for He commanded me to observe noble conduct, saying: "Be clement. Command the good and turn away from the ignorant" (Qur'an 7:199), 3. Muhyiddin ibn 'Arabi (d. 1240 CE) the Andalusian mystic and renowned teacher whose writings have greatly influenced Sufism, distinguishes four types of *adab: Adab* of the Law (*adab al-Shari'a*), *Adab* of Service (*adab al-khidma*), *Adab* of Right, (*adab al-haqq*), and *Adab* of Essential Reality (*adab al-haqiqa*). See Denis Gril, "*Adab* and Revelation, One of the Foundations of the Hermeneutics of Ibn 'Arabi," in *Muhyiddin Ibn 'Arabi: A Commemorative Volume,* ed. Stephen Hirtenstein and Michael Tieran (Shaftesbury, Dorset and Rockport, Massachusetts: Element Books, 1993), 228–263.

15.   Sulami, *Darajat al-sadiqin* in *Three Early Sufi Texts,* 120.

16.   Tor Andrae, *In the Garden of Myrtles: Studies in Early Islamic Mysticism,* trans. Birgitta Sharpe (Albany, New York: State University New York Press, 1987), 36.

17.   Sulami, *Tabaqat al-sufiyya,* 119.

18.   Brown, "The Saint as Exemplar," 11.

19.   Sulami, *Darajat al-sadiqin* in *Three Early Sufi Texts,* 126–127.

20.   On the life and works of Sulami, see Nur al-Din Shurayba's Introduction to *Tabaqat al-Sufiyya,* 11–47; Gerhard Böwering, "The *Qur'an* Commentary of al-Sulami," in *Islamic Studies Presented to Charles J. Adams,* eds. Wael B. Hallaq and Donald P. Little, (Leiden and New York: E.J. Brill, 1991), 41–56; Rkia Cornell's Introduction to Abu 'Abd ar-Rahman as-Sulami, *Early Sufi Women:* Dhikr an-niswa al-muta'abbidat as-sufiyyat (Louisville, Kentucky: Fons Vitae, 1999), 31–43; J. Thibon, "Hiérarchie spirituelle, fonctions du saint et hagiographie dans l'oeuvre de Sulamî," *in Le Saint et son Milieu,* eds. R. Chih and Denis Gril, Cahier des Annales Islamologiques (Cairo : Institut Français d'Archéologie Orientale, 2000), 13–31.

21.   For a complete translation of this work, see Sulami, *Darajat al-sadiqin* in *Three Early Sufi Texts,* 126–127.

22.   Titus Burckhardt, *An Introduction to Sufi Doctrine* (Lahore, Pakistan: Sh. Mohammad Ashraf, 1991 reprint), 110.

23.   Sulami, *Zalal al-fuqara'* in *Three Early Sufi Texts,* 132.

24.   Ibid., 132–149.

25.   Ibid., 143.

26.   Ibid., 138.

27.   Ibid., 144.

28.   Ibid., 135.

29.   Ibid., 132.

30.   Ibid., 141.

31.   Ibid., 140.

32.   Ibid., 144.

33.   Ibid., 145.

34.   Ibid., 144.

35.   The Arabic root of the verb used in this passage (*lahafa*) means, "to request or demand urgently," to solicit in such a manner that one makes a display of one's

state of need. For the Sufis, to manifest a state of need to other than for God was seen as unseemly.

36. Sulami, *Zalal al-fuqara'* in *Three Early Sufi Texts*, 130.

37. Ibid., 136.

38. Ibid., 134.

39. *Firdaws* is a synonym for Paradise. It is referred to twice in the Qur'an (18:107 and 23:11). See Duncan B. Macdonald, "Firdaws," in *Shorter Encyclopaedia of Islam*, eds. H.A.R. Gibb and J.H. Kramer (1953 repr., Ithaca, New York: Cornell University Press, 1974), 108.

40. Sulami, *Zalal al-fuqara'* in *Three Early Sufi Texts*, 147.

41. John Stratton Hawley, Introduction to *Saints and Virtues*, ed. John Stratton Hawley (Los Angeles, California: University of California Press, 1987), xi.

15

ISLAM AND BUSINESS

·

Abdulkader Thomas

Do not consume one another's wealth unjustly, be aware that lawful gain should be only through business based on mutual consent among you, and do not destroy one another.

(Qur'an 4:29)

The Prophet Muhammad, may peace be upon him, was a merchant. As a young man, he earned the nickname *al-Amin,* "The Trustworthy," for his conduct when entrusted with the business of others. On the one hand, this prophetic legacy meant that Muslims have always found honor in trade. On the other hand, Islam has established a well-developed juristic tradition governing commerce. This tradition is bounded by a concern for the believer's eternal soul. The moment trade engages in what is forbidden or opens a door that may lead to such a direction, more than just profits and losses are concerned. The Prophet Muhammad, may God's peace and blessings be upon him, said: "The lawful is self-evident and the unlawful is self-evident. However, between the two are matters that may give rise to confusion, because they are not well understood by many people. He who guards against doubtful things keeps his religion and his honor blameless, but he who indulges in doubtful things actually indulges in unlawful things."[1]

Because of such concerns, Islam imposes on Muslims rules and regulations relating to such matters as how to draw up a contract, what actions render a contract invalid, and the obligation to think of the greater social welfare in one's business dealings. Although Islam first emerged in the Arabian Peninsula, Muslims rapidly found themselves trading widely beyond their frontiers and engaging in commerce in three continents. Each new market brought with it new customs, new ideas, and new tests for the application of Islamic concepts. Until today, these challenges have required fresh investigations into the nature of Qur'anic dictates and the teachings embodied in the Prophetic Sunna. The research required to explore new Islamic responses to modern business practices is not conducted in a vacuum. In the words of the Sudanese scholar Mohammad Adam El-Sheikh, "New research should seek to meet the needs of contemporary life in light of the critical evaluation of modern experience."[2] For instance, the Shari'a as it is traditionally understood does not accommodate the corporation, which is conceived legally as a fictitious person, with rights and duties similar to that of a natural person.[3] However, all Western law codes do so. This and a variety of other legal and organizational matters pertinent to changes in global commerce require high-quality research into authentic Islamic resources in order to identify permissible commercial outcomes for the devout Muslim with respect to relevant transactions and structures. In this chapter, we examine the evolving consensus of modern Islamic scholars on the core methods of commerce within the underlying legal framework of the Shari'a. We will also look into the challenges that Muslims face in applying and understanding the Shari'a in commerce.

THE PURPOSES OF THE SHARI'A (*MAQASID AL-SHARI'A*)

Commerce is a way to improve our lives in the most basic of manners. The exchange of our surpluses, whether in money, commodities, or skills, in a mutually satisfying way allows both parties to feel that commerce has made their lives more complete. A Muslim, however, remembers that true compliance with the Shari'a means that the satisfaction of one's desires in this life may only be achieved by keeping in mind one's eternal life. Hence, the Muslim generally seeks to understand how to be guided by the Shari'a and accepts this guidance in the context of the Shari'a's purposes: "The aim of Shari'ah is to make people happier in this world and the Hereafter."[4]

For this reason, the Shari'a embodies a concept called *taysir,* which means, "making things easier." *Taysir* relates closely to the concept of the removal of hardship (*raf' al-haraj*). Such important objectives of the Shari'a are meant to assure that faith is not made distasteful by excessive or unnecessary rules and regulations in the believer's life. When it comes to commerce, these twin concepts have an inherent complementarity. Business allows for the removal of many hardships from our lives. One merely needs to examine a modern kitchen in a developed country to understand how commerce has delivered greater ease to a homemaker than could ever have been imagined by the homemaker's great-grandparents. Even in the poorest countries, commerce and the innovation stimulated by commerce have delivered modest efficiencies in the preparation of meals. Such improvements in the lives of homemakers allow them more time to devote to the care of their children, religion, or work. Is this not what is meant by making things easier or removing hardships?

The Hadith compiler Tirmidhi reported that God told the Prophet Muhammad, "You have been sent in order to make things easy, not to make them difficult."[5] An important anecdote tells of the opposition to television in the Kingdom of Saudi Arabia. In the face of ultraconservative opposition, King Faisal of Saudi Arabia pointed out two great benefits of the new invention. On the one hand, it could be used to transmit religious knowledge. On the other hand, television could be a tool to advise people of impending danger or important news. The concepts of "making things easy" and "removing hardship" are cornerstones of the concept of public interest (*maslaha*) in Islamic law. Thus, a pious Muslim businessman is necessarily bound by a sense of what the public good is in this life and how one's actions have consequences that affect others in their daily lives and may even affect one's own prospects for the afterlife.

Islam denies its adherents the opportunity to secularize personal behavior. One cannot manage a liquor store from Saturday through Thursday and devote Friday to prayer and charity. The believer is obliged to seek knowledge of what is permissible and not permissible in Islam and to have at least a rudimentary knowledge of the Shari'a rules that govern business life. Most important, the Muslim should know that it is wrong to sell or facilitate the sale of what is forbidden in Islam, such as liquor, or to obscure the essence or important elements of a transaction.

A Muslim must have a rudimentary understanding of the theological and philosophical underpinnings of the Shari'a, as these govern one's eternal life. The first principle of Islamic theology is *tawhid,* acceptance of the oneness of God. This is the most stringent approach to monotheism and constitutes the fundamental message of the Qur'an. Adherence to "Tawhidic" theology means that the Muslim accepts the rules established by God and His Messenger, the Prophet Muhammad, may peace be upon him. These rules seek to define the Tawhidic lifestyle and protect the most important values relating to this life, namely, human life, human intellect, property, honor, and conscience.[6] The safeguarding, in order of priority, of these five values allows each human being to live a quality of life in which she is free to exercise her conscience and worship God in the most uninhibited and loving manner. The protection of these five values leads to two clear principles that are repetitive themes in the conscience of the Muslim businessperson. First, within the specific framework of the Shari'a, the individual has substantial freedom of choice in almost every aspect of life, including commerce. Second, personal property may be freely held, sold, or traded.[7] These principles help give clarity to the notion of the goals or objectives (*maqasid*) of the Shari'a.

An understanding of the objectives of the Shari'a leads one to understand why Islamic law gives considerable leeway for the exercise of discretion or permissibility (*ibaha*). This is a defining principle of the law of interpersonal relations (*mu'amalat*) and commerce in Islamic jurisprudence. The Muslim businessperson is obliged to pay attention to the details of a contract.

However, she can find comfort in the opinion of the classical Islamic scholar Ibn Taymiyya (d. 1328 CE) about the permissibility of contracts. For Ibn Taymiyya, nothing was forbidden unless God and His Messenger had decreed it to be so. This principle allows considerable latitude in drawing up new types of contracts that reflect changing economic conditions: "God Most High has never prohibited a contract in which there is a benefit for the Muslims and does not inflict any harm upon them."[8] Modern juridical scholars such as Mohammad Hashim Kamali have taken this statement by Ibn Taymiyya to mean that there is no need to seek affirmative evidence in the scriptural sources to declare a transaction valid, so long as one has taken care to observe the basic rules of what one may buy and sell, and the general terms of contracts.[9]

SPECIAL OBLIGATIONS OF STEWARDSHIP

The freedom that Islam gives to the practice of commerce and the drawing up of contracts is bounded by the Qur'anic notion of the human being as *khalifa*, God's warden or trustee of the created world. According to this notion, businesspeople have a broader obligation than just the profit motive. Like other morally conscious human beings, the businessperson must consider the impact of his actions on all aspects of creation. Not only must the objectives of the Shari'a be protected, but the stewardship with which God has charged us also enjoins us to prevent waste (*israf*).[10] When the believer's obligation of stewardship is combined with the obligation to prevent waste, one finds that a Muslim businessperson is obliged to share the concerns underpinning many modern, secular movements of planetary reform, such as those to protect the environment, to defend wildlife, and to understand the ethical implications of genetic modifications. Such global thinking may be nontraditional, but it is fully in accordance with the message of the Qur'an.

God's infinite wisdom leads us to practice mercy, for human beings find it difficult to avoid exaggeration when selling, negotiating profits to an unnecessary degree, and taking shortcuts with their responsibilities when engaged in industry and commerce. This human inclination to overdo things in a way that may cause noncriminal harm is checked to a certain extent by the Qur'anic prescription of *Zakat*, the "purifying" tax on wealth that must be paid by every Muslim. These purifying dues are a balancing feature that reminds the Muslim of his role as custodian or steward of God's creation. Since wealth and the ownership of property are bestowed on us only temporarily, we are obliged to manage such benefits in a way that is beneficial to all, without causing harm.[11] The petty harms that businesspeople and others find so difficult to avoid require a direct and simple form of purification. *Zakat* "purifies" the giver by providing a social outlet for the wealth that one accumulates. This tax is paid only by those with a minimum level of wealth and is assessed in most cases as a 2.5 percent tax on such wealth.

The Zakat tax must be paid every year, even if it means selling assets to free cash for the payment of Zakat. However, this wealth tax is not meant to burden those in severe financial difficulty and who may be unable to afford a home or cannot sustain themselves and their families. The practice of Zakat has a number of complicated rules for those who are actively engaged in commerce or agriculture. These rules are the subject of substantial treatises and allow for business and agricultural managers to make specific decisions that may increase or decrease the amount of Zakat that is due. For instance, the Zakat on a herd of animals is different from that on a crop, which must be stored for significant periods. Also, the Zakat on inventory held for sale is different from that on equipment that is leased or supplies used in the ordinary course of business operations.

A rather intriguing phenomenon is the behavior of individuals residing in countries where Zakat is formally collected by the state. These persons may seek to reduce as much as possible the amount to be collected by the state for diverse reasons. They may fear that the state will not spend Zakat funds in a Qur'anically mandated manner. Or, they may prefer to direct their Zakat payments to a charity chosen by them. As with tax management strategies in a nonreligious environment, there is no Islamic restriction on structuring one's business to minimize one's taxes within the law. However, the same Muslim businesspeople who try to reduce their Zakat payments are often substantial donors to charities. The reduction of the Zakat obligation does not reduce their desire to help others in need. Therefore, they may engage in additional, nonmandatory acts of charity (*Sadaqa*). This term is derived from an Arabic root word meaning "truthful" or "righteous." The Qur'an encourages *Sadaqa*, whether given openly or secretly, as an important, self-imposed obligation for those who have succeeded in commerce.

Sadly, one of the results of the horrific attacks of September 11 has been the so-called War on Terror in which charitable contributions made by Muslims are called into question by various Western governments. The abuse of some charities by supporters of terrorism has tainted one of the most profound religious obligations in Islam. Two trends have evolved in response to these allegations, one of which is not to anyone's benefit. Many donors now feel it necessary to give their charity secretly and in cash, making it more easy for criminals to abuse the Zakat and *Sadaqa* obligations. A second response has developed whereby major Muslim businesspeople, Islamic charities, and governments have partnered to assure that transparent and auditable donations are made legitimately to lawful charities serving the needy. This latter approach is increasingly recognized by Muslim businesspeople as the only way to both fulfill their obligations to help the needy and assure that the architects of the War on Terror do not find a way to make it into a War on Islam.

ETHICAL INVESTMENT IN ISLAM AND THE WEST

Many of the limitations on investment that Muslim businesspeople embrace are similar to approaches that are becoming common in many
Western markets and in some developing economies. These are the ethical
business, finance, and investing movements, which are gaining popularity
around the world. As a result, it should not be surprising that Islamic and
Western ethical approaches to investment have strong parallels. The Shari'a
sets specific standards for commercial interaction and the avoidance of
sinful behavior. Whether or not Muslims have fully lived up to Qur'anic
standards, the ethical component of business life is seen as increasingly
important. Rodney Wilson, a leading analyst of global investment trends,
has compared the charters of Islamic banks and ethically focused conventional banks and has found a convergence between the two.[12] However,
there are differences between the Islamic and ethical business movements.
For example, the concern not to overinnovate when applying Islamic law
and the focus on correct contractual form have kept Muslims from understanding the spirit of ethical finance. Many Muslims are concerned about
the methods of transacting such investments, the sources of their funds,
and the quality of juristic opinions about these matters. Beyond Zakat
and voluntary charity, the medieval Islamic concept of the charitable
foundation or endowment (*waqf*) has yet to be adapted to modern conditions in the Islamic finance movement. Although Jordan and Bangladesh
have explored innovative means to fund and expand such endowments, this
subsegment of financial activity remains underdeveloped in modern Muslim
societies.

One of the great achievements to take place in ethical investing in a Muslim
country is the refinement of micro-finance by the Grameen Bank of
Bangladesh. This has been a curious development because Grameen's value
orientation is more in line with classical capitalism, although it has been
adapted to local social values. In recent years, a more authentically Islamic
alternative was developed by Islami Bank Bangladesh and is now widely
emulated by many Muslim institutions in Africa, Asia, and the Middle East.
The differences between the Grameen Bank and Islami Bank models reflect
the desire of Muslims to operate in an interest-free environment and to offer
services in a manner that is in accord with more traditional Islamic family
values, such as empowering the male head of a household to exercise his financial responsibilities as implied in the Qur'an. This approach imposes upon the
male head of household the obligation to provide for younger family
members, mothers, sisters, and others who are deemed to require care and
protection. In the Shari'a, this seemingly paternalistic approach grants the
so-called weaker members of a household a legal claim on the "stronger"
member. However, even under Islamic law, women who are financially

independent or who have resources sufficient for investment are allowed to invest their resources as they wish.

SOURCES OF COMMERCIAL LAW IN ISLAM

The nature of rights and obligations in the Qur'an and the Shari'a is based upon the capacity of different parties to fulfill their obligations or properly claim their rights. In many cases, the Shari'a must take into account different circumstances and conditions. Commerce finds three spheres of application of the Shari'a: (1) ethical and moral guidance for the businessperson, (2) resolution of disputes, (3) rules and regulations that govern money. Qur'anic verses that make precise injunctions and offer specific guidance are called *ayat al-ahkam*, "verses of legal rulings." With regard to commerce, three fundamental injunctions are established by the *ayat al-ahkam:* (1) the prohibition of *riba*, (2) the prohibition of inappropriate consumption of wealth, and (3) the requirement of written contracts.[13]

Since much Qur'anic legislation on commerce is of a general nature, Muslims also turn to the authentic sayings and reports of the Prophet Muhammad. Collectively, these traditions are termed the Sunna. The source for this term is a hadith of the Prophet that says, "Follow my Sunna...and that of the rightly guided caliphs who will succeed me. Hold onto it firmly and guard yourself against innovation, for every innovation is mischief."[14] The early Muslims qualified the reliability of the Hadith through a process of critical inquiry:

> Since the *hadith* was passed verbally from one generation to another, the science of *rijal* was developed for the critical examination of the life-histories and the trustworthiness of the hadith transmitters. The narrator of a hadith, for instance, ought to state his source. If the source was not an original companion of the Prophet, the narrator had to state the secondary source from which he received the hadith. Each hadith, therefore, had to be prefixed by a chain of narrators of authorities, *sanad,* that went back to the original narrator. This process was called *isnad* (unbroken chain of transmission).
>
> The method of criticism which the scholars of hadith followed helped them in discovering the degree of accuracy of a particular transmitter of a particular hadith. Jurisprudentially speaking, there are many restrictions for considering a hadith suitable to furnish the ground for a legal precept. Jurists categorized Sunna into two major categories: *maqbul* (accepted) and *mardud* (rejected). The accepted Sunna is divided into two groups: *sahih* (authentic) and *hasan* (agreeable). The vast majority of jurists regard the first category as the only valid part of the *Sunna* for serving legitimate grounds for law.[15]

Although some scholars believe that the Hadith are subject to controversy, the rigor of Hadith analysis has meant that the core body of the Sunna has been free from controversy since the ninth century of the Common Era. Although matters of worship are highly detailed within the Sunna, matters of commerce are less detailed. Of less weight than the Hadith are the *athar*, the sayings of the Companions and immediate generations following the Prophet, may peace be upon him. Accepted *athar* are seen as supplementary traditions that illuminate the Hadith and provide evidence of practices that were observed or tolerated during the Prophet Muhammad's lifetime.

According to Dr. El-Sheikh, Islamic jurisprudence (*fiqh*) is the exercise of intelligence to solve practical problems in the absence of a specific command from the Qur'an or the Sunna. The practice of *fiqh* requires intelligence and independent judgment.[16] Whereas the Qur'an and the Sunna are the primary sources of law, Islamic tradition embraces other forms of legislation and practical guidance as well. However, this exercise of human discretion is limited. According to the noted Islamic scholar Seyyed Hossein Nasr, "Divine law is an objective transcendent reality, by which man and his actions are judged, not vice versa.... To attempt to shape the Divine law to the 'times' is, therefore, no less than spiritual suicide because it removes the very criteria by which the real value of human life and action can be objectively judged and thus surrenders man to the most infernal impulses of his lower nature."[17]

However, in practical terms, says Dr. Fathi Osman, "Legal rules in the Qur'an and Sunna are limited in number, although they cover extensive areas of life. Many of these rules offer general principles and guidelines. Justice is ordained for essentially all human activities: in family, in business, in the whole society, between rulers and the ruled, and in all universal relations in general. In the field of transactions, for example, the Qur'an and Sunna emphasize the essential requirements for mutual consent for any contract and the prohibition of exploitation, fraud and usury."[18]

Most historians of Islamic law state that *ijma'*, the consensus of the jurists, is the third source of legislation in Islam. In reality, however, the proper term is *ijtihad*, literally, the "struggle" to apply the law in specific cases. One may consider *ijtihad* to be the third source of legislation because it is the result of either individual scholarly effort or collective scholarly and juristic analysis.[19] This latter, collective form of *ijtihad* is *ijma'*. The areas in which *ijtihad* operates include analogical reasoning (*qiyas*), juridical preference (*istihsan*), public welfare (*istislah*), and custom (*'urf*).[20] The purpose of *ijtihad* is to make life easier within the bounds of the permissible (the concept of *taysir* discussed above), to protect the public interest, to eliminate hardship (the concept of *raf' al-haraj* discussed above), and to address the issue of necessity in the context of meeting the objectives of the Shari'a.[21]

Certain forms of contract are not in general agreement with the accepted principles of contract in the Shari'a. However, it is through juristic preference, giving way over time to consensus, that such contracts are permitted.[22] For instance, some Muslim jurists worry about the lack of commercial trust among obligors and allow the assessment and collection of penalty interest so long as it is given to charity. This modern issue reflects a unique intersection between the Qur'anic ban on interest and the fear that Muslims do not currently live up to the standards of morality mandated by the Qur'an and the Sunna. Since the amount paid as a penalty may not be taken as a profit, modern jurists who exercise their juridical preference in this matter oblige the recipients of penalty interest to donate these funds on behalf of the defaulting borrower to a charity of the borrower's choice. Other scholars are not comfortable with this approach, but they have not voiced outrage or deep opposition to this practice because they find that there may be an overriding public benefit (*istislah*) to it.

Customary usage (*'urf*) is also accepted as a basis for rulings and judgments, provided it does not contravene or contradict Islamic values and principles.[23] For instance, when we examine Islamic mortgage alternatives, we learn that one provider has secured a ruling allowing a shareholder to pay real estate taxes on the property, even though she is not the primary or majority owner of the property. This is consistent with local usage and is justified in that the real estate taxes inure almost exclusively to the benefit of the consumer. The systematic study of modern commercial legislation in the West and its applicability to the objectives of Islamic law have begun only recently. This fact was pointed out by Yusuf DeLorenzo in a paper delivered before the International Islamic Financial Standards Board: "In the classical system, custom (*'urf*) played an important role. The legal maxim that 'all transactions are to be considered lawful as long as they include nothing that is prohibited' went hand in hand with custom and mercantile practice in clearing the way for innovation in trade and commerce. However, when the Shariah boards of the modern Islamic banks began their work in the 70's, there was no significant Shariah-compliant trade taking place, and thus no customary practice in regard to it."[24] In matters of *ijtihad*, once the collectivity of Muslim scholars (*ulama*) have formed a consensus about the soundness of an interpretation on a point of law, the differing opinions of one or a few scholars are not sufficient to overturn or invalidate the consensus.

Inductive reasoning by analogy (*qiyas*) is not popular with some modern Muslims as a means of determining legal precepts.[25] However, an authentic hadith of the Prophet Muhammad reports the verbal instructions of the Prophet to Mu'adh ibn Jabal when he was appointed as governor of Yemen. The Prophet asked how he would determine affairs. Mu'adh replied that he would first turn to the Book of God; if he could not find the answer there, he would apply the Sunna of the Prophet; and if he could not find an answer there, then he said, "I shall decide according to my own opinion." The Prophet was pleased with his answer, for it meant that Mu'adh's opinion would be an informed one. Mu'adh's appointment was confirmed and with it the acceptance of reasoning (*qiyas*) as a means of legislating practical matters in Islam.[26] As DeLorenzo summarizes: "It is the nature of Islamic jurisprudence itself to insist on the freedom of qualified jurists to formulate and hold their own opinions. In fact, the inner dynamic for renewal known as *ijtihad* ensures the relevance of Islamic law to changing circumstances by empowering jurists to constantly revisit points of law and to improve upon them when and where necessary."[27]

Ijtihad is the most flexible interpretive tool that Muslims can apply in their continuous reinterpretation of authentic scriptural texts.[28] However, the flexibility available to Muslims in commerce means that they should not lean too heavily upon *ijtihad* as a tool to seek rulings that help them achieve goals that push the outer limits of what the Shari'a permits. Especially since determinations made under this approach are susceptible to modification or replacement by a future interpretation.[29]

Consensus (*ijma'*) is as much an outcome as a source of juristic principle. Once the community of jurists are in broad agreement about the *ijtihad* of one or more of their members—the *qiyas* of a qualified scholar, the public benefit that comes from an action or application of a rule, or the validity of a custom—then their common commitment to such a decision constitutes *ijma'*. However, one must be cautioned that many times, Muslims have confused *ijma'* with their local customs, which may or may not have a basis in the core sources of Shari'a. Such customs may even introduce innovations that are contrary to precepts enshrined in the primary sources of the Shari'a.[30] *Ijma'*, as practiced by qualified jurists, has been a fundamental tool of Islamic jurisprudence and points toward the necessity of consultation (*shura*) among scholars, jurists, various experts, and the people as a whole. In commerce, the challenge for Muslims is to understand that such tools are meant to facilitate compliance with the Shari'a as opposed to circumventing it.

Collectively, the methods of "law-finding" discussed above are referred to as *usul al-fiqh*, the roots of Islamic jurisprudence.[31] They provide the methods whereby Muslims derive guidance for everyday life, including commerce, in accordance with the Qur'an and the Sunna. Historically, the approach of Muslim scholars has been to avoid codification of the results of *ijtihad*. For this reason, the evolution of *fiqh* interpretations has closely paralleled the Anglo-American tradition of Common Law in the building of judicial consensus upon the interpretive endeavors of individual judges.[32]

For ordinary Muslim, a simple understanding of *fiqh* allows the individual to distinguish among five categories of activity: obligatory, recommended, permitted, discouraged, or forbidden. Neither commerce nor finance is an obligatory action (*fard* or *wajib*). However, every Muslim looks upon the example of the Prophet Muhammad, may peace be upon him, and his beloved wife Khadija as inspirations to engage in commerce. Muhammad was a merchant who was so honest that he earned the honorific *al-Amin*, "The Trustworthy One." When Khadija, a local businesswoman, employed him, he so impressed her with his integrity that she proposed marriage to him. This example from the Prophet's early life teaches Muslims that honest and decent commerce is *mandub*, an act which is recommended but not required of the faithful. Taking the Prophet as their inspiration, Muslims traveled the world for commerce.

In East Asia and the far reaches of Africa, Islam spread with the positive impression made by Muslim merchants. As often as not, the honesty that was a trademark of the Prophet was the calling card of Muslim merchants. On the one hand, the unique class of faith-driven merchants would typically devote themselves to the kinds of commerce that were considered *mubah* in Islamic law: acts about which the Shari'a is neutral. Such acts make up the preponderance of commercial behavior. In other words, most goods and business practices that one may find in the market do not violate the rules that guide Muslims. On the other hand, those same Muslim merchants would have likely avoided activities considered *makruh*—behavior that is discouraged for the believers, but not explicitly forbidden. When it comes to the *makruh*, this might mean avoiding things that may lead to forbidden behavior or commerce. For instance, if a merchant brokers barley in the food industry, this is permissible behavior. But, what if the merchant has good reason to believe that his buyer would sell the grain to a brewery? The trade would not be forbidden, without proof or evidence that the purpose of purchasing barley would be to brew beer. But, it would certainly be discouraged.

All Muslim merchants and financiers who observe the faith avoid the *haram* or *mamnu'*—forbidden activities that constitute major sins for the believer. The Shari'a provides clear guidance about the forbidden. For instance, Jabir ibn Abdallah reported that the Prophet Muhammad forbade the sale of wine, the carcasses of animals that had died, swine, and idols. All of these are forbidden to Muslims in the Qur'an, but this hadith adds the further proviso that Muslims should avoid making a profit on forbidden things, even by selling them to those for whom they are not forbidden.[33]

In the world of investing, the Islamic perspective allows Muslims to buy stocks listed in the global markets so long as the company in which one invests is not engaged directly in forbidden activities. Determining this requires a processes similar to that used by the socially responsible asset manager.[34] Income derived from forbidden or doubtful transactions must be purified and may be taken from the dividend or gains upon sale prior to distribution to investors. The screening process follows two general procedures. The first procedure is applied at the industry level and the second at the financial level. From the perspective of the Shari'a, Muslims are not allowed to enrich themselves in ways that are contrary to the rights of God, to the rights of the contracting parties, and even to the rights of third parties. In asset management, this means first and foremost avoiding specifically forbidden areas of investment, which include those banks and insurers that are involved with *riba* (discussed below); the sale, production, and distribution of alcoholic beverages; gambling; unsavoury entertainment; and the like.[35]

Although it is relatively straightforward to identify *haram* or non-permissible businesses, the screening of financial instruments is only beginning to evolve. For example, a growing plurality of modern scholars permits one to invest in a company so long as its exposure to interest is limited to five percent or less of revenues, because it is incidental and the core income is permissible.[36] But, what if a stock represents an investment in a company with significant borrowings at interest?

When it comes to deciding how much debt may be carried by a company in which one invests, modern Islamic scholars look to a hadith in which the Prophet Muhammad stated that "one third is big or abundant." A further ruling relating to "mixture" (*khalut*) has been adapted to govern the modern mixture of borrowed funds with nonborrowed funds in a company's capital structure. As a result, Islamic scholars have concluded, "The majority deserves to be treated as the whole thing."[37] Thus, a listed company borrowing more than 33 percent of its capital is not a permissible target for investment, and a listed company that has cash and monetary equivalents of 50 percent or more is treated as if the assets are cash: its sale is impermissible as it is buying money for money at a different price.

Thus, over more than 1400 years since the Qur'an was revealed, Muslims have become adaptive, yet they have remained committed to the application of the Shari'a in the regulation of commerce. However, even though one usually finds pluralities or majorities of scholars agreeing on a particular interpretation, seldom is the majority great enough to constitute a true consensus, or *ijma'*.

Some have argued that the traditional schools of Islamic jurisprudence are incapable of addressing modern problems. This is because of a prevalent view among Western scholars of Islam and some Muslims that traditional *ijtihad* has ceased to inform civil law and commerce. However, the traditional schools of jurisprudence have well-defined methods to analyze classical texts and prior scholarly views and provide a clear approach to problem solving and legal decision making on the basis of each school's approach to *usul al-fiqh*.

When we examine modern legal rulings and scholarly research, we find that *ijtihad* remains a viable and lively tool, albeit applied with great care. When a Muslim jurist or Islamic scholar engages in *ijtihad*, he realizes that an error in judgment not only affects him but also has repercussions that may affect many other people as well. Thus, he pursues *ijtihad* with great caution. In Islam, the role of the *mufti*, the person eligible to issue a *fatwa*, is fundamentally a marriage of the spiritual and the legal.[38] The qualifications of a *mufti* require a broad mastery of skills: "The prerequisites for being a mufti are that a person be knowledgeable of the law with regard to primary rules, secondary rules, disagreements, and [legal] schools; that he possess the tools of independent reasoning (*ijtihad*) in their entirety; and that he be familiar with whatever he needs in order to derive judgments; namely, [Arabic] grammar, biographical information, and commentary on the verses that are revealed with respect to the laws and the narratives in them."[39]

When it comes to the *fiqh* of commerce, the emphasis of the various schools is on assuring that the businessperson knows the boundaries of permissibility and illegality relating to the chosen practice. The businessperson must behave with decency and fairness and he must seek a mutual benefit for all participants in a transaction. The Prophet Muhammad, may peace be upon him, said, "The accepted [pleasing to God] transaction is the transaction that takes place with mutual benefit for both the buyer and the seller."[40]

CENTRAL CONCERNS OF THE SHARI'A IN COMMERCIAL LAW

The concept of secularism—the separation of worldly life from religious life—is not the same for Muslims as it is for most Westerners. If a person is truly a steward of the created world on behalf of God, its true owner, then that person's freedoms are constrained by the responsibilities of stewardship in such areas as sociology, politics, economics, and law. In other words, under the Shari'a, all social sciences are interdependent.[41] However, in most Muslim societies, much of the time, life is similar to the way it is in a so-called secular society. Tolerance and the rule of law are meant to pervade Islamic social life just as they are in the West. An intriguing example is the Islamic marriage contract, which is a civil contract defining rights and obligations and not a holy sacrament.

In commerce, the starting point for this interdependence of faith and secular life is the belief that all worldly wealth is a trust given to humanity by God. As a result, a businessperson never truly transacts with his or her "personal" property; rather, the transaction is with property entrusted to one's control for the duration of one's life. This means that the Shari'a necessarily interferes in the dynamics of transactions to assure that each party acts in accordance with God's justice. Historically, this has meant that Muslim jurists have placed great emphasis on the terms and procedures of contract law and contractual relations, and the nature of contracts remains a matter of great concern for Muslims today. This is because violations of the rules of contracts are among those areas that are most liable to cause injustice in commercial dealings.

Unlawful Interest (Riba)

The Qur'an explicitly bans a practice called *riba* in four separate verses. Each of these Qur'anic verses affirms the absolute nature of the prohibition. However, the details of what *riba* entails in actual practice are not clearly defined.[42] In order of revelation, the verses of the Qur'an that forbid *riba* are the following:

That which you give as *riba* to increase the people's wealth increases not with God; but what you give in charity, seeking the goodwill of God, multiplies many-fold.

(Qur'an 30:39)

For taking *riba*, even though it was forbidden to them, and their wrongful appropriation of other people's property, We have prepared for those among them who reject faith a grievous punishment.

(Qur'an 4:161)

Oh Believers, take not *riba*, doubled and redoubled, but fear God so that you may prosper. Fear the fire, which has been prepared for those who reject faith, and obey God and the Prophet so that you may receive mercy.

(Qur'an 3:130)

Those who benefit from *riba* shall be raised like those who have been driven to madness by the touch of the devil; this is because they say that "trade is like *riba*," while God has permitted trade and forbidden *riba*. Hence, those who have received the admonition from their Lord and desist [from taking further *riba*], may keep their previous gains, their case being entrusted to God; but those who revert shall be the inhabitants of the Fire and abide therein forever.

(Qur'an 2:274)

The Qur'an warns that anyone who is involved with the practice of *riba* faces the wrath of God and His Messenger on the Day of Judgment. The details that allow one to determine what this term means are found in the Hadith. The attempt to create lending practices that do not depend on *riba* has led to the development of the field of Islamic banking, which has achieved exceptionally high growth rates in recent years.[43] Unlike commercial banks in the West, an Islamic bank is obliged to erect screens against the practice of *riba* and seek socially beneficial returns. Modern Islamic banks rely on *ijtihad* to adapt classical opinions on sales and leasing to the development of a process of ethical and socially responsible banking that respects the Qur'anic ban on *riba*. The development of Islamic banking has not been without controversy or challenge. A major reason for this disagreement is the fact that there are only six hadiths that give clues to the meaning of *riba* in a modern context.[44] However, a scholarly consensus is beginning to emerge, especially in the Gulf region, about the current state of Islamic banking and about the best ways to improve the system.

The scholarly view of *riba* turns on traditions like that of Anas ibn Malik in the "Book of Sales" in the *Sunan* of Bayhaqi, who reported that the Prophet Muhammad said: "When a person grants a loan and the borrower offers him a dish [in payment for something other than a dish], he should not accept it; and if the borrower offers a ride on an animal [in payment], he should not ride, unless the two of them have been previously accustomed to exchanging such favors mutually."[45] The classical interpretation of *riba* is that there are two forms of *riba: riba al-nasiyya,* which is interest on a loan of money; and *riba al-fadl,* which is a repayment in excess when commodities of the same type are traded.[46] According to the concept of inductive reasoning by analogy (*qiyas*) in Islamic law, these interpretations of *riba* are applied to any monetary commodity, whether it is mentioned in the Hadith or is a new custom that is found in modern commercial markets. According to the classical understanding of *riba,* the trading of money for money, whether it is in the form of a hand-to-hand transaction or a loan over time, is not an approved business practice under the Shari'a. This notion is based on the idea that money is not a "commodity" in itself, merely reflecting a "time value" for a return. Rather, money is a measuring tool and value determinant, devoid of its own integral value.

Deception in Business Transactions (Gharar)

The Prophet Muhammad, may peace be upon him, said, "Do not contract to buy merchandise on the way to the market, but wait until it is brought to the market [so that its fair price is established]."[47] The Prophet also said, "It is impermissible to sell a thing if one knows that it has a defect, unless one informs the buyer of the defect."[48] These traditions are examples of ethical exhortations against the practice of *gharar*. The majority of Islamic scholars consider *gharar* as "both ignorance of the material attributes of the subject matter of a sale, and uncertainty regarding its availability and existence."[49] The description of *gharar* in the Hadith is broad and implies an insistence on contractual transparency, full relevant disclosure, and fairness in the transacting environment. Restrictions on the practice of *gharar,* which may range from explicitly forbidding certain actions to tolerating an incidental oversight, are important means of preventing one party from improperly consuming the wealth of another.

Gharar literally means "deception." Hence, the best definition of *gharar* in business is "deception based on preventable ambiguity or uncertainty." In Shari'a, for *gharar* to invalidate a contract, the deception must not be trivial, it must relate to the object of the contract, and it must conflict with established business practice. However, in the view of many jurists, certain forms of *gharar* may be tolerated if an overriding public interest or benefit (*maslaha*) is involved.[50] The key to the assessment of *gharar* is that the deception that is to be prohibited must be based on a *preventable* uncertainty. This does not apply to the idea of risk in general, which is normal in the ordinary course of business.[51]

The practice of full disclosure and the maintenance of open and transparent markets are some of the best ways to prevent *gharar*. As a result, many Islamic scholars take comfort in the forms of disclosure and consumer protections that are utilized in modern Western markets. Many scholars believe that these highly regulated consumer markets should be emulated in the developing economies of the modern Muslim world.

CONTRACTS

The Arabic word for contract is *'aqd,* which comes from a root that means "to bind or tie tightly." The strength of the "binding" defined by this word is given in its Qur'anic usages, which refer to the highest order of mutual binding, whether among believers or between God and human beings: "Oh you who believe, fulfill your contracts" (Qur'an 5:1). The concept of the contract in Islamic law is similar in many ways to that in Western legal systems. The Shari'a distinguishes among contracts, promises, commitments, dispositions, and expressed intentions.[52] Whenever one or more of these actions are undertaken, it becomes an object of law and is thus subject to specific rules in the Shari'a.

In order to be valid according to the Shari'a, a contract must be a freely undertaken mutual binding of two legally competent parties. Typically, a contract in Islam relates to the exchange or use of property (*milk*) or money (*mal*).[53] The contract is binding so long as its object is not repugnant to the Shari'a. In addition, a valid contract must offer a provision for the contracting parties to withdraw from the agreement. 'Abdallah ibn 'Umar reported that the Prophet Muhammad said, "There is no [binding] transaction between two persons that undertake a transaction until they separate [after concluding the transaction], but only if there is an option to annul it."[54] If one party fails to abide by the terms of the contract, his action may be subject to a penalty. Although Islamic jurists prefer written contracts to unwritten agreements, unwritten agreements have specific rules that affect the enforceability of the contract.

Islamic law bestows extensive rights and privileges upon contracting parties. According to a famous hadith, "Everything that is not prohibited is permissible."[55] However, a contract should not contain any stipulation that frustrates the nature and purpose of the contract itself.[56] For instance, payment for a good or a service or delivery of a good or a service may be deferred, so long as the stipulation is properly recorded and witnessed.[57] The leading schools of Islamic law differ somewhat over the nature of contracts and contractual obligations, but they do not differ over the key principles of a contract. Moreover, when a jurist finds an invalid stipulation in a contract, like most Western judges he will usually limit his action to requiring the removal of the invalid stipulation. If a single invalid stipulation does not affect the overall terms of a contract, the contract is allowed to remain in force.

Unilateral assertions, such as verbal promises made during a negotiation, imply an obligation to act in a certain way. However, they do not have the legal stature of a contract, in which two parties make specific commitments to one another. Under Islamic law, a promise is not regarded as an implied contract; rather, it is seen as a unilateral expression of the promisor's willingness to perform an act, transfer a right, or refrain from doing something. A contract entails both a legal and a moral duty to carry out its provisions and is fully enforceable under the law. A promise, however, is solely a moral obligation, and thus may not be enforceable.[58]

In order to be legally valid, an Islamic contract must include a formal offer (*ijab*) and a formal acceptance (*qabul*). Once written or verbal statements confirm the offer and the acceptance, the contracting parties are liable for their obligations under the contract.[59] A valid contract under the Shari'a, however, also requires that the terms of the contract must be permissible under the Shari'a: an object of sale must be specific and free from *gharar*, and generally, the object should exist at the time of the contract.[60] The Islamic law of contracts accepts certain modifications due to unavoidable contingencies. The theory of contingencies is based on a core concept of equity and justice at the heart of the Shari'a.[61] Likewise, certain options allow contracting parties to validate the offer and acceptance of their proposed counter-parties. The key principle is that the contract should be transparent. According to DeLorenzo, "By insisting that Muslims transact by means of a specific set of well-defined contracts, the Shariah ensures that all parties have every opportunity to understand what they are getting themselves into when they transact. The classical Islamic system of *mu'amalat* (transactions) is so highly articulated for precisely this reason. While the scriptural foundations of that system may be abbreviated, owing to their delineation of principles rather than specifics, the dynamic of *ijtihad* inherent to *fiqh* has ensured that Muslim jurists, and especially Shariah boards, continue to comment and build upon the theoretical constructs."[62]

In general, Islamic scholars and jurists have been traditionally quite comfortable with allowing a business-friendly approach to contracting and contract fulfillment. For instance, one party may appoint a third party to fulfill his or her obligations as an agent. This gives rise to the broad concept of agency (*wakala*) in Islam. Muslim jurists have granted substantial liberty for the contracting parties to appoint an agent to complete a transaction. This might even include a seller appointing the buyer as an agent to outsource goods for sale to the buyer as the seller's agent.[63]

Possession (Qabd)

Wealth, in every conceivable form, is created by God and is thus His property. This view is derived from the following Qur'anic verses: "Give to them from the property of Allah which He has bestowed upon you" (Qur'an 24:33); "Have they not seen that, among the things made by our own hands, We have created cattle for them, and thus they acquired the right of property over them?" (Qur'an 36:71). Clearly, the rights we hold over "our" property are subject to divine injunction and guidance.[64] The punishment for those who take property unlawfully is significant: "He who wrongly takes a span of land will be made to wear it around his neck...on the Day of Judgment."[65] From verses and traditions such as these, it is reasonable to conclude that the possession of private property is permissible in Islam.

Ibn 'Abbas reported that the Prophet Muhammad said, "He who buys food grain should not sell it, until he has weighed it [and then taken possession of it]." Ibn 'Umar reported that the Prophet said, "He who buys food grain should not sell it until he has taken full possession of it."[66] Thus, the provenance of things to be sold must be made clear, as should the specific disclosure of the contract's objects.

Shari'a scholars define two forms of possession: physical (*haqiqi*) and constructive (*hukmi*). The former is self-evident and means that an object is within the physical control of a party with all the attendant rights and liabilities.[67] Possession, whether physical or constructive, means that one is able to deliver a good as contracted. Historically, Islamic courts have been willing to vouch for contracts of sale, no matter the distance required for delivery, so long as the provenance of the object and the capacity of the seller to deliver the object could be validated.[68] Although most traditional scholars were of the opinion that possession requires the existence of the object to be contracted, the Hanbali scholar Ibn al-Qayyim al-Jawziyya pointed out that the prohibition of the sale of nonexistent objects was meant to be a prohibition only of those things that are subject to excessive or nontrivial forms of deception (*gharar*).[69] The exception from this rule of other forms of *gharar* facilitates forms of commerce that meet public need without entering into types of transactions that are repugnant to the Shari'a.

Accountability

According to Shaykh Yusuf al-Qaradawi, "The market, its prices and sales, should be left free to respond to internal economic forces and natural competition without manipulation." This juridical opinion is based on the following hadith of the Prophet Muhammad: "If people are left alone, God will give them provision from one another."[70] This point leads us to understand that merchants are to be accountable in Islam and that governments have the responsibility to oversee markets as fair and level fields of competition. This is an important point because many types of contracts are either explicitly forbidden according to their form or are centered on a forbidden object or purpose. Often, merchants seek to disguise such activities. For example, many Muslims engage in fictitious sales that emulate a loan of money at interest. Such sales are known as *hila* ("legal fictions") and entail a buyer selling an object to another person and then buying it back at a different price. The difference is the amount of interest that would have been accrued in an interest-based transaction. Such deceptive contracts are meant to disguise a forbidden transaction as if it were permissible. Although the merchant who contracts a *hila* is accountable to God, the historical view of Muslim scholars has been that governments should prevent such deceptions to the best of their ability.

IJTIHAD UNDER MODERN CONDITIONS
OF COMMERCE

According to the hadith that states, "Everything that is not prohibited is permissible," much of what we transact in modern commerce is permissible in Islam, with the caveat that we must not engage in *riba* or *gharar*. On the one hand, this rule means that one must study modern commercial and financial arrangements carefully to determine their validity and consistency with Islamic principles. On the other hand, contemporary society has some new needs, new customs, and many blends of cultures and rules. As a result, once the analysis of contemporary commercial and financial arrangements is complete, modern Muslims need to construct authentic Islamic alternatives, not *hiyal* that circumvent the purposes of the Shari'a. For such a purpose *ijtihad* is required. The context for *ijtihad* is that "the door is wide-open for the adoption of anything of utility, of whatever origin, so long as it does not go against the texts of the Qur'an and the Sunna."[71] The great classical jurist Ibn al-Qayyim al-Jawziyya established three rules for *ijtihad:* (1) it may be applied in the absence of specific guidance in the Qur'an and the Sunna; (2) it should not contravene the Shari'a; (3) it should not lead to such a complicated expression that people either lose their attachment to the Shari'a or become confused about its established principles.[72]

As a practical matter, the outcome of modern innovation in the financial markets is a corpus of *fatawa* (the plural of *fatwa*), legalistic rulings by contemporary Muslim scholars that enable financial institutions, investors, and consumers to engage in commercial transactions. These *fatawa* are examples of *ijtihad* and are executed by scholars on the basis of their analysis of authentic sources, the facts of a proposed financial or commercial instrument or transaction, and prior precedents.[73] One hadith is particularly helpful in tempering the use of *ijtihad:* "Do not permit an error of opinion to become a tradition for the community."[74] To this end, we are reminded that the Qur'an itself warns us that even inspired judges are subject to error.[75]

The culture of Islamic business relies on a close interaction between the legal and spiritual aspects of religion. For complex reasons, Muslims have allowed themselves to become less proactive in the modernization of commerce than they have been in other areas of modern endeavor, such as technology. This inactivity has included less engagement in the problems of finance and commerce by Islamic scholars and thinkers. As a result, the modern Muslim businessperson faces unique challenges when operating in the modern marketplace. What should one do, for example, if one's business model is valid according to Shari'a principles, but the market generates risks of interacting with businesses that are not Shari'a compliant? How does one engage in finance if Shari'a rules governing finance are unknown in the market and, perhaps, alien to regional customs? Muslim communities have dealt with similar challenges in the past. The outcome of their struggles has been documented in the works of the leading schools of Islamic jurisprudence. The results of these endeavors are now being revisited and adapted to modern circumstances. The majority of these developments have been invisible to the greater public, but some are influencing business practices around the world as Islamic investing is providing new alternatives in the ethical investing market. For emerging markets that are deeply in need of reform, there is a clear advantage in reviving the Prophet Muhammad's model of honesty or integrity.

NOTES

(Ed.) following a note signifies that the note was added by the general editor of this set.

1. *Sahih al-Bukhari,* trans. Dr. Muhammad Muhsin Khan (Beirut: Dar al-'Arabiyya, n.d.), vol. 3, 151–152.

2. Mohammad Adam El-Sheikh, "The Applicability of Islamic Penal Law (*Qisas* and *Diyah*) in the Sudan" (Philadelphia, Pennsylvania: Temple University unpublished Ph.D. dissertation, Department of Religion, 1986), xviii.

3. Muhammad Taqi Usmani, "The Principle of Limited Liability," in Muhammad Imran Ashraf Usmani, *Meezan Bank Guide to Islamic Banking* (Karachi, Pakistan: Darul Ishaat, 2002), 223–232. Although predisposed to the concept, Justice Usmani has not finalized his view.

4. Abdur Rahman Doi, *Shariah: The Islamic Law* (London, U.K.: Ta Ha Publishers, 1984), 449.

5. Mohammad Hashim Kamali, *Islamic Commercial Law: An Analysis of Futures and Options* (Selangor, Malaysia: Ilmiah Publishers, 2002), 73.

6. El-Sheikh, "Islamic Penal Law," 15–18.

7.   This is independent from the separate theological argument that property is not owned by the individual, but is held by human beings in trust for God, who is the actual owner; thus, human beings are merely the caretakers of this world and its contents.

8.   Kamali, *Islamic Commercial Law,* 67; Kamali deduces from this that it is not sufficient to presume that a contract is forbidden if its type or terms are not explicitly forbidden.

9.   Ibid., 69.

10.   Lakhdar O'Barrett, "Towards a Green Planet: Why Islam Holds the Keys to a Sustainable World," *Al Jumuah* 16, no. 12, Dhu al-Hijja 1425 (March 2005), 34.

11.   John L. Esposito and John O. Voll, "Khurshid Ahmad: Muslim Activist-Economist," in *Islamic Resurgence,* ed. Ibrahim M. Abu-Rabi (Islamabad: Institute of Policy Studies, 2000), 50. For an exhaustive discussion of *Zakat,* see Yusuf al-Qaradawi, *Zakat* (London, U.K.: Dar Al Taqwa, 1996). Another outlet for wealth that is used to help others is the charitable trust (*waqf*), which is not discussed in detail in this article. A useful resource on *waqf* is Dahi Al-Fadhli and Abdulkader Thomas, *Characteristics of the Historical Formation of Awqaf* (April 16, 2005), accessed at www.ajif.org.

12.   Rodney Wilson, "Parallels between Islamic and Ethical Banking," *Review of Islamic Economics,* no. 11 (2002): 51–62.

13.   Said Ramadan, *Islamic Law: Its Scope and Equity* (Kuala Lumpur: Muslim Youth Movement of Malaysia, 1992), 43. Ramadan indicates that there are ten specific economic and financial injunctions in the Qur'an, which I have reduced to three primary categories.

14.   Ibn Maja, *Sunan Ibn Maja* (Cairo: Issa Al Halabi Press, 1952), 42–43. Often, this hadith is cited as proof that Islam is against any form of innovation. In fact, the specific reference is to innovation in the defined beliefs and practices (*'aqida*) of Islam. Muslims have historically understood that the prohibition of innovation relates to matters of belief and worship, but not to science and commerce.

15.   El-Sheikh, "Islamic Penal Law," 41–42; see also, Harald Motzki, *The Origins of Islamic Jurisprudence: Meccan Fiqh before the Classical Period,* (Leiden and New York: E.J. Brill, 2002).

16.   El-Sheikh, "Islamic Penal Law," 1.

17.   Seyyed Hossein Nasr, *Islamic Life and Thought* (London, U.K.: George Allen & Unwin, 1981), 26.

18.   Fathi Osman, *Sharia in Contemporary Society: The Dynamics of Change in the Islamic Law* (Los Angeles, California: Multimedia Vera International, 1994), 19.

19.   Ramadan, *Islamic Law,* 33; Ramadan believes, unlike Nasr, that the traditional order is not immutable. The root of *ijtihad* is *j-h-d,* which means, "to strive or make a strenuous effort." *Ijtihad* is the eighth form intensification of this root, which also gives us the third form term *jihad* or "defensive effort."

20.   Classically, following the *Risala* of Imam al-Shafi'i (d. 820 CE), the four sources of Islamic law are listed as Qur'an, Sunna, *ijma',* and *qiyas.*

21. Fuad Al-Omar and Munawar Iqbal, "Some Strategic Suggestions for Islamic Banking in the 21st Century," in *Review of Islamic Economics*, 9, 2000, 49.

22. See Kamali, *Islamic Commercial Law*, 99.

23. Besim S. Hakim, "The Role of *'Urf* in Shaping the Traditional Islamic City," in *Islam and Public Law*, ed. Chibli Mallat (London, U.K.: Graham & Trotman, 1993), 141; Hakim sees *'urf* as a subset of *'ada* (habitual practice), which was the basis for not overturning local customary practices in the opinions of the early Muslim jurists (144). See also, Kamali, *Islamic Commercial Law*, 79–81.

24. Yusuf DeLorenzo, "Shariah Boards and Modern Islamic Finance: From the Jurisprudence of Revival and Recovery to the Jurisprudence of Transformation and Adaptation" (paper presented to the International Islamic Financial Standards Board, London, U.K., May 2004).

25. This applies almost in equal measure to the political Rejectionists of our time in the Al Qaeda movement and some young Western educated Islamic reformists as well as some traditionalists residing in the West.

26. 'Umar S. Al-Ashqar, *al-Qiyas* (Kuwait: Dar al-Salafiyya, 1979), 44–5.

27. DeLorenzo, "Shariah Boards and Modern Islamic Finance."

28. El-Sheikh, "Islamic Penal Law," 28; however, as we shall see below, *ijtihad* requires significant training, and established religious authorities have been at pains to point out that modern rejectionist groups like Al Qaeda's Egyptian predecessor *al-Jama'a al-Islamiyya* have no right to apply *ijtihad* on the basis of their relatively limited learning and their narrow political aims. See Bernard Botiveau "Contemporary Reinterpretations of Islamic Law: The Case of Egypt" in *Islam and Public Law*, ed. Mallat, 274.

29. Osman, *Shari'a in Contemporary Society*, 23. Osman goes on to propose that the role of *ijtihad* may result in distinct rulings applicable in Muslim majority societies as compared to Muslim minority communities in the West, p. 26.

30. El-Sheikh, "Islamic Penal Law," 49.

31. See Motzki, *The Origins of Islamic Jurisprudence*, in which Motzki aligns the *usul al-fiqh* approach to Imam Shafi'i in the second century of the Hijra.

32. DeLorenzo, "Shariah Boards and Modern Islamic Finance.

33. *Sahih Muslim bi-sharh an-Nawawi*, (Cairo: 1924), 830; see also, *Sahih al-Bukhari*, trans. Dr. Muhammad Muhsin Khan, 233–236 and 241.

34. Muhammad Elgari, unpublished interview with Omar Fisher for *The American Journal of Islamic Finance* (January 24, 1997).

35. Munawar Iqbal, "Wealth Creation: An Islamic Perspective" (presented at the "Seminar on Wealth Creation," Durham University, Durham, United Kingdom, July 2003).

36. Usmani, "The Principle of Limited Liability," 211–212.

37. Ibid., 214–215; See also, Introduction by Muhammed Imran Usmani, 208–209.

38. Barber Johansen, "Legal Literature and the Problem of Change: the Case of Land Rent," in *Islam and Public Law*, ed. Mallat, 35.

39. David S. Powers, "Legal Consultation (*Futya*) in Medieval Spain and North Africa," in *Islam and Public Law*, ed. Mallat, 89, citing Abu al-'Abbas Ahmad b.

Yahya al Wansharisi (d. 1508 CE) *al Mi'yar al-Mughrib wa jami' al-mu'rib 'an fatawa ahl Ifriqiyya wa al-Andalus wa al-Maghrib* (Rabat: Ministry of Endowments and Islamic Affairs, 1981–1983), vol. 10, 31.

40.   Houcine Chouat, "Guidelines for Marking up Goods for Profit," *Al Jumuah* 17, no. 3 (July 2005): 20.

41.   The idea that Islam is a system or order (*nizam*) in which the social, economic, and political sciences are interrelated developed among Muslim reformist thinkers in British India around the time of the Second World War. In 1943, Mawlana Hamid al-Ansari Ghazi described Islam as an integrated political system. In 1942, Abu al-'Ala al-Mawdudi (d. 1979) used the Urdu term *Islami nizam* ("Islamic order") in a speech about Islamic ideology. The Egyptian Muslim Brotherhood ideologist Seyyid Qutb (d. 1966) derived the concept of the Islamic System from Mawdudi. In his influential manifesto *Ma'alim fi al-Tariq* (Milestones), written in 1964, Qutb warns Muslim youths to avoid Western theories about "the interpretation of human endeavor...the explanation of the origin of the universe, [and] the origin of the life of man." This concern led to the development of an intellectual movement known as the "Islamization of Knowledge." First set out in Chapter 8 of *Ma'alim fi al-Tariq* ("The Islamic Concept and Culture" [*al-Tasawwur al-Islami wa al-thaqafa*]), the Islamization of Knowledge was promoted in greater detail by Ismail Faruqi in the United States and Muhammad Naquib al-Attas in Malaysia. See Seyyid Qutb, *Milestones* (Damascus: Dar al-'Ilm, n.d.), 109–110, and the Arabic edition of this work, idem., *Ma'alim fi al-Tariq* (Beirut: Dar al-Shuruq, 2000), 139. On the origin of the concept of the Islamic System, see Wilfred Cantwell Smith, *The Meaning and End of Religion* (1962; repr., Minneapolis, Minnesota: Fortress Press, 1991), 274 n. 10. (Ed.)

42.   On the subject of *riba*, see Abdulkader Thomas, ed., *Interest in Islamic Economics: Understanding Riba* (London and New York: Routledge, 2006). This book provides a detailed analysis from legal, economic, and historical perspectives about the concept of *riba* and why it is forbidden. A key conclusion of the book is that interest on a loan of money is clearly *riba*.

43.   See Abdulkader Thomas with Stella Cox and Bryan Kraty, *Structuring Islamic Finance Transactions* (London, U.K.: Euromoney, forthcoming). Islamic banking has developed at a growth rate of approximately 17 percent per year in the Arabian Gulf region. The growth rate has been less robust, but strong nonetheless, in other parts of the Muslim world, such as South and Southeast Asia. Although the field of Islamic banking has developed rapidly over the last two decades, most Muslims around the world continue to use commercial banks as people do in the West. In addition, some countries, such as Iran, make a distinction between internal banking practices, which operate on Islamic principles, and international banking, which operates on commercial banking principles. (Ed.)

44.   Usmani, "The Principle of Limited Liability," 39–44.

45.   Ibid., 41.

46.   Many scholars view the prohibition of *riba al-fadl* as "blocking the means" to *riba,* rather than as a prohibition of *riba* itself. In Thomas, *Interest in Islamic Economics*, Shaykh Wahba al-Zuhayli reviews rules relating to the restriction of unlawful gain in the trading of food commodities as distinct from monetary commodities.

47. *Sahih Muslim*, trans. Abdul Hamid Siddiqi (Lahore: Sh. Muhammad Ashraf, 1992), vol. 3, 800. In *Sahih al-Bukhari*, trans. Dr. Muhammad Muhsin Khan, 199, the concept of *gharar* is characterized as the sale of that which is not present at the moment of sale.

48. *Sahih al-Bukhari*, trans. Dr. Muhammad Muhsin Khan, Vol. 3, 166.

49. Kamali, *Islamic Commercial Law*, 85; elsewhere, Kamali compares *bay' al-ma'dum*, the sale of a nonexistent object, to *gharar* in that both take undue advantage of the ignorance of the purchaser.

50. Ibid., 85.

51. Ibid., 88.

52. Ala' Eddin Kharofa, *Transactions in Islamic Law* (Kuala Lumpur, Malaysia: A.S. Noordeen, 1997), 7.

53. Doi, *Shariah*, 356.

54. *Sahih Muslim*, trans. Siddiqi, 804.

55. Ramadan, *Islamic Law*, 68.

56. Kamali, *Islamic Commercial Law*, 131 and 76.

57. Ibid., 142; this interpretation is one of a variety of interpretations of Qur'an 2:276 ("Allah has blighted *riba* but has made acts of charity fruitful").

58. Kharofa, *Transactions in Islamic Law*, 26; however, according to some scholars, a verbal promise may be enforceable and subject to sanction. See Usmani, "The Principle of Limited Liability," 119 and Usmani, Introduction, 88.

59. Kharofa, *Transactions in Islamic Law*, 12.

60. Certain permissible contracts relate to objects that may not yet exist or are yet to be produced. They are permitted because of the limitation of intentional deception and the public good that they enable.

61. Kharofa, *Transactions in Islamic Law*, 42–43.

62. DeLorenzo, "Shariah Boards and Modern Islamic Finance."

63. *The Mejelle*, trans. C. R. Tyser et al. (Kuala Lumpur: The Other Press, 2001), 239–254.

64. Usmani, "The Principle of Limited Liability," 18.

65. *Sahih Muslim*, trans. Siddiqi, 847–848.

66. Ibid., 802; the rules of possession for grain and money are distinct from and more restrictive than those concerning other goods, as these are explicitly cited in the traditions governing *riba*. See also, *Sahih al-Bukhari*, trans. Dr. Muhammad Muhsin Khan, 192–195.

67. Usmani, "The Principle of Limited Liability," 79.

68. See Nelly Hanna, *Making Big Money in 1600: The Life and Times of Isma'il Abu Taqiyya, Egyptian Merchant* (Syracuse, New York: Syracuse University Press, 1998), 51.

69. Cited in Kamali, *Islamic Commercial Law*, 100.

70. Yusuf al-Qaradawi, *The Lawful and the Prohibited in Islam*, trans. Kamal El Helbawy et al. (Indianapolis, Indiana: American Trust Publications, n.d.), 258–259.

71. Ibid., 71.

72. Ibid., 78.

73.   Johansen, "Legal Literature and the Problem of Change," in *Islam and Public Law*, ed. Mallat, 32. *Fatawa* often take the form of a reduction of a legal school's view on a specific matter for public consumption; or they may be a view of the *mufti* (the person authorized to issue a *fatwa*), legitimized by the *mufti*'s standing and without specific indications of precedent or pointers to the authentic texts.

74.   Ramadan, *Islamic Law*, 84.

75.   Mohammad Hashim Kamali, "Appellate Review and Judicial Independence in Islamic Law," in *Islam and Public Law*, ed. Mallat, 64; in the Qur'an, the Prophet David, not Solomon, is the paradigmatic model for a judge. After describing the settlement of a dispute in which David's judgment proved to be a test of David by God, David is told: "Oh David, We have made you a vicegerent (*khalifa*) on Earth; therefore, judge between people in truth and do not follow the passions that would distract you from the way of God" (38:26).

INDEX

———————————————— • ————————————————

About the Editors and Contributors

————————————————— • —————————————————

VINCENT J. CORNELL is Asa Griggs Candler Professor of Middle East and Islamic Studies at Emory University. From 2000 to 2006, he was Professor of History and Director of the King Fahd Center for Middle East and Islamic Studies at the University of Arkansas. From 1991 to 2000, he taught at Duke University. Dr. Cornell has published two major books, *The Way of Abu Madyan* (Cambridge, U.K.: The Islamic Texts Society, 1996) and *Realm of the Saint: Power and Authority in Moroccan Sufism* (Austin, Texas: University of Texas Press, 1998), and over 30 articles. His interests cover the entire spectrum of Islamic thought from Sufism to theology and Islamic law. He has lived and worked in Morocco for nearly six years and has spent considerable time both teaching and doing research in Egypt, Tunisia, Malaysia, and Indonesia. He is currently working on projects on Islamic ethics and moral theology in conjunction with the Shalom Hartmann Institute and the Elijah Interfaith Institute in Jerusalem. For the past five years (2002–2006), he has been a key participant in the Building Bridges Seminars hosted by the Archbishop of Canterbury.

VIRGINIA GRAY HENRY-BLAKEMORE is the director of the interfaith publishing houses Fons Vitae and Quinta Essentia. She is a writer and video producer under contract with the Book Foundation, U.S. director of photography and children's book publisher Dar Nun, and cofounder and trustee of the Islamic Texts Society of Cambridge, England. She is an accomplished lecturer in art history, world religions, and filmmaking. She has taught at Fordham University, Cairo American College, and Cambridge University. She is also a founding member of the Thomas Merton Center Foundation. Virginia Gray Henry-Blakemore received her BA from Sarah Lawrence College, studied at the American University in Cairo and Al-Azhar University, earned her MA in Education from the University of Michigan, served as Research Fellow at Cambridge University from 1983 to 1990, and is scheduled to receive her PhD from Canterbury, Kent, in 2008.

SARWAR ALAM received his doctorate in Public Administration from the University of Arkansas, Fayetteville, in 2006. He previously obtained baccalaureate and postbaccalaureate degrees in Political Science from the University of Chittagong, Bangladesh. He also obtained a postgraduate diploma in Development Planning from the Academy for Planning and Development, Dhaka, Bangladesh, and an MA in Human Resource Development from Pittsburg State University, Kansas. As a civil servant and magistrate in Bangladesh, he worked in the ministries of education, cabinet division, and women's and children's affairs.

JANE FATIMA CASEWIT holds graduate degrees in education and works on the USAID education team in Rabat, Morocco. Her lifelong interests and personal studies have centered on Islam, comparative religions, and perennial philosophy. She has written several articles on gender and Islam and has translated books about Muslims living on the periphery of Dar al-Islam. Two of the books she has translated are *Islam in Tibet: Tibetan Caravans* by Abdul Wahid Radhu and *The Life and Teaching of Tierno Bokar* by Amadou Hampaté Ba.

RKIA ELAROUI CORNELL is Senior Lecturer in Arabic at Emory University. For the previous six years (2000–2006), she was Research Associate Professor of Arabic Studies at the University of Arkansas, Fayetteville. A native of Morocco, she obtained a degree in secondary education from the Women's Regional Normal School in Meknès, Morocco, and finished an eight-year contract with the Moroccan Ministry of Education. From 1991 to 2000, she was Assistant Professor of the Practice of Arabic at Duke University. In 1999, she published *Early Sufi Women* (Louisville, Kentucky: Fons Vitae), a translation of an early work about Sufi women by the Persian mystic Abu 'Abd al-Rahman al-Sulami (d. 1021 CE). Cornell has given numerous lectures and conference presentations on the subjects of Qur'anic exegesis, women in Islam, and language pedagogy. She is currently preparing a book on the woman saint Rabi'a al-'Adawiyya and an advanced reader in premodern Arabic literature.

SUSAN L. DOUGLASS writes and researches in the fields of education and curriculum development and designs instructional materials for public and private schools. She earned an MA in Arabic Studies from Georgetown University and is presently working on a PhD at George Mason University. She has published several books and over a dozen teaching resource collections as curriculum specialist for the Council on Islamic Education. She is a regular contributor to the online world history curriculum, *World History for Us All*, supported by the National Endowment for the Humanities and San Diego State University. She authored the report, *Teaching About*

Religion in National and State Social Studies Standards (Council on Islamic Education and First Amendment Center, 2000), and was the general editor for the textbook, *World Eras: The Rise and Spread of Islam, 622-1500* (Farmington Hills, Michigan: Thompson/Gale Publishers, 2002).

SEEMI BUSHRA GHAZI is Lecturer in Classical Arabic at the University of British Columbia. She majored in Religion and Intercultural Studies at Bryn Mawr and Haverford Colleges and pursued further studies at the University of Chicago, the American University in Cairo, and Duke University. Her recitations of the Qur'an and of devotional music in Arabic, Persian, Turkish, and Urdu have been featured on PBS, BBC, and CBC. She is active in the Muslim, Sufi, and Interfaith communities of Vancouver, British Columbia, and is a founding board member of the InterSpiritual Centre Society of Vancouver.

KENNETH LEE HONERKAMP is Associate Professor of Religion at the University of Georgia, Athens. He is a graduate of al-Qarawiyyin University in Morocco and obtained his doctoral degree from the University of Aix-en-Provence in France. His research interests are in the fields of teacher–disciple relationships in formative Sufism, Islamic law, Qur'anic sciences, and the study and translation of letters of spiritual guidance written by Moroccan Sufis. He has edited and translated several previously unpublished works of Abu 'Abd al-Rahman al-Sulami (d. 1021 CE). His critical edition of *al-Rasa'il al-Kubra* of the Spanish Sufi Ibn 'Abbad of Ronda (d. 1390 CE) was published by Dar el-Machreq, Lebanon, in 2005.

DANIEL ABDAL-HAYY MOORE is a widely regarded American Muslim poet. His first book of poems, *Dawn Visions,* was published by Lawrence Ferlinghetti of City Lights Books in San Francisco (1964). He became a Sufi Muslim in 1970, performed the Hajj in 1972, and lived and traveled in Morocco, Spain, Algeria, and Nigeria. Upon his return to California, he published *The Desert is the Only Way Out* in 1985 and *Chronicles of Akhira* in 1986. A resident of Philadelphia since 1990, he has published *The Ramadan Sonnets* (1996) and *The Blind Beekeeper* (2002). He has also been the major editor for a number of works, including *The Burda of Shaykh Busiri* (2003), translated by Hamza Yusuf, and *State of Siege* (2004), the poetry of the Palestinian poet, Mahmoud Darwish, translated by Munir Akash.

FEISAL ABDUL RAUF is the Founder and Chairman of the Cordoba Initiative, a multi-faith organization whose objective is to heal the relationship between the Muslim World and the West. He is also the Founder of

ASMA Society (American Society for Muslim Advancement), serves as the Imam of Masjid Al-Farah in New York City, and is an active member of the World Economic Forum's C-100, which works to promote understanding and dialogue between the Western and the Islamic worlds. He was recently awarded the Peacebuilder Award by the Alliance for International Conflict Prevention and Resolution. Imam Feisal frequently interviews with various media and has appeared on CNN, CBS, NBC, ABC, PBS, and BBC. His published writings include *Islam: A Search for Meaning* and *Islam: A Sacred Law*. His latest book, *What's Right With Islam: A New Vision for Muslims and the West,* was chosen by the *Christian Science Monitor* as one of the top four nonfiction books of 2004.

KRISTIN ZAHRA SANDS is Mellon Fellow and Assistant Professor of Islamic Studies at Sarah Lawrence College and Research Scholar at New York University's Center for Religion and Media. Her research interests include Sufism, religion and suffering, and Islam and the media. She is the author of *Sufi Commentaries on the Qur'an in Classical Islam* (Oxford: Routledge, 2005).

ALIAH SCHLEIFER completed her PhD at Exeter University in the United Kingdom. Her thesis was the basis for her second book, *Mary: Blessed Virgin of Islam.* Her first book, *Motherhood in Islam,* was a response to the absence of definitive literature for American Muslim women seeking guidance in their lives as wives and mothers and to offset the denigration of motherhood that is fashionable in certain circles in the West. She taught from 1974 until her death in 1995 at the American University in Cairo, where she received her master's degree in Islamic and Arabic studies. She was born in New York City and received her BA from Barnard College in Spanish Language Studies. She worked as a coordinator for an antipoverty program prior to her embracing Islam and traveling with her husband and children to the Middle East. She lived in Jordanian Jerusalem (before 1967), Amman, Beirut, and finally Cairo.

ABDULKADER THOMAS is President and CEO of SHAPE Financial Corporation of Arlington, Virginia, and Kuwait. A graduate of the Fletcher School of Law and Diplomacy in International Trade, Thomas earned a BA with honors in Arabic and Islamic Studies from the University of Chicago and is an Islamic banking consultant. He is currently a PhD candidate in the International Center for Education in Islamic Finance in Malaysia. He is known for his regulatory work in the United States and the United Kingdom and is a frequent speaker and author on Islamic financial and banking matters. His recent books include *Islamic Bonds: Your Guide to Issuing, Structuring and Investing in Sukuk* with Nathif Adam (London:

Euromoney, 2004), *Structuring Islamic Financial Transactions* with Stella Cox and Bryan Kraty (London: Euromoney, 2005), and *Interest in Islamic Economics: Understanding Riba* (Oxford: Routledge, 2005).

NARGIS VIRANI is Assistant Professor of Arabic and Islamic Studies at the New School in New York City. She earned her PhD from Harvard University. During the course of her Arabic Studies, she studied at the University of Jordan in Amman, the Bourguiba Institute in Tunis, and Al-Azhar University in Cairo. At Al-Azhar she studied the Qur'an under the Shaykh of Al-Azhar and holds a *shahada* (certificate) and an *ijaza* (permission to teach the Qur'an) from the Shaykh. Dr. Virani is currently revising and expanding her dissertation on the relationship between Jalaluddin Rumi's multilingual verses and his mystical discourse. She is also working on a second monograph analyzing the use of the Qur'an in Muslim literary writings.